REA

ACPL ITEM
DISCARDED

3 1833 02189 7241

306.8
Wright, H. Norman
Family is still a great

D0532086

$4-12-93$

DO NOT REMOVE
CARDS FROM POCKET

ALLEN COUNTY PUBLIC LIBRARY

FORT WAYNE, INDIANA 46802

You may return this book to any agency, branch,
or bookmobile of the Allen County Public Library.

DEMCO

# FAMILY IS *STILL* A GREAT IDEA

# Family Is *Still* a Great Idea

### H. Norman Wright

VINE
BOOKS

Servant Publications
Ann Arbor, Michigan

Allen County Public Library
900 Webster Street
PO Box 2270
Fort Wayne, IN 46801-2270

The names and characterizations in this book drawn from the
author's counseling and personal experience are rendered pseudony-
mously and as fictional composites. Any similarity between the names
and characterizations of these individuals and real people is unin-
tended and purely coincidental.

Copyright © 1992 by H. Norman Wright
All rights reserved.

Vine Books is an imprint of Servant Publications especially designed
to serve evangelical Christians.

Scripture quotations are from *The Amplified Bible* (AMP), copyright ©
1958 by the Lockman Foundation; *The Holy Bible: New International
Version* (NIV), copyright © 1973, 1978, 1983 International Bible
Society, Zondervan Bible Publishers; *New American Standard Bible*
(NASB), copyright © 1960, 1962, 1963, 1971, 1972, 1973, 1975, 1977
by the Lockman Foundation, Zondervan Bible Publishers; and *The
Living Bible* (TLB), copyright © 1971 by Tyndale House Publishers, all
used by permission.

Published by Servant Publications
P.O. Box 8617
Ann Arbor, MI 48107

Cover design by Barry Littman
Text design by K. Kelly Nelson

92 93 94 95 96 10 9 8 7 6 5 4 3 2 1

Printed in the United States of America
ISBN 0-89283-785-3

**Library of Congress Cataloging-in-Publication Data**

Wright, H. Norman.
    Family is still a great idea / H. Norman Wright.
      p.  c.m.
    Includes bibliographical references.
    ISBN 0-89283-785-3
    1. Family—United States.    2. Family—Religious life.
I. Title.
HQ536.W69   1992
306.85'0973—dc20

92-26138

*Dedication*

This book is dedicated to the following who have enriched my life in so many ways:

To my mother and father, Amelia and Harry Wright, and the rich legacy they have given to me, which included an abundance of time, love, Christian values, and a love of life in so many ways.

To the families from whom they came, the Corneliuses from Germany, and the Wrights from England.

To the multitude of my relatives spread throughout this country.

To my steadfast and encouraging brother, Paul Fugleberg and his family.

To my gracious, loving, and supportive wife, Joyce.

To Irma and Julius Archinal for the heritage of Christian values they gave to their daughter, Joyce.

To my son Matthew, whom God used to change my life so much, and who now abides with his heavenly Father.

To Sheryl, my creative daughter, and her supportive husband, Bill Macauley.

To our friends who have become like family over the years, Don and Billie Latva, Rex and Eve Johnson, Fran and Warren Holthaus, Gary and Carrie Oliver, Doug and Pat Weaver, and Dale Dukellis.

May this book cause families to discover their heritage and legacy, discover the abundance of riches they have and can experience in Jesus Christ, and may their lives draw others to Jesus Christ.

# TABLE OF CONTENTS

# The Tie
# that Binds

**F**ILLED WITH THE JOYOUS enthusiasm of youth, Kim could hardly wait for her wedding day! Sweet dreams filled her mind about the warm coziness of married life, like snuggling together in front of a crackling fire. Sure, her own family had gone through some tough times, but hadn't they emerged all the stronger because of them? Learning to support and love one another even when it hurt helped them to believe in one another at a very deep level. Kim cherished the thought of passing on this positive legacy to her own children.

Plagued with doubts and fears, Bill often felt a dark cloud hovering over his future. After watching his parents constantly bicker and put each other down, he wasn't at all sure he even wanted to have any children. Painful memories of family life still festered in his heart, like some deep wound that wouldn't seem to heal. As a matter of fact, Bill hadn't seen many families that had it all together. He silently wondered if getting married was such a smart idea after all.

The random thoughts of two people off the street? Perhaps. But this particular young man and woman were getting married in just three months... to each other! How would they ever be able to merge such totally opposite images of family? What would they create together? How could they capture a shared vision of the joys of marriage and children? Indeed, how could they even agree on the basic question of bringing new life into two such different worlds?

Yet I have seen it happen time and again. It is possible. One of the delights of my family counseling practice is to rejoice with those who *do* make it work, even in the face of incredible odds. Kim and Bill did. Seventeen years later, this beautiful couple and their three children are busy creating their own image of family life, their own legacy. Their shared life has not been without pain, of course, but still rich with the joys of love. Bill has discovered that family is *still* a great idea.

## FAMILY PORTRAITS

All of us carry an image of what a family should be. And since so many varied factors merge together to shape our perceptions, our family portraits are rarely simple and well-focused. Our own images may be distinct or fuzzy, but few of us stop to reflect on all that went into creating our own ideals.

ﾞﾑ

*What images fill your mental family photo album?*
*What do you equate with the ideal family?*

Take a moment and think back. When someone mentions family to you, what do you think about? What images fill your mental family photo album? What do you equate with the ideal family? Where did your dreams come from? You probably developed your ideals and dreams in the context of your own family, as well as through your experience of society and the media—especially during your impressionable adolescent years.

3 1833 02189 7241

In response to a national survey, here are the comments of five different men and women:

"When I think of family, I like to think of things like support and love and guidance."

"One thing about my family and my family's values is that my parents love me no matter what."

"[I think of] an ideal family as being one in which there's love, mutual respect, and communication. I don't care if there's one parent, two parents, etc. If those things are there, that's an ideal family. On the other hand, where the children don't feel love and they don't communicate with each other, that's not a very ideal situation. I think you need to define it in those contexts, not just the physical structure of who and where."

"I have the best memories of my childhood. When I was younger, every night my mom would come in after I was put to bed and she'd kiss me good night and she'd sit there for a couple of minutes and we'd talk a little bit and she would leave. Then my dad would come in and kiss me and we'd talk a little bit and he'd leave. And I used to look forward to their coming into my room for those few minutes. I remember that like it was yesterday. I know my parents love me. I know that. They've said it. And I feel comfortable telling them that, and I think they feel comfortable telling me."

"Self-confidence comes from emotional support, because if you've got someone who's always putting you down, you're going to have this much [very little] self-confidence and you're not going to be worth anything to anybody, but if you get support from the family, that helps."[1]

Families have always been the wellspring of strength and stability in any society, often the source of our deepest sorrows as well as our greatest joys. In the crucible of modern culture, are families becoming stronger or weaker?

My adolescent journey took place during the fifties, just as television moved out of infancy and began to shape the beliefs and values of a nation. When I entered a high school of two thousand students in 1952, little did I know that two of my fellow students were part of a family whose image would provide a focal point for the next half a century.

Who could possibly carry such influence? David and Ricky Nelson—two brothers, one a year younger and the other a year older than me. As seen each week on TV by millions of Americans, the two teens added lots of zip and spice to the lives of Ozzie and Harriet. These two parents and their two sons portrayed a typical American family of the times.

I'm sure the producers of "Ozzie and Harriet" never realized the extent to which society, psychologists, and sociologists would fixate on this foursome. The Nelsons came to reflect the ideal family portrait, even as family life began to change during the turbulent sixties and the fragmented seventies. Consider some of these typical reflections from the late eighties:

It used to be so simple, it seems in retrospect. Dad at the office or factory and Mom at home nurturing the next generation.... But the return of those days is about as likely as a prime time comeback of "Ozzie and Harriet." Less than ten percent of U.S. families are "traditional"—father at work and mother at home.[2]

Most of us were raised in a typical nuclear American family.... But today, there is no such thing as a typical family. And only a distinct minority (seven percent) of America's population fits the traditional family profile.[3]

Today, less than ten percent of the population lives in the "Ozzie and Harriet" two-parent family where Dad is the sole financial support.[4]

There is only one in ten American families today where you have Mom at home and Dad at work—only one in ten. "Ozzie and Harriet"... are gone.[5]

At a hearing before the Legislature, [State Representative Mary Jane] Gibson noted that fewer than ten percent of

American families resemble the familiar "Ozzie and Harriet" model of mother as caregiver and father as breadwinner.[6]

Inspired by [Blankenhorn's] op-ed piece in the Washington Post, we sidled up to Nexis the other day and nonchalantly asked how many news stories in 1989 included the phrase "Ozzie and Harriet." Startling answer: eighty-eight stories. Usual context in which those names from the fifties were being invoked: A politician was on stage reciting the news that the traditional nuclear family—the kind symbolized by the Nelsons during their marathon stint on black-and-white TV— was dead or dying.[7]

෨

*If the traditional nuclear family typified by*
*Ozzie and Harriet Nelson is dying, what is family today?*
*Indeed, can we still point to such an entity?*

## BLURRED IMAGES

If the traditional nuclear family typified by Ozzie and Harriet Nelson is dying, what is family today? Indeed, can we still point to such an entity? Morris Massey made some insightful comments in his book, *The People Puzzle:*

It's only been until recent times that a family's role and re-sponsibilities and processes were automatically handed down from one generation to another. It isn't only today that writers are crying out over the decline of the family. That has been going on for thousands of years.

But the American family unit is in a precarious position. There are definite changes in the family unit today as we "ex-pect" it to be. The norm that we have had for the family is the nuclear family unit which is father, mother, and children living together. This was an American invention of the past several decades.

If you look at the patterns of families in Europe and other countries, you find many variations from what we believe is the ideal. Historically, an extended family included parents, children, and other relatives, especially elders.

The reason the nuclear family developed here was mobility, education, and economic independence. And as these elements change, the nuclear family content is going to change as well.[8]

Is family a mother, father, and children? Or is it a grandmother, mother, and daughter living in the same household? Is it a never-married man raising his five-year-old son by himself? Is it a divorced mother with four children? Or could it be a home with four teenagers cared for by a twenty-year-old sibling because both parents were killed in a traffic accident?

Family can be all of these, and more.

For years we have used different terms to describe two types of families: the "intact family" and the "broken family." But today a great variety of family forms have sprouted to life. Our entire society has changed, with each new year showing a rapidly accelerated pace. "Mom, Pop, and the kids" is fast becoming the minority form of family life today. I've heard children say, "Am I odd? In my class at school, two other kids and I are the only ones who have a family with both Mom and Dad at home. All the others have just a mom or dad."

With the exploding divorce rate, one author raised the delicate issue of denial in this puzzling equation of family life:

> We need to question the level of denial in the society when we believe that divorce results in dysfunctional adults and children, while giving less weight to the numbers of intact families where affairs are common, marriages feel dead, and abuse is an everyday occurrence.
>
> In many cases, divorce is not the main issue. It is not even the cause of the dysfunction. Divorce was the result of previously existing dysfunction.
>
> We also need to question our persistence in believing that the intact family is the norm and divorce is the problematic exception.[9]

But just because "intact" families are fast becoming the minority, should we abandon this ideal? I believe God's plan and desire is that a family unit include both a man and woman, faithful, healthy, and together for life. It can happen and does happen. Perhaps our magazines and media would do us a greater service by recounting more stories about such stable families—rather than focusing on abusive and disintegrating marriages and families.

But I also think we should eliminate the phrase "broken family," which attaches a negative stigma or label to a person or family. Many "non-intact" or "non-normal" families are very healthy and function quite well. I have seen healthy and dysfunctional intact families, as well as healthy and dysfunctional divorced families.

No matter what state your own family is in, or your relatives' families, or even your own children's families, you can all be whole and healthy. People in all kinds of varied circumstances can demonstrate the healing and refining power of God at work in their lives.

## NEVER ENOUGH TIME

Most family specialists believe the modern American family is increasingly less able to fulfill its basic functions. They view this venerable institution as at least becoming weaker if not dying. Let's consider some of the new twists in family that have proliferated over the last twenty-five years.

One modern reality is that fewer people are getting married at all, and those who do tend to marry later in life. How old were your grandparents when they married? What was the age of your parents when they tied the knot? Your own children are likely to marry later than you did. Joyce and I married at age twenty-two, but our daughter waited until she was twenty-seven. Many of the couples I am now seeing in premarital counseling are in their late twenties or early thirties.

Another change is reflected in the diminishing number of children couples are having today. Even the decade of the sixties to the seventies showed a drop in the average number of children per family. The quality of life for our children also seems to be declining. Many are no longer able to relish the innocent joys of childhood in the midst of tormenting strife or abuse.

Are these the rantings of a fired-up television speaker or an ultra-conservative organization devoted to a highly traditional set of family morals and values? No. Simply the findings of a group of secular sociologists concerned about the direction of family life today. A 1989 investigation of family and family values by the Massachusetts Mutual Life Insurance Company indicated that the family's basic function is endangered. They described "family" as the base for caring and nurturing and the place where values are taught and learned.[10]

But the average person in our country also sees the family under attack. And what do many identify as the major threat? *Lack of time.* Most families suffer from never spending enough hours together as a group. Instead of developing close, significant, intimate relationships, many dwell under the same roof more like unrelated boarders. Quality family time can be even more rare for a single parent struggling to just make ends meet.

ᡒᬞ

*Most families suffer from never spending enough hours together as a group. Instead of developing close, significant, intimate relationships, many dwell under the same roof more like unrelated boarders.*

A major reason for this time crunch is the increasing economic pressure of our times. When Mother and Father labor for huge chunks of the day or night just to pay the bills, the quality of family life inevitably declines.[11] Many have been forced to shift back to a survival posture.

One result of this lack of time is a de-emphasis on the *formal structures* of family relationships. Spending quality time together is the current focus. Having a satisfying and fulfilling marriage often becomes more highly valued than just being or staying married. Partners feel more free to split if the relationship is not meeting their own personal needs, further contributing to family disintegration.

## UNTIL DIVORCE DO US PART

Unfortunately, the likelihood of divorce continues to steadily increase. Marriage has become almost like a revolving door, a relationship that people can make and break at will. And as the divorce rate climbs, the more normal this pattern becomes. Negative sanctions against divorce are diminishing and people tend to not take seriously the detrimental effects that are so blatant.[12]

When the trend of living together prior to getting married started, people assumed it would be healthy for a marriage relationship. Sometimes in an honest attempt to "test the waters," modern men and women often choose to get to know one another intimately without the pressures of a marriage contract. Such couples are usually shocked to learn that cohabitation has tended to have just the opposite effect.

What researchers have discovered is couples who live together first also tend to get divorced first. A study at the University of Wisconsin reported that 38 percent of couples who lived together before they married were divorced within ten years, compared with 27 percent who married without cohabiting first. Such a finding surprised even many experts, who had also assumed that living together helped iron out potential marital problems and thus diminish the chances of eventual divorce.[13]

An article entitled "Marriage: The First Years, What Holds You Together..." states this fact another way: "If a couple lived together before marriage, they were twice as likely to have trouble later on. A little over one-third of the couples in the study had lived together before marrying. Of those marriages, more than one-quarter—27 percent—were found to be 'distressed' after thirty months." Of the 64 percent who did not live together beforehand, only 13 percent reported later distress.[14]

## THE GOOD LIFE

Many of the changes taking place in the family are positive. But we see a rising concern—even among those without strong religious beliefs—that much in these new trends is feeding the decline of the family. Raising children in today's world presents perhaps the ultimate challenge. Past generations assumed certain elements were necessary for success in this noble endeavor, such as the following:

1. A relatively large family that did lots of things together.
2. A family with numerous routines and traditions and a good amount of quality time together between the adults and the children.
3. A family that had regular contact with relatives and lived in a supportive neighborhood.
4. Children with little or no concern that their parents would divorce.

How many families do you know today who still fit this model of the good life? Since World War II, we have witnessed dramatic changes in technology, values, and traditions. With each passing year, the intensity and speed of the changes almost leaves us breathless.

In the sixties and seventies especially, the family received a staggering blow from the enormous social changes in our country. America's streets and homes overflowed with racial strife, generational conflict, the growing influence of drugs, the anti-war debate, gay power, gray power, environmental concerns— just to name a few trouble spots. The American dream seemed to be literally suspended for a time—as though we all needed to take time out and catch our breath.

Those who had pulled themselves up by the bootstraps out of the depression set their faces like flint to make life better for their kids. Many succeeded, but at what price? The "Material Good Life" eventually reached a peak without any obvious avenues for improvement. VCRs, cellular phones, two cars in every garage, and a microwave in every kitchen... was this all that life had to offer? Just "getting ahead of the Joneses next door" no longer seemed enough.

While we built more elaborate houses chock full of labor-saving devices, we simultaneously seemed to find life less enjoyable. In the mad rush to accumulate material possessions, many people seemed to have lost not only the meaning of life but their individual identity as well. American society was rapidly changing, but was it for the better? What good was comfort when the traditional source of stability—the family itself—seemed to be disintegrating?

## OLDIE GOLDIES

Yet another change started to take place in the seventies. People began spending less time anticipating an improved lifestyle, and more time yearning for the good old days. The lure of the past seemed to promise sharper guidelines for life and a clearer definition of success.

The theme of nostalgia actually became big business. Families searched their basements or attics for remnants of yesteryear. Junkyards were no longer junkyards, but hunting grounds for valuable antiques. Reproductions became the trend, along with clothing and music of the past. Radio stations began playing the "oldies" of the fifties and sixties. The "Happy Days" television program a number of years ago transported many to a time of innocence, when life seemed simpler and better. Radio programs from the thirties and forties—once a major family event full of laughter or suspense—were being rebroadcast.

Why? Feeling so threatened by the instabilities of the present and the future, people naturally hungered for the emotional security offered by tangible objects from the past.

The family in the seventies needed lots of reassurance. More marriages were ending and both parents often worked outside the home just to stay afloat. Drug and alcohol use increased among all members of the family unit. Increased mobility separated more and more families, along with a growing trend of shifting the elderly toward retirement homes. For example, southern California's "Leisure World Retirement Centers" offer two locations, each housing ten thousand folks over the age of fifty-five.

Few would deny that the family was changing in form, function, and purpose. Feeling helpless in the face of such insurmountable odds, many parents became more dependent upon the growing number of "helping professionals." Lacking confidence in their own wisdom, mothers and fathers often fell victim to the advice of these supposed experts in raising children. The modern-day abundance of parenting resources can overwhelm and confuse many of us.

Media images continued to powerfully mold our images and dreams. Old and young alike were fascinated by "The Waltons" television program, even though critics labeled it as "too idealistic." I personally felt their very realistic portrayal of family life conveyed deep spiritual truths about living and surviving together.

By speaking to the heart as well as to the mind, the Waltons successfully demonstrated strong family values and a more supportive lifestyle than many viewers seemed to be experiencing. Although made up of many different personalities, this family modelled that secret ingredient that many lack and wish for: bonding.[15] Do you watch any specific programs which reflect those same strong, positive family values? Fewer and fewer are available.

During the eighties and into the nineties, individual family members have become much more autonomous. Even while the family system remains a source of strength, we often drive, work, jog, eat, pray, and even die in isolation. Personal fulfillment and independence have become our primary goals, often to the neglect of family involvement. Individual members do not feel so bound by the family group, nor do they often choose to band together as in the past.

ಇ

*Even while the family system remains a source of strength,
we often drive, work, jog, eat, pray,
and even die in isolation.*

Many social functions have shifted from the family to other institutions, to the detriment of the glue that once held us together. Federal, state, and other agencies have assumed many functions that were once reserved for close relatives. Families have grown smaller, break up more frequently, and have a shorter life span. People seem less willing to invest time, money, and energy in keeping the family strong. The individual rather than the family unit has become the recipient of that investment.

During the past quarter of a century, we have witnessed a definite weakening of the family structure as we have known it. With all the talk and apparent emphasis on the importance of family, why has this undeniable disintegration occurred?

As we go on to discuss some of the possible factors contributing to the demise of the traditional family unit, reflect upon your own experience. Have any of these trends enveloped you as well?

## THE PARENT DEFICIT

In the opinion of most family life specialists, the greatest negative effect of today's trends falls upon the younger generation. The future of any culture, society, or country is the children. Yet the quality of life enjoyed by our youth has significantly deteriorated.

We quickly agree with such a thesis when we glance at the inner cities and impoverished slums of America. Yet in the midst of the plentiful material goods and opportunities enjoyed by so many children, how do the rest suffer? The major problem with today's children is the "parent deficit."

Many of today's parents relegate childrearing to others, or even to the television. As one author put it, "I think the thing that affects family values, currently, is the fact that there are no more full-time parents any more. The economy is forcing more two-income families, there are a lot more single parents, a fifty percent divorce rate. You're going to have a lot of kids that aren't getting any parental guidance. They're getting all their guidance from a video game or TV."[16]

Scripture talks about having a mother and a father in the home. That doesn't mean that both cannot work outside the home—often a necessity in times of economic recession. For others, such a decision is sometimes purely a matter of choice. I see many young couples in premarital counseling who want to begin their married life at exactly the same economic level as their parents. In fact, many of them accomplish just that by holding dual careers and running up massive debts on multiple credit cards. They end up making themselves slaves to their comfortable lifestyle for the next decade or two.

Could it be that both men and women have contributed to the demise of the traditional nuclear family? This deterioration offers serious cause for concern for everyone. Even secular research indicates that childrearing is most successful when it involves two parents who both carry the same level of concern for their calling.[17] Our challenge is to accomplish such a feat in the midst of a rapidly changing society.[18]

Our social upheaval is mirrored in other ways as well. As I approach my mid-fifties, I'm doing more reflecting about what it's going to be like for the next generation. On a recent trip to Yosemite National Park, I walked down a path with my son-in-law, fighting the enormous crowds. We both wondered, "What will it be like for children of the future when they visit this park?" Will they have to make a reservation months in advance just in order to see it? What national resources will be left? The park service is doing their best to preserve what we have, but will that be enough?

Apart from the massive federal deficit, looking around at Yosemite made me ponder the enormous environmental changes we have seen. What will the children of the future inherit from us? The more we cut down the giant forests of the world, the more our world changes for the worse. Perhaps the next nuclear disaster or massive oil spill will carry even worse consequences than the Chernobyl accident or the Alaskan oil spill. And centuries pass before the results dissipate.

As I finished this book, I witnessed the Los Angeles riots which erupted after the Rodney King verdict. An all-white jury acquitted the four white policemen accused of using excessive force in the arrest of this black motorist. I couldn't even drive around Long Beach one night because we were still under a curfew.

I was frightened to watch beatings and looting on television while it actually happened. Over forty people died and hundreds were injured in the worst urban strife since the Civil War. Over three hundred businesses were burned in the city I call home.

Los Angeles may not recover from this disaster for two or three decades. And those hurt the most are the individuals and families who live here, especially those who feel stuck in hopeless surroundings.

Officials worry that many cities around our country are just waiting to ignite the same way. Many people wonder, "Do I want to raise children in this kind of society?" We are leaving our legacy for the next generation to face, not only indelibly marked on the environment but also in the lives of our own families.

## SITTING ON DADDY'S KNEE

In his excellent book, *Father Memories*, Randy Carlson offers a very graphic illustration from the environment of the lasting impression fathers can leave on their offspring:

Fathers leave a lasting impression on the lives of their children. Picture fathers all around the world carving their initials into their family trees. Like a carving in the trunk of an oak, as time passes the impressions fathers make on their children grow deeper and wider. Depending upon how the tree grows, those impressions can either be ones of harmony or ones of distortion.

Some fathers skillfully carve beautiful messages of love, support, solid discipline, and acceptance into the personality core of their children. Others use words and actions that cut deeply and leave emotional scars. Time may heal the wound and dull the image, but the impression can never be completely erased. The size, shape, and extent of your father's imprint on your life may be large or may be small but it is undeniably there.[19]

Due to overwork or other pressures, more and more men have abandoned the parenting arena. Some say we are now seeing a disappearing act by fathers. Besides being simply absent from the home for longer hours, larger numbers are even denying paternity and avoiding their fathering obligations altogether.

Willard Gaylin, author of *Feelings*, describes the unique and definite role fathers can have in shaping the future of their children:

If we experience something too strongly in the past, we may anticipate it where we ought not and perceive it where it does not exist. If, for example, we were intimidated by a punitive father who terrified us, we may approach all authority figures with the bias of that early dominant memory. The memory of that authority may possess a greater reality to us than the actual authority figure with whom we were involved. Regardless of how gentle and unchallenging the authority figure is, we may approach each teacher, each employer as though he had both the power and the personality of that dominant father who once ruled our life.[20]

When we consider the father-daughter relationship in particular, we know that dads have a unique way of shaping a girl's future. Some instill in their daughters an expanded view of their potential, as related to me by one successful business woman: "When I was very young, my father would sit me on his knee and tell me there wasn't anything I couldn't do. I could accomplish anything I chose to attempt. He gave me a belief in myself and my abilities."

Sadly, other fathers allow their daughters only a limited view of their role in the world. They communicate that women must follow the prescribed roles of wife, mother, housekeeper, volunteer, etc. No doubt these are excellent roles—as long as they are a daughter's personal choice from among a variety of options for women today. But many daughters are not encouraged to be all they could be.

Corrie Ten Boom describes her experience of her early years with a loving father and how this sustained her years later in the Nazi prison camps:

My security was assured in many ways as a child. Every night I would go to the door of my room in my nightie and call out, "Papa, I'm ready for bed." He would come to my room and pray with me before I went to sleep. I can always remember that he took time with us and would tuck the blankets around my shoulders very carefully, with his own characteristic precision. Then he would put his hand gently on my face and say, "Sleep well, Corrie... I love you."[21]

Corrie Ten Boom recalls in vivid detail the way her father's care was demonstrated. Her father's warm and gentle touch filled her with security and love. Clear boundaries were set. Her value as a person was held high.

And that's exactly the way Corrie saw her heavenly Father. The words she used and the feelings she attached to her childhood memories reveal much about the kind of woman she became. When Corrie and her sister Betsie were being held in a concentration camp, she reached back into that store of father-memories for strength.

۶۰

*Her father's warm and gentle touch filled her with security and love. Clear boundaries were set. Her value as a person was held high.*

In the most horrid conditions one can imagine, Corrie recalls: "I sometimes remembered the feeling of my father's hand on my face. When I was lying beside Betsie on a wretched, dirty mattress in the dehumanizing prison, I would say, 'O Lord, let me feel Your hand upon me... may I creep under the shadow of Your wings.'"[22]

## CUSTOM-DESIGNED ROLES

When your parents began their marriage, who taught them what their family roles were to be? For that matter, who taught you? You and your parents perhaps accepted the prevailing societal norms. Culture taught you what a mother was supposed to do, what a father, daughter, or son could do or be. Most individuals adopted the clearly defined roles of their parents.

Today's world is disruptively different. Most families face overwhelming ambiguities which often create stress and confusion. Studies have shown that marriages are more stable when couples have clear and similar role expectations. Family roles today are more often *custom-designed* than *predetermined,* usually defined within the framework of each individual unit. Of course, such a trend can be positive as well as threatening.

As one man explained, "My role as a father seems to be defined more by the expectation my wife and children have for me than what society says. I could be in another family and my role there would be much different than here. Yeah, it's true this gives me lots of freedom and personal fulfillment, but I'm concerned because my performance is based on other people's expectations and whether I measure up or not!"[23]

And so the changes and the problems continue to mushroom out of proportion. When we read the paper or watch the news or even talk to our own neighbors and relatives, we hear about divorce, spouse and child abuse, children on drugs, unfaithfulness, couples living together before marriage, and homosexual marriages. These issues make the news; they are serious cause for concern.

But what about the millions of families who make it work? They're out there as well—homes where love, joy, fulfillment, and forgiveness are lived out every day. Yours may be one of them. Families who have learned to be hopeful in spite of riots, disasters, and poverty. Father and mothers, sons and daughters who have learned to be servants to one another.

Such families certainly aren't perfect. Each member has no doubt experienced his or her fair share of pain and disappointment. But they have learned how to survive in tough times, how to get up after they've been knocked down, how to hold one another up in areas of weakness. These courageous families have discovered the vision of Philippians 2:1-5 (AMP):

So by whatever [appeal to you there is in our mutual dwelling in Christ, by whatever] strengthening and consoling and encouraging [our relationship] in Him [affords], by whatever persuasive incentive there is in love, by whatever participation in the [Holy] Spirit [we share] and by whatever depth of affection and compassionate sympathy,

Fill up and complete my joy by living in harmony and being of the same mind and one in purpose, having the same love, being in full accord and of one harmonious mind and intention.

Do nothing from factional motives—through contentiousness, strife, selfishness or for unworthy ends—or prompted by conceit and empty arrogance. Instead in the true spirit of humility (lowliness of mind) let each regard the others as better than and superior to himself—thinking more highly of one another than you do of yourselves.

Let each of you esteem and look upon and be concerned for not [merely] his own interests, but also each for the interests of others.

Let this same attitude and purpose and [humble] mind be in you which was in Christ Jesus. Let Him be your example in humility.

Does such a family portrait sound like an impossible ideal? On our own, absolutely. But nothing is impossible with God. Jesus Christ, the Son of the heavenly Father, can teach us how to help our families to function in healthier ways! And the Holy Spirit, the third person who flows forth from their love, can empower us to make it happen.

No family has ever been perfect and none ever will be in this sin-filled world. None of us relates perfectly or lives out perfectly defined roles. Every family is "dysfunctional" in some way. In fact, the moderately dysfunctional family is probably closer to normalcy than a so-called "perfect" family.

Spending time lamenting what was wrong with our own families of origin won't help us to make any significant changes in our present families. I believe God does want to take an honest look at the positive legacy we have inherited, as well as the areas of weakness or lack. Armed with such knowledge, we will be able to develop a clearer vision for our own legacy.

ॐ
## BRINGING IT HOME

How can this vision for a vibrant family become even more of a reality in your own life? To help you work toward an answer, here are perhaps the two most crucial questions of this book:

1. What do you want your family to become?
2. What steps do you need to take to make it happen?

When you plan a vacation, you usually decide where you want to go and then determine how you're going to get there. Travel agencies are happy to help with maps and brochures galore. It's no different in the journey of a family. Those who know where they are going have the greatest opportunity of arriving safely and quickly at their destination. They're less liable to drift or become side-tracked by dangerous detours.

If you want to arrive at a particular destination with your family, you need both a goal and a plan. No one can define your goals for you. And until you know what you're aiming for, you're less likely to ever hit the target squarely in the middle.

First you need to honestly consider what your family is like right now. The following questions are certainly not a test, but just another way for you to gain a clearer perspective on the current status of your family. Read each statement below and circle the number that most accurately describes your family right now.[24] Remember, your answers are neither right nor wrong. No family is perfect across the board. Don't be disappointed when you don't feel like the "perfect ten."

The most helpful approach involves each member of the family responding to these questions. Significant differences will probably surface between individual family members. You need to allow for these differences and not even try to convince the others of your own opinion. An honest and thorough discussion will help you decide together what can be done to move ahead. Then you can all finally take action in a united effort to improve your life together.

1. Our family is together as a unit at least once or twice a day either for meals or talking together. If some family members live outside the home, we see them fairly frequently and they are present at holiday gatherings or significant family events.

| 0 | 1 | 2 | 3 | 4 | 5 | 6 | 7 | 8 | 9 | 10 |
|---|---|---|---|---|---|---|---|---|---|----|

almost      seldom      sometimes      much of      almost
never                                  the time      always

Here is one step we could take as a family to improve this area of our family life:

2. Our family is able to function evenly and smoothly without experiencing disruption or stress or pressure. We have a reasonable schedule and tend to stick with it. When absent family members return, it is a comfortable adjustment with everyone together.

| 0 | 1 | 2 | 3 | 4 | 5 | 6 | 7 | 8 | 9 | 10 |
|---|---|---|---|---|---|---|---|---|---|----|

almost      seldom      sometimes      much of      almost
never                                  the time      always

Here is one step we could take as a family to improve this area of our family life:

3. Our family handles differences and disagreements on a rational and reasonable basis. We allow feelings to be expressed but logic and reason is involved in decision-making. Different family members take responsibility for resolving issues.

| 0 | 1 | 2 | 3 | 4 | 5 | 6 | 7 | 8 | 9 | 10 |
|---|---|---|---|---|---|---|---|---|---|----|

almost      seldom      sometimes      much of      almost
never                                    the time      always

Here is one step we could take as a family to improve this area of our family life:

4. Our family shows respect for our family heritage, relatives, older members in the family and attempts to understand one another's generational perspective.

| 0 | 1 | 2 | 3 | 4 | 5 | 6 | 7 | 8 | 9 | 10 |
|---|---|---|---|---|---|---|---|---|---|---|

almost           seldom        sometimes       much of      almost
never                                            the time      always

Here is one step we could take as a family to improve this area of our family life:

5. When our family experiences problems which stem from outside influences over which we have no control, we pull together as a unit. Everyone does their share without blaming one another and becoming stuck on the unfairness of life.

| 0 | 1 | 2 | 3 | 4 | 5 | 6 | 7 | 8 | 9 | 10 |
|---|---|---|---|---|---|---|---|---|---|---|

almost           seldom        sometimes       much of      almost
never                                              the time      always

Here is one step we could take as a family to improve this area of our family life:

6. Each person in our family is a contributing member who adds rather than drains the family resources.

| 0 | 1 | 2 | 3 | 4 | 5 | 6 | 7 | 8 | 9 | 10 |
|---|---|---|---|---|---|---|---|---|---|---|

almost           seldom        sometimes       much of      almost
never                                              the time      always

Here is one step we could take as a family to improve this area of our family life:

7. Each person in our family takes the initiative and proper steps to reconcile relationships when disagreement arises. We do not have any "withdrawers" or "grudge collectors" who build up resentment and pay others back later.

| 0 | 1 | 2 | 3 | 4 | 5 | 6 | 7 | 8 | 9 | 10 |
|---|---|---|---|---|---|---|---|---|---|----|

almost      seldom      sometimes      much of      almost
never                                  the time     always

Here is one step we could take as a family to improve this area of our family life:

8. We have a common faith in Jesus Christ and seek to put him and his teachings first in our individual and family lives. We discuss spiritual matters together and pray together as a family. Each person has their own personal devotional life.

| 0 | 1 | 2 | 3 | 4 | 5 | 6 | 7 | 8 | 9 | 10 |
|---|---|---|---|---|---|---|---|---|---|----|

almost      seldom      sometimes      much of      almost
never                                  the time     always

Here is one step we could take as a family to improve this area of our family life:

9. We tend to recover fairly quickly when we experience a family crisis or loss. We encourage one another to fully express their personal grief. We have discovered the uniqueness of each individual's personality and needs, and have learned to adapt our responses accordingly so that they feel understood and supported.

| 0 | 1 | 2 | 3 | 4 | 5 | 6 | 7 | 8 | 9 | 10 |
|---|---|---|---|---|---|---|---|---|---|----|

almost      seldom      sometimes      much of      almost
never                                  the time     always

Here is one step we could take as a family to improve this area of our family life:

10. We take pride in our family as a whole. We accept one another based upon who each person is, rather than basing approval upon performance. We have learned to rely upon our

family life as a source of strength and are learning to allow God's grace to flow more freely in our family.

| 0 | 1 | 2 | 3 | 4 | 5 | 6 | 7 | 8 | 9 | 10 |
|---|---|---|---|---|---|---|---|---|---|---|
| almost never | | seldom | | | sometimes | | much of the time | | | almost always |

Here is one step we could take as a family to improve this area of our family life:

# ROOTS RUN DEEP

THE WORLD SEEMED TO STAND STILL as people stared at the clock hands inching closer and closer to midnight. Five, four, three, two, one! The sound of guns shooting into the air suddenly shattered the silence. Sirens blared and fireworks fractured the sky.

New Year's Eve in Times Square? More than that. That single second marked the greatest event in a hundred years: the turn of the century. Nineteen-hundred seemed like a whole new era. People were beginning to experience new inventions and changes which totally amazed them. We now stand less than ten years away from the turn of the millennium. The changes in the last fifty years should render us speechless, except that many of us have become too jaded by technology to stand in awe.

Only the elderly have any personal experience of the world in the early 1900s. You may have vague memories of what you learned from school, TV specials, or novels. Spectacular events such as the sinking of the Titanic or World War I are perhaps the most widely known. Especially vivid in my mind are scenes from the classic movie, *All Quiet on the Western Front,* which portrayed the devastating years suffered by the Allied soldiers in the trenches of France. In fact, one of my uncles inhaled mustard gas released by the Germans against his infantry unit and suffered the ill effects for the rest of his life.

Few survivors of that major conflict are still alive. Do you remember the decade in which World War I happened—1910-1920? Do you remember why it happened? Very few do. We're too caught up in the challenges of today. Yet our own family issues and values had their roots in the past decades. Tensions between the various generations exist for definite reasons. Examining these reasons will help us to better understand what is happening today, as well as what might happen in the future.

## THE DEFICIT DRIVE

Do you remember what life was like when you were ten years old? Was it during the seventies, the fifties, the forties, or earlier? I myself turned ten during the decade of World War II and the recovery years.

Perhaps you don't realize why this fact is so important. Around age ten, most children begin to internalize the values which they have been learning from parents, school, and church. It has been suggested that about *90 percent* of every generation's inner reactions solidify during this particular period of their development!

ɛ

*Around age ten, most children begin to internalize the values which they have been learning from parents, school, and church.*

I was introduced to this concept a few years ago by Dr. Rick Hicks in his presentation at Forest Home Conference Grounds. What I learned was an eyeopener. As I further studied the book upon which he had based his presentation, *The People Puzzle,* by

Morris Massey, many of my questions began to be answered. Why we are who we are today made more sense.

The values expressed by our own culture and the world during that crucial age of ten continue to influence us throughout our adult life. In many ways we are a product of our environment. We are all exposed to positive and negative values, too much of some things and not enough of others.

*Human beings are particularly driven by the early deficit in their lives.* As Massey put it, "People strive to achieve as adults what they feel they were deprived of in their early stages of life. Thus, what we grow up without is what is likely to become important to us. What we grow up with, we can accept, reject, not pay any attention to, or take for granted. It is particularly those things which we were deprived of that may become very important for us in later life."[1]

We can observe the impact of deficits whether it be in the area of economics or in our family life. People constantly come to counseling hungry for love, acceptance, affirmation, and encouragement. Since they didn't experience enough of it in their childhood, their primary direction in life is to discover what they missed.

In what ways might you feel driven? Can you identify some significant lack from your past which might help to explain this drive? These deficits tend to shift from decade to decade. As each generation is influenced in different ways, a discernible shift occurs in what the next generation thinks they want. The prior generation typically resists such changes.

Consider your own experience. Aren't your values somewhat different from your parents' generation? And aren't your children's values and perspectives different in some significant way from yours? Have you ever reflected on why you hold certain values? And why others born in different decades seem to cling to other values?

Here are some enlightening exercises you may want to try in your own immediate family, or better yet at an extended family gathering. Ask everyone to choose three things from their wallet or purse that communicate something about his or her values. Ask each person to share why they selected what they did. Then ask each person to choose the one item they would keep if they could only select one. What does this choice say about each person's values?

Next ask each person what three belongings they would grab if their home were threatened by a flood or fire. Ask why they selected the three. What does this say about what they value most?

Another way to reveal values involves listing ten items in your home that require electricity. Assume that because of an electrical shortage, you have to eliminate four which are no longer useable. Then select three of the remaining items that you feel you must have. Why were these three selected? What does each person's selection say about their values?[2]


## QUESTIONING ABSOLUTES

Let's take a look at the decades of this century one by one. If you are in your seventies or early eighties, you were probably ten years old during the 1920s. This decade was largely an extension of the values of the previous generation, a very patriotic period because of the aftermath of World War I. Men begged to enlist and fight in Europe, but fifty years later, the male youth expressed a totally different response to the Vietnam War.

The twenties was a time of absolutes. Within each family, authority was held by the parents, who trained and indoctrinated their children. Relationships reflected the classic nuclear/ extended family. Women basically functioned as mothers and housewives who raised the children without much help from babysitters or daycare. The man was the breadwinner, often willing to work long hours at a boring job. Why? Simply because he needed the money to survive.

But the twenties also reflected a subtle shift in values. Americans began searching for more excitement. People found new thrills in almost anything. A sense of visible hedonism began to appear as puritanical American values were challenged. Hair and dress styles began to change. The forerunners of the hippies, "the flappers," wanted to change the world and express their individualism. And they did, eliciting the same response from older adults as did the hippies a few generations later.

Prohibition became the law of the land, but breaking that law was the norm for many. Bootlegging boomed as an industry, giving rise to FBI figures like Elliot Ness. Films provided an escape into fantasy and opened the eyes of many middle-class folks to a larger world. Movies also presented a new set of heroes. Little did the originator of films realize how this invention would shape our society. The cult of materialism started in the twenties, especially in the cities, while life seemed to proceed as usual in the more rural areas.

Do you know anyone who was ten during this decade? Have you ever interviewed a person from the Roaring Twenties to discover what they experienced and believed? What their values were? Question someone in their late seventies or eighties if possible. You could learn a lot about the origins of your own worldview.

## SURVIVAL SOCIETY

If you entered the thirties as a ten-year-old, you suffered through the throes of the Great Depression. Twenty-five percent of our population endured extended unemployment. My mother became a widow during this decade. Many wore old clothes, reinforced old shoes with cardboard, missed meals, stood in line for watery soup, and struggled just to stay alive.

The values of those who received the brunt of that experience were warped forever. They were a survival society. The generations coming out of this decade grew up without economic security. As they grew older, what motivated them? Money and security. They became serious savers who planned for the future. This generation is a classic example of the idea that what we grow up without can become a driving force in our lives.

An interesting aspect of the thirties were the heroes portrayed in radio, comics, and movies. Children were taught the traditional value of virtue by heroes who repeatedly demonstrated that you would get the most out of life by "good, clean living." In contrast, the villains usually paid a stiff price for their ill-gotten gains. Who are the heroes and heroines of this current decade?

What do they portray and how is it affecting what children believe today?[3]

By the end of the thirties, economic recovery had been stimulated by the winds of war spreading across Europe. Who do you know that was ten during the thirties and what were some of their values? How might they differ from someone who is twenty years away from them in age?

## MAKING WAR AND BABIES

The forties are the decade in which I turned ten, and my values were shaped by many events during that time. Our nation was suddenly plunged headlong into war. The newspapers, magazines, radio, and newsreels reflected America's all-out war effort. Families pulled together, helped at the USO, planted "victory" gardens, and bought war bonds.

Our family did all of those things. My father served as an air-raid warden for our street during blackouts. Mom helped serve food to the servicemen at the Hollywood USO. No lights could be reflected from our home at night. We purchased gas not only with money but with gas coupons. The main value during these years was an intense national commitment to win the war.

Woman-power emerged at this time as three and a half million females went to work on assembly lines. The homefront began to change rapidly in terms of customs, ideas, economics, and relationships between men and women. The once cohesive family unit began to disintegrate. Kindergartens began to teach children rather than Mom. The government started day-care programs to fill in the gap. Because of the shift in values that occurred during the war years, America was forever changed.

❧

*Especially after the sacrifices of the war,*
*the "good life" was something everyone felt they deserved.*

Did you know that the term "teenagers" came into existence during the forties? When men over eighteen had gone off to war, the younger adolescents discovered they had become the elite group. They learned how to earn money and were catered to commercially. During the early forties they listened to their parents, but by the end of the decade, their ears had grown dull. They tuned in more to their own peer group rather than the old fuddy-duddies at home. Sound familiar?

Following the war, the newly created war industry shifted gears to meet consumer demands. Especially after the sacrifices of the war, the "good life" was something everyone felt they deserved. Pleasure seeking and accumulating material things became the number one priority after those bleak war years.

One of the most significant occurrences was the population revolution begun in 1945 and 1946. World War II ended and the servicemen returned. Nine months after V-day, Americans delivered over two hundred thirty thousand births in one month! By the end of 1946, 3.4 million babies had been born—the beginning of the biggest baby boom in U.S. history.

A "Baby Boomer" is by definition someone born between 1946 and 1964 in one of four countries: the United States, Canada, New Zealand, and Australia. By the end of the forties, that crop of babies had grown to 14.5 million. By 1954, new births were occurring at the rate of 4 million a year. This rate continued until 1964 when some of the first Baby Boomers began getting married. Can you imagine what all these babies did to the diaper industry, baby food processing plants, and school enrollment? And then they flooded the job market.[4]

Did you know that Baby Boomers currently compose about half of the U.S. population? They head up approximately forty-four percent of households, control an estimated fifty-five percent of consumer spending, and oversee a massive power block. The Baby Boomers are the first generation to grow up with television and computers. They are the largest, richest, and best-educated generation we have ever produced. *High expectations and short-term thinking* characterize their philosophy, with sacrifice and savings almost dropping out of their vocabulary.

This huge chunk of our population tends to look inward for strength and solutions to problems. Flexibility and changeability are common, along with resistance to rigidity and traditions. Boomers will often challenge tested methods and say, "Let's try this." Rather than being joiners, they often resist loyalty to traditional organizations or groups. They prefer innovation and tolerate social diversity. This generation is the first whose careers will not remain stable over their lifetime—some due to their own choice and others to the rapidly changing job market.

Early Boomers born before 1957 were strongly influenced by events of the sixties and seventies, especially the Vietnam War and the accompanying social upheaval within our society. These classic Baby Boomers are the most idealistic and the most easily disappointed of any generation.

Boomers want relevance, asking, "What's in it for me?" They tend to focus on themselves and show an intolerance for mediocrity. Such values can have quite an impact on churches and worship style as well as family life and economics. Can you imagine what happens when one church combines a large group of Baby Boomers with a large group of Survivors (the grandparents of Baby Boomers who were raised during World War I and the Great Depression)? Would they be able to blend or else show signs of combustion? I've seen churches do either or both simultaneously.

Baby Boomers enjoy being actively involved and tend to avoid passive spectator activities. They prefer interacting with others. This is also a very accepting group who will tolerate situations that would easily shock their parents and grandparents. Boomers tend to feel that people should be free to believe whatever they want to about God, religion, sex, lifestyle preferences, or politics. This acceptance is often reflected in warm expressions of love to others.

Perhaps the Baby Boomers are best known by two characteristics: lack of commitment and a desire for instant solutions. One of the criticisms of this group has been that they seem to be committed just to themselves. Even their commitments to marriage are often short lived.[5] The cry of "I want it now" reflects the way in which this generation was raised. Fast food, one-hour cleaners, television programs that solve problems in thirty minutes, ads which constantly reflect "have it now, you deserve it" have all exacted a price.

I have seen these same sentiments frequently expressed by couples who come to me for premarital counseling. One of my assignments is for each of them to write out their goals in life at different stages. I discover that many of them want to start out their life at the same economic level as their parents, even though the older generation spent thirty years to attain that standard of living. And they expect to retire at age fifty with sufficient money to do as they wish.

ঽ

*Fast food, one-hour cleaners, television programs
that solve problems in thirty minutes,
ads which constantly reflect "have it now, you deserve it"
have all exacted a price.*

Some of the Baby Boomers like marriage. The difficulty has been making it work for a lifetime. Half of them will experience at least one divorce, but it doesn't always stop there. One in five will experience two divorces. I have seen a number of these people in my counseling who carry a heavy weight of residue from two family breakups. Unfortunately, about 5 percent will divorce three times or more.[6]

Baby Boomers define a traditional family quite differently than the previous generation. They usually think of a family as two wage earners with one or two children who are cared for outside of the home during the day. They accept couples living together (even Christian couples), as well as their right to have children, to remain childless, to have abortions before or after marriage, and to delay childbearing for many years. They are also more accepting of homosexual relationships, roommates of the opposite sex living in the same household, as well as adoption occurring by a single person or a homosexual couple.

## "BOOMERANG KIDS"

Have you ever heard the term "boomerang kids"? These are young adults who leave home for awhile and then decide to return to live with their parents. Is it because of intense love for their parents and a renewed desire to be part of the household? Usually it's strictly economics. Today some children return home after going through a traumatic divorce, bringing along their own children as well.

Joyce and I have experienced this boomerang effect four times with our own daughter... and we're not even Baby Boomers. After leaving home at nineteen, Sheryl came back a year and a half later. Our daughter said, "Wouldn't you enjoy having me live at home with you again?" Talk about being put on the spot! I didn't know what to say since we happened to be really enjoying our empty nest. But return Sheryl did, with her cat. After four months she moved out again, but this time she left her cat!

Several months later our daughter moved back and then after awhile left again. A few months after that she moved back in with another cat, Alex. Now the dynamics of our home really went through a transition. Our two Shelties saw the new cat as another creature to dominate, but little did they know that Alex had been raised with a large Doberman pinscher. And the cat had dominated the dog! In two days' time, Alex was running the household. When Sheryl left for the fourth time and willed us her cat again, Alex turned out to be one of the best cats I have ever "adopted."

The week after Sheryl left, one of my nephews came to live with us for "two weeks until he found a job." Five months later he moved out and I felt a loss because Mark had filled an empty place in my life. My own son was profoundly retarded. Having a normal boy around the home was a new and fulfilling experience for me.

Then just before our daughter was about to be married she said, "I would really like to live at home the last three months before I'm married, so that we can experience everything together as a family." Translation: "I want to save money!" We learned what revolving doors meant as Sheryl moved in and out. But I wouldn't change that experience for anything.

## THE FOUR "E"S

Baby Boomers had the unique opportunity to be raised in homes which were characterized by four potent factors. And even though some aspects have changed over the years, these four elements continue to have a profound impact.

The first "E" is *Entitlement*. Baby Boom children were given everything they wanted by their parents. Because of this they feel they are entitled to the best for themselves and their own children. Does this fit anyone you know?

*Entertainment* is the second "E." Being the first generation to be raised on television, this ever-present form of entertainment has heavily influenced what they expected elsewhere, including at school and at church. TV has also affected their reading ability and diminished their interest level in other recreational opportunities. They feel entitled to receive enjoyment in life. Does this describe anyone you know?

*Enlightenment* means Baby Boomers feel they can have and enjoy and know it all. They can obtain any information they feel they need. Some parents have pushed their children too much and too fast to devour all of this information.[7] Do you know anyone in this category?

The last "E" stands for *Enchantment*, being enraptured by independence. In many families, the old value of conformity has been replaced by the romance of independence and self-reliance. Unfortunately, such a shift tends to create isolated individuals. We now find that families are tending to focus more on interdependence and mutual support, values which are far more biblical. Do you know anyone who is enchanted with independence?

Where were you in the swirling forties? Where were your parents? What do you remember? How have your values been shaped because of that decade?

## ROLLING DOWNHILL FAST

As we entered the second half of the century, America was like a car rolling downhill, quickly picking up speed. Sometimes we seemed to have lost the braking mechanism. What happened in the fifties? Just about everything. The values people learned during this decade were different from any previous generation. The rate of change in every area of life grew rapidly. Most people wanted to live, enjoy, and consume.

Approximately 60 percent of all families began to experience a middle-class income level. They lived on easy credit with no major concerns about debts. Spending was much more fun than saving. Americans rushed to gratify all of their desires especially in consumer goods. Living in a house in the suburbs with two cars in the garage became the standard.

Working on the assembly line became replaced by corporate life for many. Casual living grew into a way of life. Civil rights gained a foothold during this decade. Family life was hit with huge changes as well. Permissiveness was growing and the belief that "it's my right" had taken hold.

Traditional sex roles were starting to change in the fifties. Women began marrying earlier. Sex appeal was now out in the open. Parents indulged their children with things and even used their kids to compete with others. They wanted to make sure their child had everything he or she needed. Of course the expected outcome came to fruition: the spoiled children demanded all the more.

The innocent spontaneity of childhood was soon usurped by a wealth of planned activities. And parents lost the concern for helping their children develop their own unique individuality. Socialization was reinforced in the schools, namely "getting along with others at all costs." Education was accelerated when Sputnik was launched by Russia. I remember standing outside my dorm one night at Westmont College, my friends and I searching the skies for a glimpse of the first satellite.

Children in the fifties had a multitude of material goods and plenty of opportunities, but in many ways they felt emotionally abandoned. They were taught to expect and to take, but not to give to others. The outcome of this teaching has been felt for the past two decades in our society.[8]

🙶

*Children in the fifties had a multitude of material goods*
*and plenty of opportunities, but in many ways*
*they felt emotionally abandoned.*

Do you see the results of this tumultuous decade anywhere in your life? In your family? How are your values different from those which typified the fifties?

## VIOLENT UPHEAVAL

Many of us would like to just forget the sixties. The children of the previous decade were now adolescents or adults and American values were in an upheaval. The relative stability of the fifties was quickly replaced by the new theme of change. The media itself was transforming the world as we began to discover insane inconsistencies in our society. Those who were completing their value solidification or had already established their values were disillusioned by the hypocrisies, discrepancies, and untruths which they discovered.[9]

Civil rights surged throughout society. A young president was assassinated before our eyes. A bloody war fought far away in a small Asian country by the name of Vietnam fragmented both our political and educational systems, as well as polarized countless family members. Violence was becoming a part of everyday life.

The older folks who had waded through the muddy flats of the depression or else sacrificed for their children during the fifties were often angered to see how these adolescents and young adults were behaving. American youth had the gall to challenge the ethics of hard work, respectability, and competition. They declared the American dream worthless and threw their parents' values right back into their faces.

Behavior once considered off limits in terms of morality, sex, and language became commonplace. Women became more open about their sexuality and older generations could not understand or handle the blatant disregard for morality of this new generation. As a youth pastor in a church for seven years during this decade, I saw such value shifts played out many times.

Generational gaps began to widen into uncrossable chasms. When one generation felt threatened by another, they began to isolate themselves. Because they couldn't understand each other, they began to polarize into factions according to their own values. Examples of this behavior are often seen in the gathering of seniors into their own communities and retirement centers.

Singles apartment complexes and clubs further isolated groups. Grandparents used to be at home helping with their grandchildren, but now this tended to happen only in more rural areas. And fewer and fewer farming families survived because of technology and falling farm prices.

Blame became rampant. Somebody had to be responsible for this blitzkrieg of American values. Parents blamed schools and schools blamed parents for the wealth of problems. Liberals were blamed as well as the Civil Rights movement and the politicians. Our country's spending policies came into question as society became more concerned with erasing poverty.

Children gained more power and expressed their opinions in family decisions. We were dominated by youth who yelled obscenities and refused to be ignored. They became the "now generation" and were overindulged. A tremendous gap emerged between the values of adolescents and their parents. Young folks didn't see why they had to contribute to society because they were catered to so much. Those who came from an affluent background believed, "Let others take care of them."[10]

What did you do in the sixties? Whom did you listen to and whom did you believe in? Did you have any heroes or heroines? How did you interact with people older than you? What did you want out of life during the sixties? How have your values solidified or changed since that decade?

## THE DECADE OF DISINTEGRATION

The seventies seemed to be a decade of disintegration for people in their fifties and sixties. Their good life was disappearing. The news was flooded with ugly words like "inflation, pollution, crime, the war that divided our nation, the stock market, the generation gap, immorality, riots, traffic, strikes against the public, racism, and skyjacking."[11]

Much of the common confusion once again centered around values. Children who were ten during this decade received a big hit from this upheaval. It seemed as though a new culture was being superimposed upon an old one. Young adults seemed wary of the world they were entering, their optimism dulled by seeing the Vietnam War constantly on TV.

Discovering how the government officials had lied and then living through the heartbreak of Watergate didn't help this generation overcome their pessimism. The effects of Watergate and the coverups had a profound effect on the moral development of children in our country. They learned that the importance of honesty, trust, responsibility, and truthfulness is superseded by that of power, money, pull, and position. They learned not to trust anyone in authority—be they politicians, scientists, educators, police, or even leaders of the church.

The seventies also saw a search for spiritual fulfillment by those who hungered for certainty. But modern day cults began to emerge which reflected broader values from around the world. When a country undergoes a significant distortion in cultural values, cults tend to proliferate.[12]

People became even more sexually promiscuous and the drug culture escalted, which further shook an already wobbly economic system. The good life of the previous decades was slipping as we discovered there were shortages after all.

## A CHRISTIAN COUNTERCULTURE

What will be the outcome for the generations of the eighties and nineties? What values will we end up reflecting and what will the next generation reflect? Christians are called to be counter-culture people. God wants us to be deeply concerned for those around us rather than committed to individualism. We are called to be people of character rather than accumulators of earthly goods.

When I myself look at this brief sketch of history, the rapidity of change seems almost unmanageable. Can we find any way to stabilize ourselves as individuals and families? Can we find any way to resist the overwhelming pressures of society? Is there any way to pattern our lives differently so that we are less a product of our culture?

Yes, as expressed quite simply in the words of Jesus. As individuals and as family members, our calling is clearly stated in three very basic concepts:

1. Don't be conformed to this world but be transformed.
2. Be the salt of this world. Refine it. Influence it. Purify it. "You are the salt of the earth, but if salt has lost its taste—its

strength, its quality—how can its saltness be restored? It is not good for anything any longer but to be thrown out and trodden under foot by men" (Mt 5:13, AMP).

3. Be a brilliant light to show others who God is. "You are the light of the world. A city set on a hill cannot be hid. Nor do men light a lamp and put it under a peck-measure but on a lamp stand, and it gives light to all in the house. Let your light so shine before men that they may see your moral excellence and your praiseworthy, noble and good deeds, and recognize and honor and praise and glorify your Father Who is in heaven" (Mt 5:14-16, AMP).

When Jesus Christ comes into our lives, we are called to step outside of the circle of cultural influence and reflect a new standard—one which may not always be appreciated or respected. Any minority population will struggle with this lack of acceptance. Our character, values, and morals will come into conflict with our society.

The apostle Paul carried this message to other parts of the Mediterranean world. As he wrote in his letter to the Romans:

I appeal to you therefore, brethren, and beg of you in view of [all] the mercies of God, to make a decisive dedication of your bodies—presenting all your members and faculties—as a living sacrifice, holy... and well pleasing to God, which is your reasonable (rational, intelligent) service and spiritual worship.

Do not be conformed to this world—this age, fashioned after and adapted to its external, superficial customs. But be transformed... by the [entire] renewal of your mind—by its new ideals and its new attitude—so that you may prove [for yourselves] what is the good and acceptable and perfect will of God, even the thing which is good and acceptable and perfect [in His sight for you]. (Rom 12:1-2, AMP)

Think for a moment. How can you and your family reflect this biblical value system? What can your church do to make a difference in the world, along with your community, your schools, and your government? If you want a cause and a challenge for your life, a way to direct your energy outward rather than inward, the opportunity certainly lies near at hand.

I have seen many people in my generation and Baby Boomers and Baby Busters willing to make a difference. Twenty to thirty-year-olds from my church congregation joined a group called City Dwellers. In some of the worst spots of Hollywood, they serve the people in both action and word—among the hookers, street people, gay prostitutes, and poor Hispanic families.

❧

*If you want a cause and a challenge for your life, a way to direct your energy outward rather than inward, the opportunity certainly lies near at hand.*

I have a young doctor friend who can't wait to finish his residency so he can work with poor families in a third world country. One of my associates hits sixty-five this year and will quit his counseling practice and use his social security income to support himself on the mission field training others to counsel.

The Jensens sold their large expensive home, reinvested in a smaller one which proved adequate and used the money to purchase two smaller older homes near them for both sets of parents. They had decided that they wanted them close at hand for their children to benefit from extensive exposure to them as well as to be able to monitor their health and day-to-day functioning themselves rather then seeing them become isolated in a retirement community.

I have friends who take their children with them each Sunday afternoon to their church where over three hundred homeless gather to be fed and assisted in whatever way possible. These children are learning at a young age to minister as well as discover another side to life. Not everyone lives in a home or has sufficient food and a job. Their level of appreciation has definitely been changing.

Recently my wife's cousin and his wife who are with Campus Crusade sold their home and moved to Mongolia to bring the gospel of Jesus Christ to these people. They described Christmas in this foreign land: "No lights, no trees, no special food, no cele-bration, for these people don't know about this special occasion. We're learning to eat their food and live as they do."

I know a family that has a savings account in the name of each of their children. Both parents and children match each other in the amount they put into this account each month, beginning on the child's tenth birthday. It's not for a car, nor for college, but to pay for a summer mission trip when each child turns sixteen. As they travel to some third world country and serve alongside the missionaries, their lives have been directed more toward fulfilling our call to servanthood. Yes, we can all be different and have a profound impact upon our culture.

ð

## BRINGING IT HOME

Your parents attempted to impart their values to you. Have you ever sat down and tried to remember what they held dear, what they believed about certain topics or areas of life? Spend a few minutes reflecting on how your parents' values have affected and influenced your life and how you are passing on your values to your family members.

Listed below are several important life issues. You may want to follow this procedure with additional topics you think are impor-tant. Think carefully about what your father and mother (or another significant person) believed about each issue. Then com-plete the statement which begins with "My mom/dad always said...," as it pertains to each issue.

Then summarize your position on each issue by completing the statement which begins, "What I believe now is..." Then com-plete the statement "What I say to my children is..." Look to see how your values and beliefs parallel your parents' and what you say to your own children.

You may want to have your spouse complete this exercise as well, and then ask your children to respond to the questions based on what they hear you saying. You may be amazed at the varied responses you get! Consider the responses in light of the decade in which each person grew up.

## WHAT MY PARENTS AND I BELIEVE

1. *About money:*
   Examples: Mom always said, "Money is to be spent. Enjoy it when you have it. But when you don't have it, don't spend it. Don't ever use a credit card." Dad always said, "Money is hard to come by. Save it!"

   My mom/dad always said, _____.

   What I believe now is _____.

   What I say to my children is _____.

2. *About food:*
   Examples: Dad always said, "Be sure you eat the right foods." Mom always said, "Be sure you clean up your plate."

   My mom/dad always said, _____.

   What I believe now is _____.

   What I say to my children is _____.

3. *About sex:*
   Examples: Mom always said, "Sex is a gift from God. But it has its place only in marriage. Be sure you wait." Dad always said, "Watch out."

   My mom/dad always said, _____.

   What I believe now is _____.

   What I say to my children is _____.

4. *About the opposite sex:*
   Examples: Dad always said, "Women are too emotional and flighty." Mom always said, "Men just aren't emotional enough."

   My mom/dad always said, _____.

   What I believe now is _____.

   What I say to my children is _____.

5. *About Jesus:*

Examples: Mom always said, "Your faith in Christ is your most important decision in life." Dad always said, "Always let him guide you."

My mom/dad always said, _____.

What I believe now is _____.

What I say to my children is _____.

6. *About work:*

Examples: Dad always said, "You're not old enough to have a job yet." Mom always said, "Do the best you can and be loyal to your employer."

My mom/dad always said, _____.

What I believe now is _____.

What I say to my children is _____.

7. *About school:*

Examples: Mom always said, "Do your best and I'll be proud of you regardless of your grades." Dad always said, "Why go to college? Not everyone needs it."

My mom/dad always said, _____.

What I believe now is _____.

What I say to my children is _____.

8. *About career:*

Examples: Dad always said, "Just get a job that makes money." Mom always said, "Find something you enjoy."

My mom/dad always said, _____.

What I believe now is _____.

What I say to my children is _____.

9. *About self-esteem:*

Examples: Mom always said, "Don't be too hard on yourself." Dad always said, "I wasn't much good."

My mom/dad always said, _____.

What I believe now is _____.

What I say to my children is _____.

10. *About fears:*

Examples: Mom always said, "There is a lot to be afraid of in this world." Dad always said, "I'm afraid you won't turn out like Mom and I want."

My mom/dad always said, _____.

What I believe now is _____.

What I say to my children is _____.

11. *About anger:*

Examples: Mom always said, "Don't get angry. It will get you into trouble." Dad always said, "When you're angry, let it rip. I do."

My mom/dad always said, _____.

What I believe now is _____.

What I say to my children is _____.

# LOOKING IN THE REARVIEW MIRROR

HAVE YOU EVER BEEN ON A TRIP OUT WEST? You fight your way out of city traffic, cross the great Mississippi River, then cruise along an endless stretch of highway through the wheat fields of Kansas. As you drive through Colorado, the terrain begins to change dramatically. The prairies give way to steppe lands, then to the forests and foothills.

Suddenly the Rocky Mountains loom in the distance. Higher and higher you climb as the air becomes thinner and thinner. The dramatic scenery often makes it difficult to keep your eyes on the road. The spectacular canyons of Utah take your breath away. Finally your overheated car chugs past parched desert land of Nevada, through the lush greenery of California, and finally to the precipitous cliffs of the Pacific.

Living in a family can feel somewhat like that westward journey. The scenery keeps changing with each season of life. The boring plains of daily drudgery give way to mountainous difficulties which suddenly come out of nowhere. Desert dryness and impatience end in overheated arguments, vast canyons seem impossible to cross, and intermittent pastures of warm affection keep you going, until you finally look out over the ocean of eternity.

On such a stressful journey, we can sometimes forget where we've come from. Looking in the rearview mirror from time to time is one way to refresh our memory and improve our perspective of the present.

You may have come from a "traditional family" made up of two parents and a number of children. But what used to be nonconventional isn't anymore. The family is being redefined. Dual career, Mom working and Dad at home, blended families, single parents, the never-married parent—all of these variations and more are becoming accepted forms of family life. Family used to mean just those related by blood or marriage, but now a family may be made up of a group of friends who help and support one another in times of need.

Tina shared with me her own family experience. "I think I experienced every variation of family life in my twenty-eight years," she said. "I was born into a traditional nuclear family, then lived in a single-parent family after my parents divorced. A few years later I became a member of a blended family when Mom married a man with two children. I lived as a single person for awhile, joined a commune, adopted a baby and raised her by myself for three years, and then married. What's left to experience?"

Tina isn't alone. Many people experience different terrain in their family journey. Each of us passes through various stages as we grow. Families do the same. Some phases of family life are easier than others.

## SCENERY FROM THE PAST

When we begin families of our own, our relationships to those individuals and other friends can easily become closer than those with our family of origin. But we will also continue to relate to the family from which we came. We carry a lot of the scenery from our growing up years into the present.

We don't spring out of the air fully formed. We are all rooted to a vast underground network of family relationships, family patterns, family rules, and roles that are evident in the family personality and the family system. And we carry this network with us into any new family we form. The family we grew up in, the family that teaches us more than we'll ever know, is our family of origin. And when we leave to make our own way in the world or to marry, we attempt to re-create that family in some way.[1]

ક્ર

## *We "inherit" behaviors, interactions, roles, and perceptions of others from our family.*

We all tend to repeat what we know best—including certain behaviors that we learned in our family of origin. I catch myself walking through the house turning off the lights in various rooms and echoing the words of my father, "Let's not leave the lights on when we're not in the room." We "inherit" behaviors, interactions, roles, and perceptions of others from our family.

Think about it—whom do you echo in your life? Take a moment and reflect on some of the typical behaviors or phrases of your parents and siblings (or any other significant person that you considered family). On a separate sheet of paper, list the names of three of these people along with five common behaviors or statements that you remember.

Do you see any of these showing up yet in your family life? If not, just give them time. Either these or some others will. Some families play out certain behaviors at dinnertime or every Sunday after church, rituals that continue for years. Then the children marry and scatter across the country. Two decades later, one of those same rituals has been resurrected in one of the newer households. But this family seldom stops to determine why this ritual "just happened to be reestablished."

Your family instilled in you a pattern of thoughts, expressions, and behaviors. Some are like seeds which may lie dormant for years and then suddenly spring into life. Some may be negative, some neutral, and some positive. We all need to do some "weeding" in each generation in an effort to eliminate the negative from overwhelming our positive legacy; we need to fertilize the good seeds so they will flourish and benefit everyone.[2]

## FAMILY SCRIPTS

In Hollywood, California, the movie capital of the world, the major studios have a department called major casting. This group is primarily responsible for finding particular people to play certain roles. A call goes out and many people come in for auditions. The trick is to meld the various parts into a believable and smoothly functioning cast.

A family is like one of the major studios. Families inevitably cast their members in somewhat predictable roles out of necessity and convenience. But instead of being temporary, some of these casting decisions end up being permanent. Some roles are good, some are healthy. Others are not.

Even though you may not like the role you had as a child, it was deeply engraved on your memory. You are very familiar with your own script and how the other family members played different parts. These roles will tend to follow you the rest of your life unless you engage in some major surgery. You will replay these same scripts over and over again. And whether you realize it or not, you tend to be attracted to others who play and let you play the roles you know best.

Roles give your family an identity, some sense of balance. When one person makes a radical change or suddenly leaves, that intricate balance is immediately upset. Unless some sort of regrouping and recasting is accomplished, the family is in danger of going out of business.

Some roles have prescribed duties such as mother, father, or grandparent. Each different culture usually has its own script for some of the formal roles of a family. But are you aware that every family plays out a series of informal roles as well? These more spontaneous and casual scripts develop in order to maintain the balance within a family and reduce tension. Some of the roles occur because of unique personality differences and birth order characteristics.[3]

Let's consider a few of these informal roles to help you better understand your past and present family members.

*A family usually has a **mediator**, individuals they turn to when a problem needs to be settled.* Others see them as people who are fair. In most families, this person is a parent, but in some it could be a child. This individual is a problem-solver. Fred told me, "I feel like a court arbitrator. I am constantly helping my family resolve their issues. Oh well, at least it brings a sense of calm to our family."

Did your family of origin enlist the help of a mediator? How well did they do their job? If no one qualified, did chaos reign? Who is the mediator in your present family? How comfortable are you with this present arrangement? What if something happened to your current family mediator? Would the other family members be able to resolve serious problems otherwise? If a family doesn't have a mediator, others may jump in to reduce tension, such as the clown, the scapegoat, the crybaby, or the enabler.[4]

***Enablers** provide emotional and relational nurture and a sense of belonging.* Since they usually want to preserve family unity at all costs, they often go to extremes to keep the peace. Their goal is to eliminate all conflicts and help everyone get along. Unfortunately, conflicts are more often buried and perpetuated rather than resolved. Enablers tend to be driven by fear. They are afraid that family members cannot survive without their efforts, as well as afraid of being abandoned by others.

Jim was a counselee who described his role so well. He said, "I feel like I belong to a United Nations peacekeeping team whose job is to put out all the small wars which erupt throughout the world and then maintain the peace."

Was there an enabler in your family of origin? If so, who? If you were the enabler, do you carry any resentments because of the pricetag attached to such a role? Can you think of any conflicts that got ceremoniously swept under the rug? Who has assumed that role in your present family? Can you see the underlying fear that motivates such behavior? Would you like to make any changes in how this role functions in your own life?

*The **doer** in your family was the one who said, "Give it to me and it will get done."* They have an overdeveloped sense of responsibility which often drives them unmercifully. They provide most of the maintenance functions in a family. Doers are also called the "responsible ones" who make sure bills are paid, people are fed, clothed, chauffeured, and so on. Sometimes they take this sense of responsibility too far and try to orchestrate the lives of other family members.

We usually remember the doers in our family of origin because they always took up the slack. Who assumed this role in your growing-up years? How did your family benefit from their efforts? Did that person carry that sense of responsibility gracefully or did he or she tend to whine about the unfair distribution of labor in the family? Any doers in your present family? Do you like this present arrangement? If not, what changes would you like to make?

· ❧

### *We usually remember the doers in our family of origin because they always took up the slack.*

*Still others are the family **clowns** who bring humor into the family through play, fun, and even silliness.* They're always joking and cutting up, especially when confronted by difficult situations. Their fun-loving nature is a great cover for any deep pain or isolation. Humor brings the attention that clowns may feel unable to merit in other areas. Hank told me, "I always got a lot of attention. Even when Mom was really upset with me, I'd get off the hook. I could always make her laugh."

Clowns are usually the most lovable ones, but often at great cost to themselves. Any clowns in your past family? Do they still make you laugh and feel good? What about your present family? What do you see as some of the results of having a clown in the family?

***Manipulators** are the clever controllers in the family who learned early on how to get others to do what they wanted.* They know how to seduce, to charm, to play sick, or to appear weak. They can and often do use every trick in the book to get their way.

Think back. Anyone come to mind who played that role during your childhood years? What feelings arise if you were among those being manipulated? Any unresolved anger or resentment? Do you experience manipulation in your present family? Is this role clearly focused in anyone in particular? How do you feel about this person?

*Critics are the fault-finding negativists in the family who always see the glass as half-empty instead of half-full.* Their behavior is characterized by sarcasm, hurtful teasing, and complaining. They prefer to use their energy to tear others down than build themselves up. Critics are not very pleasant to be around, but some families end up enduring them.

Think about your past family. What about Mom? Dad? Siblings? Grandparents? Children? Any painful memories of unfair criticism? Some families are so permeated with fault-finding that not even the tiniest mistake escapes notice. Did you ever feel like you were walking around on eggshells? How about your present family? In what ways is this person fulfilling a destructive or a useful role? What can be done to improve this situation?

*Scapegoats are the family victims who actually end up as the family blame-collector.* Their misbehavior makes everyone else in the family look so good that they can say, "If it weren't for him or her, our family would be all right." If the scapegoat tries to change roles, other family members are not likely to let him or her off the hook. As long as they're around, they have someone to blame for their own irresponsibility.

Even though scapegoats don't seem to care what's going on, they actually tend to be the most sensitive people in the family. Because they are sensitive, they notice the hurt in the family, and often act out the resulting stress through misbehavior. Their negative actions may be a cry to the rest of the family to do something about the hurtful things that are happening in the home.

When scapegoats are the children in the family, they often feel responsible for keeping their parents' marriage together. If they sense problems between the adults, misbehavior may be used to unify the parents in attacking them.

Scapegoating is very destructive. Unfortunately these victims learn when to take the blame and sometimes purposefully create situations in which they can be blamed in order to reduce tension in the family. Scapegoating can be predicted to some degree. If it happened in your family of origin, it will tend to be carried on in your present family.

Only children tend to end up in this particular role since they have fewer inner resources than the adults. Scapegoating may also be determined by the birth order of the parents. First-born parents are likely to protect their own firstborn; second-born parents will protect their secondborn, and so on. A child from a difficult labor or a handicapped child may be protected and the other children are cast into the scapegoat role.[5]

Did someone serve as a scapegoat in your family of origin? Can you see how they collected the family garbage, even unintentionally? What useful purpose did they fulfill? How do you think they may have suffered as a result? Who is the usual scapegoat in your present family? Has that person ever expressed a desire to step out of that role? Do any changes need to happen in this area of your family life?[6]

## WHO MAKES THE CASTING DECISIONS?

How do roles become assigned to family members? Many different factors may come into play, such as family expectations, birth order, gender, or the changing needs of the family. Even physical resemblance or personality characteristics which remind people of another relative may play a significant part in assigning roles.

Have you ever been compared to or compared someone to a family member? "You're just like your father." "You look and talk just like Uncle Lyle." "You remind me so much of my sister when she was your age." Naming a child after someone will also tend to generate comparisons. Even the selection of a particular name may cast a person in a role.[7]

Often the various roles hold a family structure together. Some families are so inflexible that they don't allow for any change in the assigned roles. The children are then more likely to perpetuate those same roles in their future family. I've seen the youngest child in a family referred to as "my little baby" by her parents— even well into her thirties! Do you have any memories like this involving yourself or your siblings?

Fortunately, some families become aware of their tendency to cast people in various roles and decide to allow family members greater flexibility. This is a healthy move! Sometimes pet names or nicknames are purposely dropped at a certain age. Children may ask to be called by a different name or even declare they are tired of being the one to solve all the problems. Parents often make a declaration of what they will continue to do and what they will no longer be doing within the family.

While you cannot change your past, you do have something to say about the family that you have or will have. Looking in your rearview mirror will help you determine what you want and what you don't want for the future. Are you comfortable with the roles you play in relationship to your spouse, your children, or other significant people in your life? What ways of responding would you like to give up or change? Why not write out the role you would like to play and begin to rehearse a different script? It's worth considering.

One of my counselees shared with me his decision to change. Stu said, "I began to envision not being a critic anymore. I actually wrote out in advance how I really wanted to respond, wrote out positive encouraging comments, practiced saying them out loud, prayed about the change... and in time it worked! The hardest part was being consistent and not letting others force me back into the old role."

We are heavily influenced by our past upbringing and we do tend to repeat patterns of parenting—whether we want to or not. But we can choose to glean the best from our past experience and toss out the rest. Why not use the best and the worst lessons from your family of origin as fodder for the future? Evaluate and then select and envision how you would like to respond in your own family.

Remember that when you were a child, you saw your parents through childish eyes. Now you have the opportunity to reevaluate what occurred in your childhood through an adult's eyes.

Much of what you remember may be only brief and vague sketches about how you felt about things. Unfortunately, too many people tend to fixate on the negative experiences rather than balance them out by discovering what went well.

❧

> *Remember that when you were a child,*
> *you saw your parents through childish eyes.*
> *Now you have the opportunity to reevaluate what*
> *occurred in your childhood through an adult's eyes.*

Many parents tend either to repeat patterns thoughtlessly, or else to strongly react against the way they were raised and end up overcompensating. In either case, you are still not in charge of what you are doing in your family. Why not take charge by determining what worked, what didn't, and what you want for your own family?

## DOOMED TO REPEAT THE PAST?

You might feel predestined to be a certain way because of your experiences. Your future is never cast in concrete. I have seen people who were raised in abusive homes who did not turn out to be abusers themselves. They chose to reject that style of parenting and learned not to assimilate abusive behavior into their own lives.

Counseling is often required to help us work through such a shift. I've found that people change the most when they appropriate the spiritual resources available to them. When a person allows Jesus Christ to invade their life and redevelop them as they pray and incorporate Scripture into their attitudes and behaviors, growth and significant change can occur. Spiritual transformation can have more impact on your family and parenting than any past experience or knowledge.

The adopted son of former President Ronald Reagan, shared his struggle and journey of acceptance in his autobiography, entitled *Michael Reagan: On the Outside Looking In.* "I grew up convinced that my birth mother gave me away because she didn't love me and I was bad.... It is only in the light of recent discovery that I have come to realize that my memory has been selfishly selective. My parents—birth as well as adoptive—were not villains."[8]

Reagan's story illustrates someone who was able to challenge his childhood memories. By editing out the distortions, his perception was fairly objective. For many years, he fixated on just one powerfully negative experience of his life, feeling abandoned by his mother. And every time he thought about it, the pain become more intense and more deeply entrenched in his life.

Soon we begin to generalize such feelings and fear a repetition of this past pain in our current situation. Our brain takes our experiences and creates a "memory trace" that can never be erased, though we can successfully block it out. The further we are from the actual experience, the greater the probability of distortion. We become locked in on one part of it, reinforce it, and disregard the rest. *Our memory is always selective.* Michael Reagan did this, as he later realized:

I was three days old when I was adopted. Around four years ago, I received in the mail from Dad's former business manager a hundred-dollar War Bond accompanied by a letter that said the bond was "in celebration of your coming home." The bond was bought on April 4, 1945, by Ronald Reagan for Michael Edward Reagan. Receiving that bond took me back forty years in time. I realized that my dad must have loved me dearly. If only I had known it during my childhood.[9]

The intensity and pain of his plight are further illustrated in a recurring nightmare in which Michael Reagan's family is about to enter heaven—all except him.

The gates open, and I step aside to let my family precede me. Suddenly God steps in front of me, placing His burning hand on my chest. My son Cameron turns around. "Come on, Dad," he says impatiently and starts toward me. But God is still halting my progress. He turns his back to me and takes out my Book of Life from deep within his white robes. He opens the book and shows my family a page. His voice booms in my ears. "Michael Reagan is not allowed into heaven because he is illegitimate."[10]

While focusing on his mother's act of giving him away, Reagan had ignored another crucial fact. He had been selected, chosen, wanted, and accepted by his adoptive parents. Every believer has also been adopted by God. Unfortunately, many Christians have chosen not to focus upon that life-changing truth.

## EDITING OUR MENTAL TAPES

How is your memory selective? Have any events been pumped up by injections of mental and emotional steroids? Even though others did not experience exactly what you did, could they perhaps help to fill in the vacant spaces? Others who lived through the same events tend to experience them differently.

One of the typical tricks of the mind is to make negative assumptions. Approaching an event or a memory with preconceived ideas often distorts reality. Our assumptions can block out any incoming information which doesn't fit the preconceived idea. And like a heat-seeking missile, our minds tend to go straight toward whatever we expected to find.

If the experience was a negative one, can you find anything positive about it that could be salvaged? Are you sure anyone intended to hurt you in that way? Are you sure the other person involved is even aware of what you remember as a negative experience? If you had not had this experience in your life, how do you think you would be different today?

If you didn't have this experience to blame for your present situation, what else could you attribute this to? Randy Carlson offers this sound advice:

When things go wrong in our lives we are sometimes quick to put the finger on Mom and Dad, figuring that if somehow they had done things differently we wouldn't have turned out the way we did, or wouldn't be struggling with the problems we face. Some people spend time digging up the dirt of the past in order to sling mud at someone else. But as the saying goes, "He who slings mud loses ground!"

It is time to set the record straight and look at the positive impact of the parenting you received. Let us give credit where credit is due.[11]


## SHIFTING INTO REVERSE GEAR

If you do feel shackled by a traumatic memory, perhaps these suggestions will help. Try to identify the specific loss or disappointment and grieve over it. Consider how you have related to others because of that personal trauma. Discover what else happened in your life that was positive and what you have now that is positive. Make a commitment through your relationship with Jesus Christ not to let your present life be dictated by your memory of your past.

Work to develop a vision for your family life and follow it. When you have a goal in mind, you may find yourself swimming upstream, but you can still move forward by cooperating with God's power at work in your life. When you envision your life as it could be, the odds are less likely to appear overwhelming. You will still recognize obstacles, but won't dwell on them so much. Focusing on how things could be will enable you to experience today and anticipate tomorrow.

ै।

*I often counsel husbands and wives who don't feel that they love their partners. Fortunately, some of them want to develop their love, but are stumped as to how to make that happen.*

I often counsel husbands and wives who don't feel that they love their partners. Fortunately, some of them want to develop their love, but are stumped as to how to make that happen. My advice is always the same: "Let's imagine together what it would be like if you did love your partner. Describe how you would feel about him/her, how you would treat him/her, think about him/her, support him/her, and defend him/her before others." And so we discuss this together for a while.

Then I usually say, "I would like you to write out in detail this vision you have created for loving your partner and read it over several times a day. I would like you to pray about each facet of this vision, and ask God to make this love come alive within you. And then I want you to behave toward your partner as though you actually did love him or her. Do this for the next month. You'll see a difference."

Chuck Swindoll helps us to understand what developing a vision really entails:

> Vision is the ability to see God's presence, to perceive God's power, to focus on God's plan in spite of the obstacles.... Vision is the ability to see above and beyond the majority. Vision is perception—reading the presence and power of God into one's circumstances. I sometimes think of vision as looking at life through the lens of God's eyes, seeing situations as He sees them. Too often we see things not as they are, but as we are. Think about that. Vision has to do with looking at life with a divine perspective, reading the scene with God in clear focus.
>
> Whoever wants to live differently in "the system" must correct his or her vision.[12]

Scripture tells us that our minds need to be changed before we can see with God's eyes: "Do not be conformed to this world.... But be transformed (changed) by the [entire] renewal of your mind—by its new ideals and its new attitude—so that you may prove [for yourselves] what is the good and acceptable and perfect will of God, even the thing which is good and acceptable and perfect..." (Rom 12:2, AMP). How well does your family life reflect this transformation?

Dr. Ray Guarendi talks about using "reverse resolve," which means choosing to do the opposite of the way you were raised. He includes the stories of a few parents who describe how they reached such a decision in their own lives:

> "In our house, children were seen and not heard, so I have been careful to listen to my own children.... I knew when I had

children I wanted to play and vacation with them because I had always wanted to do that as I was growing up.... My worst times with my parents were listening to them quarrel early in the morning. I hated to hear anyone raising their voice or insulting another person; so, I try to be very careful not to call names and to try to criticize in such a way that no one loses face."

"The worst time of my life was the death of my little brother. He was two and I was four. I was his little mother and even at such a young age, I felt a great void in my life. Also, the knowledge that, according to my parents, the wrong child died affected my life in many ways. The unloved feelings that I experienced, however, helped me in that I grew up determined that any children I had would *never* experience that feeling."

"I was the last of seven, of which four survived. My father was forty-three when I was born. By the time I got interested in sports at the ten/eleven-year-old age, he didn't have time for me. I wanted to do things, but he didn't have time. I said to myself then that if I ever had children of my own, I would give them a great deal of support—spiritual or whatever they needed—and I would be with them.

"I can vividly remember the day my dad died. I came home from the hospital and there was a picture of both my parents on the bureau. I went up to the picture, and I looked up at my dad and said, 'Dad, it is a shame, but I never knew you.' I made a vow to myself that this would never occur in my family, and I do spend time with the kids."

"My father was raised in an environment where sons were considered an asset and daughters a liability. Sons were a measure of a man's virility, daughters a weakness in his manhood. My worst times [as a child] were a result of the beliefs he had. I remember a family reunion where the men had gathered and were teasing one of the men for having his fourth daughter and no sons. My dad spoke up and bragged that he had three sons. He never mentioned he had a daughter.

"The impact of those attitudes affected my determination to

be better and amount to more. It made me my own person. It also affected the way our children were raised. Their sex did not enter into any decision. The only thing that mattered was that, if it was a chore, it needed attention, and if it was an activity, it only mattered whether he or she wanted to try it—that's all."[13]

After tortuous years of chaos, the children of alcoholics often firmly resolve to create a different family life. Here's the story of one such man:

Terms like "dysfunctional family" may be fairly new, but I am well-acquainted with the pain that dysfunction can cause. My drunken father was anything but a hero. My mother did her best to love my brother, sister, and me but my parents didn't have a real marriage. They didn't have a relationship. At best, they had an existence. I never once saw my father hug my mother, let alone ever experience having him hug me. I cannot remember a single time when my father took me somewhere alone and spent time with me.

I grew up on a one-hundred-and-fifty-acre dairy farm just outside a small town in Michigan. Everyone knew everyone else and, of course, everyone knew about my father and his drinking. My teenage buddies made jokes about him and I laughed at them, too, trying to cover up the hurt and pain.

Sometimes I'd go out to the barn and find my mother lying in the manure behind the cows, beaten so badly she couldn't get up. I hated my father for treating her so cruelly, and to avenge that treatment I would do everything I could to humiliate or punish him. When he would get drunk and threaten to beat my mother, or if he were in a drunken stupor when my friends were planning to come over, I would drag him out to the barn, tie him to a stall, and leave him there to "sleep it off."

As I got older—and bigger and stronger—I did this more and more often. Sometimes I'd be so enraged, I would tie my father's feet with a rope that ended with a noose around his neck. I actually hoped that he would choke himself while trying to get free.

I recall finding my father drunk and flying into such a rage that I tried to sober him up by shoving him fully dressed into a bathtub full of water. In the struggle, I found myself holding my dad's head under water. If someone hadn't stopped me (to this day I'm not sure who it was), I would have probably drowned him.

I grew up not really knowing how to give or receive love. As I went through high school and on to college, I was hungry to experience a family where real love was present.[14]

You may be surprised to know that the author of those words is Josh McDowell, an internationally known speaker with Campus Crusade and author of more than thirty-five books. His book, *How to Be a Hero to Your Kids*, reflects the transforming power of Jesus Christ at work in a person's heart.

All of these parents have demonstrated "reverse resolve." They first assessed what occurred in their childhood and made a conscious choice to move a new direction in their own family. Making a definite decision differs from just desiring to avoid parental mistakes. These parents refused to allow their childhood to dictate how they would function in the present and future.

Guàrendi defines "reverse resolve" in this way: "It is the determination to use painful memories to fuel the drive to become genuinely good parents despite a lack of childhood training. As these parents left the direct influence of their parents, they were able to reinterpret past events, no longer being controlled by them, but turning them into vivid guidelines for what not to do at all costs with their own families. In essence, they made past pain work to their family's present benefit."[15]

A person who makes such a resolve is a combination survivor and innovator. Some of you readers came from very positive families with little to sift through and discard. Others did not. But even though your past cannot be changed, you are never limited by what you experienced. How does this renewal occur?

1. Change begins with the desire for your family to be different.
2. Change takes shape as you capture a vision or a dream of how you want to be different.

3. Change is initiated when you take the steps to evict those responses from your life which you no longer want. This step-by-step process often takes months, but by applying the suggestions in this book, you can make it happen.
4. Change proceeds as you gain new insight through learning from others, from books, scriptural teaching, and the behavior and attitudes you see modelled in healthy families.
5. Change happens as you pray and envision Jesus Christ empowering you to be different and learn to accept the transformation which the Holy Spirit's presence can bring.

## BRINGING IT HOME

The following inventory can help you to evaluate where you have been and what is going on right now in your life. If you are married, it is important for both you and your spouse to answer these questions and discuss them together. If your children are adults, ask them to do the same. You may want to make additional copies to use with other family members.

Part One reviews your parents' marriage relationship, as well as your own. Perhaps your parents divorced or you were raised with a stepparent. Allow yourself latitude as you evaluate the specific marital model you experienced. Part Two focuses on their parenting skills and yours. Part Three helps you assess your past sibling relationships and your own children's relationships. Taking a close look at each of these areas will help you to evaluate how healthy your relationships have been in the past and are in the present.

Use the scale of zero to five to evaluate each statement. For your past relationships, circle the number. For your present relationships, mark an "X" to indicate your response.

0 = "rarely, if ever"
3 = "some of the time"
5 = "most of the time"

## Part One:
### The Marital Relationship

0 ——————— 3 ——————— 5   1. My parents had a strong, loving relationship.

0 ——————— 3 ——————— 5      We have a strong, loving relationship.

0 ——————— 3 ——————— 5   2. My parents were interested in each other.

0 ——————— 3 ——————— 5      We are interested in each other.

0 ——————— 3 ——————— 5   3. My parents had fun together on a regular basis.

0 ——————— 3 ——————— 5      We have fun together on a regular basis.

0 ——————— 3 ——————— 5   4. My parents spent private time together.

0 ——————— 3 ——————— 5      We spend private time together.

0 ——————— 3 ——————— 5   5. My parents had a healthy sexual relationship.

0 ——————— 3 ——————— 5      We have a healthy sexual relationship.

0 ——————— 3 ——————— 5   6. My parents treated each other like best friends.

0 ——————— 3 ——————— 5      We treat each other like best friends.

0 ——————— 3 ——————— 5   7. My parents communicated honestly and directly.

0 ——————— 3 ——————— 5      We communicate honestly and directly.

0 ——————— 3 ——————— 5   8. My parents socialized together.

0 ——————— 3 ——————— 5      We socialize together.

0 ——————— 3 ——————— 5   9. My parents resolved conflicts effectively.

0 ——————— 3 ——————— 5    We resolve conflicts effectively.

0 ——————— 3 ——————— 5  10. My parents had an effective method of financial planning and action.

0 ——————— 3 ——————— 5    We have an effective method of financial planning and action.

0 ——————— 3 ——————— 5  11. My parents maintained a home in a mutually satisfactory way.

0 ——————— 3 ——————— 5    We maintain a home in a mutually satisfactory way.

0 ——————— 3 ——————— 5  12. My parents had mutual interests.

0 ——————— 3 ——————— 5    We have mutual interests.

0 ——————— 3 ——————— 5  13. My parents showed their affection through words, gestures, and deeds.

0 ——————— 3 ——————— 5    We show our affection through words, gestures, and deeds.

0 ——————— 3 ——————— 5  14. My parents seemed willing to compromise.

0 ——————— 3 ——————— 5    We are willing to compromise.

0 ——————— 3 ——————— 5  15. My parents were faithful to each other, to the best of my knowledge.

0 ——————— 3 ——————— 5    We are faithful to each other.

If you have any low responses for your parents, do you know why that happened and what they might have done differently to correct the difficulty? If you have any "zero" responses for yourself, do you know why that has occurred and what can you do to try to correct it at the present time? If you are married, be sure to discuss these thoughts with your partner.

## Part Two:
### *The Parent-Child Relationship*

(Use a check for Mother and an X for Father.)

0 ————— 3 ————————— 5  1. My father/mother praised their children.

0 ————— 3 ————————— 5     We praise our children.

0 ————— 3 ————————— 5  2. My father/mother respected the uniqueness in each child.

0 ————— 3 ————————— 5     We respect the uniqueness in each child.

0 ————— 3 ————————— 5  3. My father/mother modelled appropriate behavior for their children.

0 ————— 3 ————————— 5     We model appropriate behavior for our children.

0 ————— 3 ————————— 5  4. My father/mother gave their children information geared to their age level.

0 ————— 3 ————————— 5     We give our children information geared to their age level.

0 ————— 3 ————————— 5  5. My father/mother provided the physical necessities.

0 ————— 3 ————————— 5     We provide the physical necessities.

0 ————— 3 ————————— 5  6. My father/mother understood and accepted what was normal behavior for children at each age level.

0 ————— 3 ————————— 5     We understand and accept what is normal behavior for our children at each age level.

0 ————— 3 ————————— 5  7. My father/mother respected their children's feelings.

0 ——————— 3 ——————— 5       We respect our children's feelings.

0 ——————— 3 ——————— 5   8. My father/mother admitted their mistakes and apologized when necessary.

0 ——————— 3 ——————— 5       We admit our mistakes and apologize when necessary.

0 ——————— 3 ——————— 5   9. My father/mother accepted their children's understandable mistakes.

0 ——————— 3 ——————— 5       We accept our children's understandable mistakes.

0 ——————— 3 ——————— 5 10. My father/mother expressed their thoughts and feelings in a nonthreatening, nonjudgmental manner.

0 ——————— 3 ——————— 5       We express our thoughts and feelings in a nonthreatening, nonjudgmental manner.

0 ——————— 3 ——————— 5 11. My father/mother set clear rules and limits and reinforced them in a kindly, consistent manner.

0 ——————— 3 ——————— 5       We set clear rules and limits and reinforced them in a kindly, consistent manner.

0 ——————— 3 ——————— 5 12. My father/mother established clear family rules.

0 ——————— 3 ——————— 5       We established clear family rules.

0 ——————— 3 ——————— 5 13. My father/mother practiced effective, humane forms of discipline.

0 ——————— 3 ——————— 5       We practice effective, humane forms of discipline.

0 ——————— 3 ——————— 5 14. My father/mother spent ample time with the children.

0 ——————— 3 ——————— 5     We spend ample time with our children.

If you have any low responses for either parent, do you know why this happened? How do you feel about each statement and how has that influenced you concerning your own role as a parent? If your children are still at home, are there any changes that you could make in any of these categories that would be helpful at the present time?

## Part Three:
### *The Sibling Relationship*

0 ——————— 3 ——————— 5 1. The children spent ample time with siblings and/or friends.

0 ——————— 3 ——————— 5     Our children spend ample time with siblings and/or friends.

0 ——————— 3 ——————— 5 2. The children had ample time to play and relax.

0 ——————— 3 ——————— 5     Our children have ample time to play and relax.

0 ——————— 3 ——————— 5 3. The children developed peaceful ways to resolve their conflicts.

0 ——————— 3 ——————— 5     Our children have developed peaceful ways to resolve their conflicts.

0 ——————— 3 ——————— 5 4. The children had secrets and information not shared with the parents.

0 ——————— 3 ——————— 5     Our children have secrets and information not shared with us (to the best of our knowledge).

0 ——————— 3 ——————— 5   5. The children turned to one another for support and information.

0 ——————— 3 ——————— 5   Our children turn to one another for support and information.

0 ——————— 3 ——————— 5   6. The children respected one another.

0 ——————— 3 ——————— 5   Our children respect one another.

0 ——————— 3 ——————— 5   7. The children had their own space where privacy was assured.

0 ——————— 3 ——————— 5   Our children have their own space where privacy is assured.

0 ——————— 3 ——————— 5   8. The children tolerated one another's differences.

0 ——————— 3 ——————— 5   Our children tolerate one another's differences.

0 ——————— 3 ——————— 5   9. The children treat one another kindly a good deal of the time.

0 ——————— 3 ——————— 5   Our children treat one another kindly a good deal of the time.

0 ——————— 3 ——————— 5   10. The children could count on one another when they were really needed.

0 ——————— 3 ——————— 5   Our children can count on one another when they are really needed.

If you have any low responses, do you know why this happened in your childhood? If your children are still at home and there are some low responses for the present, what are the reasons and the course corrections that could be implemented now?

As you consider the overall results of this past and present family evaluation, what is your overall response? Would you evaluate each family as basically healthy? In some of the areas, you may not have been able to alter the situation. In others, you may have been able to make some changes, but those could be past issues now. Living with regrets will not help you grow and be a different person in the present or future. Focus on what was positive in your past family and your present family and build upon these.[16]

# FAMILIES THAT FLOURISH

G ETTING MARRIED CAN BE A SCARY proposition these days. Yet love often conquers this healthy fear as couples forge ahead with preparations for the big day. One of the most important investments is premarital counseling, yet one often neglected in all the hustle and bustle.

I see them in my office each week, young couples in love, joyfully looking forward to their upcoming marriage. They usually spend six to ten hours with me, a grueling and enlightening experience for two people who don't know each other all that well yet. Many times I discover that their own families are not really that healthy. I always ask how their *new* family is going to be different. They sometimes reply definitely and emphatically, "Healthy! It *will* be healthy!"

But they are often thrown by my next question: "What's your plan?" They first look at each other and then back at me with a puzzled expression. "What do you mean, what's our plan?"

My reply is the same each time. "You have to have a plan to

have a healthy family. Even though you didn't like some aspects of your own family, it's what you know best and there's a level of comfort with it. Unless you have a vision of what you want for a healthy family, and a plan to get there, it will never happen." Slowly, the light begins to dawn.

No goal... no plan... no progress. The same holds true for your family and mine. Would you be able to explain to someone what the characteristics of a healthy family are? Could you describe it with specifics? Many people cannot.

We hear so much about family problems these days that many wonder if healthy home life even exists anymore. Our world is so unstable and unpredictable, changing so rapidly in both technology and values. Is a stable family really possible? Isn't every family unit doomed to be dysfunctional?

Of course. To some degree, we all fail to function well as individuals and families—the result of the fall of the human race when sin entered the world. But in spite of sin and human weakness, families can be healthy. What makes it possible for a family to function well in such a dysfunctional world? The main reason is the power of Jesus Christ to refine and reshape each individual and enable him or her to respond in healthy ways.

Scripture very clearly describes the turmoil and unpredictability of life. But God's Word also teaches that peace and stability are possible regardless of our circumstances. Many non-Christian families flourish, while many Christian families fail miserably. Christians are certainly far from perfect. But our deepest potential always resides in allowing Jesus Christ to invade our lives and begin a radical process of transformation.

Scripture often reminds us that we are "in Christ," and that he is "within us." Capturing the reality and significance of that fact translates into true change. When we allow Jesus Christ to refine our attitudes, beliefs, behaviors, and the effect of past experiences, we discover an ever-flowing wellspring for a renewed family.

## FINDING A GOOD MODEL

Have you ever helped your kids build some complicated design, perhaps a model airplane or a Tinkertoy forklift? I don't know about you, but I need a detailed plan in front of me as to what piece goes where. Surely family life is one of the most intricate designs of all, consisting of so many complicated relationships thoroughly entertwined with the world around us. Of course, not every healthy family will look like it was pressed out of the same mold. True to God's infinite creativity, diversity abounds.

Is there a model which we can work toward in building our families? I have discovered several in plowing through various books and studies on the subject. Lots of folks claim to be experts these days. Who can we trust with our most precious project?

If you told a medical doctor, "I am healthy," he would use certain basic criteria in order to determine the accuracy of your diagnosis. Let's say you went to a family therapist and asked, "Is my family healthy?" What criteria would the therapist use in his or her analysis? Here are some of the basic building blocks to be examined.

えん

## *A family always faces an uphill battle if the marriage is sick.*

*The marriage relationship.* Of the myriad of factors involved in family life, the single most important one is the marital relationship. It is the foundation stone on which all the other pieces of family structure will be built. We need to distinguish between the marital unit of husband and wife and the parental unit. Each element will have its own roles and responsibilities. Two people may be both partners and parents, yet keep the roles separate.[1]

A family always faces an uphill battle if the marriage is sick. A warm, caring, supportive relationship contains the best ingredients for nurturing children. We will explore this foundational need to build a strong marriage in greater detail later in this chapter.

*How does the family deal with power?* When you think of power, what comes to mind? For our purposes, I would define power as each individual's capacity to influence another person. Or the ability to make our own thoughts and feelings the main force in making decisions.

Power within a family can be sorted out in various ways. It could be equally shared by all members. On the other extreme, one particular person might totally dominate the rest. Within a dominated family, opportunities for developing close or intimate relationships are greatly diminished. A strongly dominant spouse or parent usually cannot handle intimacy. In a healthy family, power is shared by the spouses, while they gradually give their children more and more opportunities to learn how to use power in a healthy way.

*Family closeness.* A third characteristic that therapists look for in a healthy family is both the amount and type of family closeness. Being close as a family is important, but it must also be balanced with the freedom of each individual to express his or her own individuality and have access to some private space for retreat when necessary.

Either emotional starvation or smothering within the family can be extremely detrimental. Personal boundaries are often violated in either situation. The absence of warmth and affection can create enormous insecurity and love hunger. The other extreme of holding on too tightly and controlling others leaves too little opportunity for individuality and intimacy.

Both intimacy and autonomy need to be encouraged within the family. If not, each member and especially the children end up stunted in their capacity to form healthy relationships with adults later on. How well do family members bond together? How well are individual boundaries established and respected? All of these issues add crucial building blocks to the healthy family.

Just as families are all different, each individual also develops his or her own unique personality. The following message needs to be heard very clearly: "It's OK for you to be who you are and for me to be who I am." The next chapter will help you explore this vital area in greater detail in terms of your past and present family. (If you need special assistance in discovering personality uniqueness and accepting differences, please refer to the suggested reading list at the end of the book.)

*The pattern of communication.* The fourth area to be evaluated is the pattern of communication which occurs within the family. Is each person encouraged to talk, to share feelings, likes, and dislikes? Does everyone enjoy total freedom in expressing feelings or are some emotions on an unspoken forbidden list?

In some families, anger is all right and affection is not. In others, just the opposite may be true. Some families forbid the expression of all feelings. Some families carry a prevailing mood which seems to permeate the atmosphere—ranging from warm to polite to angry to depressed to hopeless.[2]

We all grow and function best when we live in an atmosphere of acceptance. Do the members of the family listen to each other? I mean *total listening* with both eyes and ears. Too many family conversations are nothing more than dialogues of the deaf. We are called by Scripture to be listeners. "... be... (a ready listener,)" (Jas 1:19, AMP). "He who answers a matter before he hears the facts, it is folly and shame to him" (Prv 18:13, AMP).

The parents must set the example. By adapting their own style of communication, they help everyone else to learn the principles of speaking the other's language. We all need to be especially sensitive to gender and personality differences which can create various ways of responding. (See the book list for suggested resources.)

Are family members allowed to speak for themselves? Perhaps you've been with a family in which individuals interrupt one another constantly, speak for one another, and complete sentences for other family members. Such a nasty habit can often develop without our even realizing it.

Within the framework of communication patterns, individual adeptness in problem solving and conflict resolution especially reflects the growth and progress of the family unit. Learning to negotiate is a skill couples need to learn and then teach their children.

Families who continue to grow in healthy ways focus on what works rather than on what doesn't. They look for the times when problems are resolved and discover what greased the wheels so they can do it again. They resolve to learn from their experiences, rather than getting bogged down in an unproductive fixation on what went wrong.

A number of years ago, the Chicago Cubs won their divisional championship. But as often happens, one of their leading hitters experienced a batting slump during the season. The manager noticed that this player began spending extra time in the clubhouse evaluating films of his performance. In trying to discover what he was doing wrong so he could stop striking out so much, he was scrutinizing tapes taken during his slump. Unfortunately, watching those films only reinforced his bad habits!

The manager complimented him on wanting to do something about the problem. Then he suggested to the batter that he begin watching films of when he was doing his best at the plate, really striking the ball with power. The ballplayer took his manager's wise advice. When he focused on what worked before, it began to work again.

## A DISASTROUS CRISIS OR AN OPPORTUNITY TO GROW?

Life is full of challenges for all of us. One of the most difficult is dealing with an upheaval in our lives due to some loss or tragic event. How well families handle crisis situations as well as the more frequent changes can also be a barometer of health.

Common transitions—such as a child leaving for school, or getting married, or returning home once again—offer countless opportunities for the entire family to adapt and grow. How well individuals handle their own response to these times of change and how they respond to one another are both reflections of family health.[3]

Many families are thrown into total disarray by a sudden crisis or unforeseen change. They perceive the disruption as a threatening enemy, something to be feared. Other families may recognize the difficulties presented by the crisis, but set their sights on learning from the particular problems and people involved.

The courage of one family could be a model for us all. The mother underwent surgery requiring a hospital stay of twenty-seven days. Her husband and three children—ages seven, eleven, and fourteen—had to carry on without her. They cooked, cleaned, and discovered how to complete tasks which were totally foreign to them. Mom's return home required another period of readjustment for everyone as she began to resume her former responsibilities. Fortunately, the entire family met together on several occasions to share how they felt, what they were learning, and how the family was changing because of the mother's absence.

ぶ

*Problems are the opportunities of life that allow both the individual and the family to grow.*

Such crises can either strengthen or weaken relationships. Problems are the opportunities of life that allow both the individual and the family to grow. The apostle Peter described this challenge when he said:

Beloved, do not be amazed and bewildered at the fiery ordeal which is taking place to test your quality, as though something strange—unusual and alien to you and your position—were befalling you.
But in so far as you are sharing Christ's sufferings, rejoice, so that when His glory (full of radiance and splendor) is revealed you may also rejoice with triumph—exultantly." 1 Pt 4:12-13, AMP

## HEALTHY PARENTING

Finally, the mother and father in a healthy family fulfill God's call to be loving parents. Being totally responsible for growing children is a tall order. Let's consider some of the necessary ingredients in healthy parenting.

First and foremost, parents are the primary providers for all of the basic needs of the child, such as food, clothing, shelter, and health care. You would be amazed at the number of families who can afford all of this, but funnel the funds elsewhere for various reasons.

Healthy parenting means being there when a child needs you. Coming home to an empty house day after day can have a very negative impact upon a child. He or she may feel abandoned or get into serious difficulty because of the lack of supervision. Even in the midst of work demands, parents can spend adequate time with their children.

Parents need to provide protection from the normal hazards of life, as well as information and experiences the child is not yet equipped to handle. Media exposure—including television, movies, and recordings—needs to be screened, limited, and supervised. Children are not pushed into anything that is beyond their capabilities nor prematurely exposed to certain activities and experiences.

Healthy parents are able to determine the child's developmental level so that they don't expect too much nor too little. They understand and accept age-appropriate behavior, as well as being able to identify and correct that which is not appropriate. Effective parenting takes into account every child's age and stage of development when assigning privileges and responsibilities. Both the mother and father respect the uniqueness of each child and adapt their responses according to each specific child and situation.

Proverbs 22:6 exhorts parents to "train up a child in the way he should go (and in keeping with his individual gift or bent), and when he is old he will not depart from it" (AMP). Scripture is not advocating favoritism here, but respect for the individuality of the children. Wise parents encourage the child to develop his or her special areas of giftedness.

Both physical and verbal affection are necessary expressions of love and acceptance. Regardless of their background and experience, healthy parents take care to provide a role model of healthy marital interaction, as well as giving to the children without exploitation. Children especially enjoy seeing their parents give one another some visible sign of affection like a loving kiss or a warm hug. How to make up after the inevitable arguments of married life also provide invaluable lessons for life.

Healthy parents establish rules and guidelines for their children, while also teaching them how to discern and establish guidelines when the parents are not around. These rules also need to take into consideration the ability and individuality of each child. The parents remain parents and the children remain children. They understand and respect their positions.

Independence rather than dependence is fostered in a healthy family. Throughout the parenting role is woven a thread of gradual relinquishment of authority and decision-making. The child is enabled to gracefully move from dependence to independence.

The spiritual dimension of life is lived out in word and deed. Wise parents give direction to each child for his or her spiritual growth. Such spiritual guidance must be integrated into all seven days of the week, rather than remaining a mere token expression when Sunday arrives. Personal devotions are most effectively taught—or more aptly "caught"—by what children observe happening in the everyday lives of their parents. The wisest parents endeavor to lead each child to a saving knowledge of Jesus Christ.

Healthy parenting requires working as a team whether parents are together or divorced. They publicly support each other and work out their individual differences behind the scenes. Mothers and fathers need to avoid triangulation with the children, where each parent pairs off with a particular child against the spouse with respect to some issue. Healthy parents don't use the children to communicate to the estranged spouse or get back at him or her.[4]

What about your experience with parenting? Does this sound anything like the family you grew up with? Or like your present-day family? Are there any changes you could initiate which could make these elements of healthy parenting more of a reality?

## BECOMING ONE FLESH

Now let's return to that foundation which is so vital to a healthy family—the marital relationship. Perhaps I can best sum up what constitutes a healthy marriage by referring back to a definition I have been using for years. This description reflects the purpose of marriage as well as the potential for change and growth:

Marriage is a total commitment of two people to the person of Jesus Christ and to one another. It is a commitment in which there is no holding back. It is a pledge of mutual fidelity. It is a partnership of mutual subordination. A Christian marriage is similar to a solvent, a freeing up of the man and woman to become all that God intends for them to become. Marriage is a refining process that God will use to shape us into the man or woman that he wants us to become.

A marriage relationship is many things. Marriage is a gift from God and each individual is a gift to the other. It is an opportunity to learn how to love, a journey in which we as the travelers face many choices for which we are responsible, a call to friendship as well as a call to suffering. Marriage is not an event but a way of life which involves intimacy in all areas in order to be fulfilling for both individuals.

A marriage relationship grows stronger if each person understands the stages and changes of individual development and how these might affect each other's lives. Married people also need insight into the various stages of family life in order to prepare for each of those stages in advance. Feeling adequately equipped will help couples feel less overwhelmed when they enter each of those stages.

&.

*No couple is totally compatible.*
*Years of marriage are required for a man and woman*
*to learn the skill of being compatible!*

A marriage relationship can unfold like a stunning rose blossom when each person has built his or her own personal identity and security upon an understanding of God's love. Each learns to derive values from God, rather than from performance, status, or appearance.

This may be a moot point for many of you reading this book, but extensive premarital counseling is another vital factor in establishing an intimate relationship. A couple has the best chance to make their marriage blossom when they set aside the time to consider these crucial issues prior to the wedding.

Most people today are woefully unprepared for marriage and all that it entails. No couple is totally compatible. Years of marriage are required for a man and woman to learn the skill of being compatible!

*Being servants of one another.* Of all the various concepts of the meaning and purpose of marriage, the one which is most foreign in our society is that of servanthood: the pattern of seeking to meet your partner's needs rather than being self-centered.

To put it simply, a servant's role is to make sure that the other person's needs are met. In a husband-wife relationship, being a servant is an act of love, a gift to the other person to make his/her life more full. It is not something to be demanded. It is an act of strength and not of weakness. It is a positive action which has been chosen to show your love to each other. Hence, the apostle Paul said, "Be subject to one another," not limiting the role of servanthood to the wife.

A servant may also be called an "enabler." The word enable means "to make better." As an enabler you are to make life easier for your spouse instead of placing restrictive demands upon him/her. An enabler does not make more work for the partner, nor does he/she hinder the other from becoming all he/she has been designed to become.

A servant is also one who "edifies" or builds up the other person. The English word edify is derived from the Latin word "aedes" meaning "hearth" or "fireplace." The hearth was the center of activity in ancient times. It was the only place of warmth and light in the home, and the place where the daily bread was prepared. It was also the place where people were drawn together.

Edifying is often used in the New Testament to refer to building up another person. Three examples of edifying are expressed in the verses below: 1) personal encouragement, 2) inner strengthening, and 3) the establishment of peace and harmony between individuals.

"So let us then definitely aim for and eagerly pursue what

makes for harmony and for mutual upbuilding (edification and development) of one another" Rom 14:19, AMP.

"Let each one of us make it a practice to please (make happy) his neighbor for his good and for his true welfare, to edify him—that is, to strengthen him and build him up spiritually" (Rom 15:2, AMP).

"Therefore encourage one another and build each other up, just as in fact you are doing" (1 Thes 5:11, NIV).

First Corinthians 8:1 (NIV) sums up the matter of edifying: "… love builds up."

To edify then, means to cheer another person on in life. You are to be a one-person rooting section for your spouse which can increase your spouse's feelings of self-worth. The result is that your spouse's capacity to love and give in return is enhanced.[5]

## WHAT ELSE MAKES A GOOD MARRIAGE?

Here are some additional characteristics of a healthy marital relationship. While not all-inclusive, this list will help you reflect upon the marital bond between you and your spouse and between your parents. I hope it helps you make a course correction if necessary to move toward a more positive marriage.

In a healthy marriage, a husband and wife respect each other and are mutually supportive. The relationship is definitely a two-way street, as opposed to one being a giver and the other a receiver. They are sincerely interested in one another and in reality are best friends. In an article "Marriages Are Made to Last," *Psychology Today* reported on a study of three hundred fifty-one couples. Three hundred of these stated they were happily married.[6]

The couples were asked to select from the list those statements that best reflected their own marriage. The results are shown below. Interestingly, the top seven reasons for what makes a good marriage were the same for the men as for the women. Here are the reasons respondents gave, listed in the order of frequency:

| # MEN | WOMEN |
|-------|-------|
| 1. My spouse is my best friend. | My spouse is my best friend. |
| 2. I like my spouse as a person. | I like my spouse as a person. |
| 3. Marriage is a long-term commitment. | Marriage is a long-term commitment. |
| 4. Marriage is sacred. | Marriage is sacred. |
| 5. We agree on aims and goals. | We agree on aims and goals. |
| 6. My spouse has grown more interesting. | My spouse has grown more interesting. |
| 7. I want the relationship to succeed. | I want the relationship to succeed. |
| 8. An enduring marriage is important to social stability. | We laugh together. |
| 9. We laugh together. | We agree on a philosophy of life. |
| 10. I am proud of my spouse's achievements. | We agree on how and how often to show affection. |
| 11. We agree on a philosophy of life. | An enduring marriage is important to social stability. |
| 12. We agree about our sex life. | We have a stimulating exchange of ideas. |
| 13. We agree on how and how often to show affection. | We discuss things calmly. |
| 14. I confide in my spouse. | We agree about our sex life. |
| 15. We share outside hobbies and interests. | I am proud of my spouse's achievements. |

*The friendship quality of love known as "phileo" is at the top of the list for both men and women.* In a marriage which achieves this important goal, the energy for friendship is primarily directed toward the spouse rather than outside friendships.

Give one example of how this is a part of your marriage.

*Nurturing is another important ingredient.* In a healthy marriage, the support, affirmation, and encouragement of courtship does not dissipate over time but grows. Each spouse feels loved and valued by his or her partner. They learn to express love in a way that registers with the other.

One of the best descriptions of the healthy expression of marital love I have seen was written by Mel Krantzler in his book, *Creative Marriage:*

> Marital love requires the ability to put yourself in your partner's place, to understand that the differences that divide you are the differences of two unique personalities, rather than betrayals of your hopes and dreams. The unconditional willingness of each of you to understand and resolve these differences through the sharing of your deepest feelings, concerns, attitudes and ideas is a fundamental component of marital love.
>
> Postponement of your need for instant gratification when your partner feels no such need; sharing the struggle to triumph over adversities as well as sharing the joys and delights of being together; nurturing each other in defeat caused by forces beyond our control and renewing each other's courage to prevail in the face of despair; carrying necessary obligations and responsibilities as a flower rather than as a hundred-pound knapsack; acknowledging the everyday value of your partner in a look, a smile, a touch of the hand, a voiced appreciation of a meal or a new hair style, a spontaneous trip to a movie or a restaurant; trusting your partner always to be there when needed; knowing that he or she always has your best interests at heart even when criticism is given; loyalty and dedication to each other in the face of sacrifices that may have to be made—all of these are additional components of marital love that courtship knows little about.[7]

Give one example of how such nurturing is a part of your marriage:

## INVESTING IN AN EMOTIONAL BANK ACCOUNT

One of the best illustrations I have found of healthy responses in marriage and the family is the concept of an "Emotional Bank Account." When we open a financial bank account, we try to make regular deposits. Then when a withdrawal is needed, we have built up a reserve to draw upon.

A spouse can make deposits into the Emotional Bank Account of his or her partner through courtesy, kindness, honesty, trust, open communication, and commitment. The depositing spouse builds up a good reserve to draw upon in case of emergency. The partner learns to trust the spouse more and more. When mistakes are made or lapses occur, a safety net of understanding and acceptance exists because of deposits which have built up in the bank account. Inconsistencies are easier to tolerate because they can be seen as the exception and not the rule.

But when a spouse shows discourtesy, disrespect, doesn't listen, is not trustworthy, and fails to affirm, the Emotional Bank Account is eventually overdrawn. And when this happens, little flexibility exists because people have learned to be careful around each other. They have learned to walk on egg shells, to measure words, to outsmart their partner. Trust has been evicted from the marriage.

გ

*When a spouse shows discourtesy, disrespect, doesn't listen, is untrustworthy, and fails to affirm, the Emotional Bank Account is eventually overdrawn.*

Marriages begin to deteriorate when there is no continuing reserve in the bank account. Families deteriorate when there is no reserve. Each of us needs regular deposits to our Emotional Bank Accounts.[8]

Give one example of how this is a part of your marriage:

## MORE HEALTH TONICS

*Growing marriages administer liberal doses of tolerance, patience, and acceptance.* The partners look to discover the unique qualities of one another. They learn to accept the differences and peculiar quirks which everyone brings to a marriage. They are not on a campaign to revamp their partner. Differences are tolerated and each person is not expected to be perfect.

Happy couples have learned to live out Ephesians 4:2 on a daily basis: "Living as becomes you—with complete lowliness of mind (humility) and meekness (unselfishness, gentleness, mildness), with patience, bearing with one another and making allowances because you love one another" (AMP). They've learned to say, "It's OK for me to be me and for you to be you."

Give one example of how this is a part of your marriage:

*Just laughing and having fun together are sometimes the most refreshing tonic.* I've noticed them in church, in restaurants, on the beach, or walking down the street: couples who are a delight to watch because they're having fun together. They've learned how to enter each other's world and enjoy mutual activities.

Growth of this kind usually requires one spouse to alter what he or she enjoys doing to encourage the partner to be willing to try something new. For example, a husband could limit his weekly golf outing to nine holes instead of eighteen or even thirty-six in order to make it less strenuous and overwhelming for his wife. Or the wife could temper her competitive tennis game to make room for her husband who is just learning.

My wife and I might go fishing in a boat for three hours in the warm sunshine (which my wife enjoys) instead of hiking three miles up a mountain in the snow at five in the morning to fish all day (which I enjoy). Happy couples are able to have fun together, laugh together, and be spontaneous.

Give one example of how this is a part of your marriage:

*Don't forget that magic elixir, sex.* One of God's special gifts to us is sexual expression. A healthy marriage reflects a couple who delight in their sexuality and its expression within their committed relationship. Stagnation of sexual expression has not set in and they continue to grow in their own personal ways of loving one another. This intimate area is shared only with each other and they are able to adapt their expression when necessary because of illness, stress, or aging. They have learned to delight one another.

Give one example of how this is a part of your marriage:


*Share interests and activities.* Even though each partner is involved in some separate functions, they participate in certain activities together. They are not "married singles," but nourish their special relationship on an ongoing basis. They are able to grow together socially and move in and out of each other's world. Happy couples also enjoy a life apart from the children, which means being able to leave them with a sitter and go out for an evening—and not talk about the kids![9]

Give one example of how this is a part of your marriage:


*Hold it all together with trust and confidence.* Part of a healthy marriage is being able to bounce your inner hopes, dreams, thoughts, and feelings off your spouse. Both husband and wife feel free to share joys and concerns with the other. They usually do not feel left out of the other's life during the difficult times. They are careful to keep this information and sharing between them in confidence, without inappropriately invading their children's or parent's lives with it.

Give one example of how this is a part of your marriage:


*That old bugaboo: money.* The economic realm of life seems to have mushroomed in complexity and difficulty over the past decade. How a couple functions as a financial partnership is vital to a healthy marriage. It is not the duty of just one partner to make financial decisions or to be knowledgeable. The husband and wife have worked out a mutually agreeable system for budgeting and investing.

I'm always concerned when one spouse has no idea what his or her partner earns, even though they both sign a joint income tax return each year. In a healthy marriage, even though one person may actually handle the money, the other spouse should be able to step in at a moment's notice. All their assets are held in common.

If one is employed outside the home and the other isn't, the employed spouse sees the other as contributing just as much to family life. They also seek outside advice for assistance with their finances. Money is not used as a weapon or reward in the context of their home. (See helpful resources for this area in the suggested reading list.)

Give one example of how this is a part of your marriage:

*How to fight and make up.* Being able to resolve conflicts and put them behind is a vital quality for any married couple. The existence of problems is not denied, but rather faced head on. They learn what works, what doesn't, and are creative enough to try new approaches.

I have heard so many couples complain, "We've talked about this problem for years, but nothing changes. We never resolve anything and I'm getting tired of it!" Healthy couples avoid rehashing the same agenda for months. By learning from each experience, they become better able to express whatever feelings arise without being threatened by their existence. Working together is the main element.

Give one example of how this is a part of your marriage:

## FORGIVENESS VS. RESENTMENT

The last ingredient is found in secular descriptions of quality marriages as well as Christian ones. It has to be there for a couple to deal with their humanity and live together for a lifetime. That crucial quality is *forgiveness*. Offenses and hurts inevitably occur. When you become more vulnerable within a marriage relationship, disappointment and pain cut even deeper. Learning to forgive and move ahead offers a healing balm for any marriage. Forgiveness is the practical application of experiencing and giving the grace of God in our marriage.

❧

*Unfortunately when the war of resentment*
*takes place in marriage,*
*the relationship can wind up being the orphan.*

When forgiveness is absent, resentment quickly moves into the vacuum. Resentment will cost both partners dearly, and often ends up killing the relationship. One of the tragedies of a war is the number of orphaned children left behind. Unfortunately when the war of resentment takes place in marriage, the relationship can wind up being the orphan.

Let's face facts. Hurts, unmet needs, and disappointments are bound to occur when two imperfect people marry. Embarking upon a crusade to make the other one pay for his or her misdeeds leads to marital bankruptcy. Consider the words of Leo Buscaglia and let them guide your own response to wrongdoing:

When wronged by those we love, we seem to devalue years of a relationship—a relationship that may have brought us many joys and which required much intellectual and emotional energy to have lasted so long. Still, with a single harsh statement, a thoughtless act, an unfeeling criticism, we are capable of destroying even the closest of our relationships. We quickly forget the good and set out to rationalize scenarios of hate.

We do this rather than take up the challenge of honest evaluation and confrontation. We ignore the possibility that in the act of forgiving and showing compassion we are very likely to discover new depths in ourselves and new possibilities for relating in the future. We are too proud. We engage rather in self-deferent activities which keep us from forgiving; beliefs that if we withdraw and run from the situation we will hurt the other and absence will heal us; the fantasy that in avoidance there can be closure; the naive hope that in hurting, shaming, blaming and condemning we will be made to feel better.

We fail to realize that when we refuse to engage in forgiving behaviors, it is we who assume the useless weight of hate, pain and vengeance which is never-ending, and, instead, weighs upon us rather than the wrongdoer.[10]

Forgiveness costs. Forgiveness is a risk. It takes time. It has to be given again and again. Jesus reminded us of that fact. Forgiveness cannot be given out of fear but out of love and compassion. Forgiveness is an action that lets the other person know they are loved "in spite of." Forgiveness is no longer allowing what has happened to poison you.

Again and again the Word of God calls us to be people of forgiveness. "... forgiving one another [readily and freely], as God in Christ forgave you" (Eph 4:32, AMP). "He who covers and forgives an offense seeks love, but he who repeats or harps on a matter separates even close friends" (Prv 17:9, AMP).

Forgiveness is a decision to believe the best about the other person and give him or her them the benefit of the doubt; it is the decision to wish that person well in your heart and to ask God to bless them.

Forgiveness means saying, "It is all right; it is over. I no longer resent you nor see you as an enemy. I love you even if you cannot love me in return." When you refuse to forgive you inflict inner torment upon yourself, and that makes you miserable and ineffective. But when you forgive someone for hurting you, you perform spiritual surgery on your soul. You cut away the wrong that was done to you. You see your "enemy" through the magic eyes that can heal your soul. Separate the person from the hurt and let the hurt go the way children open their hands and let a trapped butterfly go free.

Then invite that person back into your mind, fresh, as if a piece of history between you has been erased, its grip on your memory broken. Reverse the seemingly irreversible flow of pain within you.[11]

Give one example of how this is a part of your marriage:

## A LIMITLESS FUTURE

I've had some people come right out and tell me that the above list is impossible to attain. Having seen many quality marriages over the years, I can't agree. Each couple will be at different levels in how well each characteristic is functioning, but as long as they have this goal in mind, are working toward it, and are able to perceive progress, I would call their marriage healthy.

Each and every element will never be operating to the fullest degree. Such qualities are *ideals* for which we aim rather than targets on which we can score a bull's-eye. Perfection will never exist in this life, but that doesn't keep us from working toward the goal. Perhaps these elements can give you a new sense of vision. Without a vision, a person or a marriage can perish.

In the latter part of the eighties, a series of movies called "Back to the Future" proved to be popular. Unfortunately, many couples live the same way today. They create for themselves a limited future for their marriage by projecting the past and the present upon it.

By becoming stuck in the dilemmas that seem so endless, married couples can fail to remember that there is a future. Especially for Christians, that future is filled with hope. Too many overwhelmed men and women mentally condemn the future to be an unhappy continuation of the past. Norman Cousins once said, "We fear the worst, we expect the worst, we invite the worst."[12]

Scripture holds out a sure promise for our marriage as well as our individual lives: "'For I know the thoughts and plans that I have for you,' declares the Lord, 'plans to prosper you and not to harm you, plans to give you hope and a future'" (Jer 29:11). When you capture the truth of these words, your marriage and family life have a limitless future.

ॐ

## BRINGING IT HOME

The following questions are from the Marital Assessment Inventory which I created a number of years ago. I hope you will find these questions to be beneficial in determining where your marriage is at the present time and what steps could be taken to encourage further growth.

### Marriage Assessment Inventory

*Instructions:* Use an X to indicate your current level of satisfaction, with "0" meaning no satisfaction; "5" average; and "10" meaning super, fantastic, the best. Use a circle to indicate what you think your partner's level of satisfaction is at the present time.

Remember that this is not a test; no one scores ten on every scale. In fact, many couples fail to score ten on any one of them. Focus on where your marriage is for each category, rather than where it isn't. Then determine what you can do to improve.

1. Our daily personal involvement with each other.

| 0 | 1 | 2 | 3 | 4 | 5 | 6 | 7 | 8 | 9 | 10 |

2. Our affectionate romantic interaction.

| 0 | 1 | 2 | 3 | 4 | 5 | 6 | 7 | 8 | 9 | 10 |

3. Our sexual relationship.

| 0 | 1 | 2 | 3 | 4 | 5 | 6 | 7 | 8 | 9 | 10 |

4. The frequency of our sexual contact.

| 0 | 1 | 2 | 3 | 4 | 5 | 6 | 7 | 8 | 9 | 10 |

5. My trust in my spouse.

| 0 | 1 | 2 | 3 | 4 | 5 | 6 | 7 | 8 | 9 | 10 |

6. My spouse's trust in me.

| 0 | 1 | 2 | 3 | 4 | 5 | 6 | 7 | 8 | 9 | 10 |

7. How well we speak one another's language.

| 0 | 1 | 2 | 3 | 4 | 5 | 6 | 7 | 8 | 9 | 10 |

8. How power is shared.

| 0 | 1 | 2 | 3 | 4 | 5 | 6 | 7 | 8 | 9 | 10 |

9. The way we make decisions.

| 0 | 1 | 2 | 3 | 4 | 5 | 6 | 7 | 8 | 9 | 10 |

10. The way we manage conflict.

| 0 | 1 | 2 | 3 | 4 | 5 | 6 | 7 | 8 | 9 | 10 |

11. Adjustment to one another's differences.

| 0 | 1 | 2 | 3 | 4 | 5 | 6 | 7 | 8 | 9 | 10 |

12. Amount of free time together.

| 0 | 1 | 2 | 3 | 4 | 5 | 6 | 7 | 8 | 9 | 10 |

13. Quality of free time together.

| 0 | 1 | 2 | 3 | 4 | 5 | 6 | 7 | 8 | 9 | 10 |

14. Amount of free time apart.

| 0 | 1 | 2 | 3 | 4 | 5 | 6 | 7 | 8 | 9 | 10 |

15. Our interaction with friends as a couple.

| 0 | 1 | 2 | 3 | 4 | 5 | 6 | 7 | 8 | 9 | 10 |
|---|---|---|---|---|---|---|---|---|---|----|

16. The way we support each other in rough times.

| 0 | 1 | 2 | 3 | 4 | 5 | 6 | 7 | 8 | 9 | 10 |
|---|---|---|---|---|---|---|---|---|---|----|

17. The way we support each other's careers.

| 0 | 1 | 2 | 3 | 4 | 5 | 6 | 7 | 8 | 9 | 10 |
|---|---|---|---|---|---|---|---|---|---|----|

18. Our spiritual interaction.

| 0 | 1 | 2 | 3 | 4 | 5 | 6 | 7 | 8 | 9 | 10 |
|---|---|---|---|---|---|---|---|---|---|----|

19. Our church involvement.

| 0 | 1 | 2 | 3 | 4 | 5 | 6 | 7 | 8 | 9 | 10 |
|---|---|---|---|---|---|---|---|---|---|----|

20. The level of our financial security.

| 0 | 1 | 2 | 3 | 4 | 5 | 6 | 7 | 8 | 9 | 10 |
|---|---|---|---|---|---|---|---|---|---|----|

21. How we manage money.

| 0 | 1 | 2 | 3 | 4 | 5 | 6 | 7 | 8 | 9 | 10 |
|---|---|---|---|---|---|---|---|---|---|----|

22. My spouse's relationship with my relatives.

| 0 | 1 | 2 | 3 | 4 | 5 | 6 | 7 | 8 | 9 | 10 |
|---|---|---|---|---|---|---|---|---|---|----|

23. My relationship with my spouse's relatives.

| 0 | 1 | 2 | 3 | 4 | 5 | 6 | 7 | 8 | 9 | 10 |
|---|---|---|---|---|---|---|---|---|---|----|

# CONNECTED YET SEPARATE

W E ARE HEARING MORE AND MORE today about the importance of bonding between parents and children. The principle of bonding has long been observed in the animal kingdom, as well as between people and animals. A newly hatched gosling will attach to whoever is around. If the mother goose is absent and you are there, guess who becomes the mother! Instant parenthood whether you want it or not.

However, healthy closeness or attachment occurs when secure boundaries have been developed. Over the several years we raised Shelties, we learned the importance of not taking the new litter from the mother or siblings too soon, nor letting them remain past a certain period of time. The puppies seemed best able to develop a close relationship with their new owners during an optimum age range.

Sometimes this normal bonding process goes awry. I've heard people say, "My daughter and I never bonded right from the first. It's always been a struggle between us." A father said, "I was away in the service and didn't see my daughter until she was one. We never did bond!" A mother said, "I bonded more with my grandmother than with my mother for the first five years of my life." Can you imagine the painful struggle of those who were held hostage in Lebanon over a number of years? Some returned home to reestablish relationships with children they had known for just a few months or perhaps had never even met.

Is bonding that vital? Yes! Even the close relationship with a pet carries an element of healing. Heart attack victims are more likely to survive and speedily recover when they have a dog. Bonding with someone helps us to feel more secure, accepted, valued, and related to another. And the more we feel accepted, the better able we are to become independent. Healthy attachment clears away barriers to individual growth and maturity. The fear of being isolated and lonely is diminished.

Think back for a moment. When you were a child, did you bond with any particular individual? What made it possible for the bonding to occur? Do you wish you had bonded with anyone else? What was the result of your not bonding with this person then and now? How has this affected your response to people today?

How strong are the bonds between the members of your present family? Do you know how they feel? Have you ever asked them? What could you do to develop even closer relationships? In your immediate family, with whom have you bonded most closely?

When we are bonded to another person in a healthy way, we don't respond because of "oughts" or "shoulds." Our responses flow naturally and spontaneously out of care, compassion, empathy, and love. I've counseled couples who told me they didn't even feel anything when they separated. There seemed to be nothing there, which makes me wonder what was there in the first place.

In marriage counseling, I can usually tell if a couple has bonded to one another or not. I ask each to write out ten traits they appreciate about their partner. Often one of the lists reflect strong feelings about several of the partner's personal qualities. Unfortunately, their partner's list may include just tasks that they appreciate. The first spouse has an emotional investment in the relationship and has attempted to bond, whereas the partner has not. It needs to be a two-way relationship.[1]

## THE ROAD TO ALIENATION

Psychologist Dr. Henry Cloud tells the story of two highly respected multi-millionaires, both aged fifty with numerous friends. In the same week, each of these two men lost their fortunes, their wives, and their three children in the marital break-up. Those were the similarities. The differences were in their responses.

One man became depressed and suicidal. He locked himself in his house for a month. Phone calls from friends were ignored. He began to withdraw from reality and had to be taken care of by his own father. It took him a year just to recover from his emotional distress.

The second man called a group of his friends together and asked each of them to have lunch with him on different days so he could have continual support. He went to a counselor to help him deal with his grief and depression. Within a year, this man was rebuilding his life and was financially stable.[2] What made the difference between these two men? Why did one survive so well? Dr. Cloud describes it this way:[3]

The difference was not just the way they handled the crisis. It was in the nature of their attachments. The first man had never let himself need anyone, and he had no deep attachments, even to his three children. When he lost everything, he had no deep love in his life and no way to survive. He had no model for deeply abiding bonds with others. He was alone when catastrophe hit, and because of his lack of bonding, he did not know how to ask for help.

The second man was a recovered alcoholic who had been involved in a support group for years. He had learned about the nature of deep attachments with others; he knew they would sustain him along with his relationship with God. His soul was full apart from his riches and his accomplishments, for he had the love of others within. As a result, he could reach out to them and draw on their strength in his time of need. His bonds of love with others and God, as well as himself, brought him through. He vividly illustrated Jesus' word picture:

"Everyone who comes to me, and hears my words, and acts upon them, I will show you whom he is like: he is like a man building a house, who dug deep and laid a foundation upon the rock; and when a flood rose, the torrent burst against that house and could not shake it, because it had been well built. But the one who has heard, and has not acted accordingly, is like a man who built a house upon the ground without any foundation; and the torrent burst against it and immediately it collapsed, and the ruin of that house was great." **Luke 6:47-49, NASB**

One man isolated himself, which led to alienation. That happens in friendships. Unfortunately, isolation or alienation also happens even in the best of families. It may last for a brief period of time or it could persist for years.

We shouldn't be surprised if people suffer the pain of alienation from time to time. In fact, the separation between God and humanity was at the root of all of our problems. When Adam and Eve sinned, alienation came into being. The human race lost its unbroken relationship with God and others at that moment. For the first time, a deep, inner pain crept into our existence. From that point on, all humankind has struggled with this pain of isolation.

&

*Unfortunately, isolation or alienation also happens even in the best of families. It may last for a brief period of time or it could persist for years.*

When alienation involves a family, all efforts must be directed to reconciliation, the same dynamic that needs to happen between God and the human race. Scripture expresses it this way:

For it has pleased [the Father] that all the divine fullness— the sum total of the divine perfection, powers and attributes— should dwell in Him permanently.

And God purposed that through—by the service, the intervention of—Him (the Son) all things should be completely reconciled back to Himself, whether on earth or in heaven, as through him [the Father] made peace by means of the blood of His cross.

And although you at one time were estranged and alienated from Him and of hostile attitude of mind in your wicked activities, yet now has [Christ, the Messiah] reconciled [you to God] in the body of His flesh through death, in order to present you holy and faultless and irreproachable in His [the Father's] presence. Col 1:19-22, AMP

Consider two families for a moment: your own family past and family present. Rate your relationship with each family member on a scale of zero to ten, from very distant to very close. If any are very distant, what caused the alienation? What could you do about it at the present time? You could also use the same scale to evaluate your relationship with God at the present time.

## SECURELY VULNERABLE

Let's consider what you can do to enhance the closeness or intimacy within your own family. The word intimacy is derived from the Latin word *intimus,* meaning "inmost." Intimacy suggests a very strong personal relationship, a special emotional closeness which includes understanding and being understood by someone who is very special.

Intimacy has also been defined as "an affectionate bond, the strands of which are composed of mutual caring, responsibility, trust, open communication of feelings and sensations, as well as the non-defended interchange of information about significant emotional events."[4] Openness can be scary, but the acceptance each partner offers in the midst of vulnerability provides a wonderful sense of security.[5]

Intimacy means taking the risk to be close to someone and allowing that person to step inside our personal boundaries. Sometimes this can be painful. As we lower our defenses to let another person draw near, we reveal deep secrets, including our weaknesses and faults. With our real selves exposed, we become vulnerable to possible ridicule from our partners.

The possibility of pain is unavoidable, but the rewards of intimacy greatly overshadow the risk. Mike Mason, in his book *The Mystery of Marriage*, stated: "It is not intimacy itself, therefore, which is so distasteful and intimidating to the world, but rather the moral condemnation that comes with it. People crave intimacy with one another, but are repelled by the sin that such closeness inevitably uncovers in themselves: the selfish motives that are unmasked, the pettiness that spills out, the monstrous new image of self that emerges as it struggles so pitifully to have its own way."[6]

A family which bonds is not a family of clones or one congealed mass of gelatin. Individuality is still a part of each person's life. Rather, we see a balance between individuality and relationships. Each person is encouraged to be all he or she can be. Each is not threatened by the differences that prevail. Each has accessibility to every other family member and enjoys considerable flexibility within the family. Both parents are usually responsible and dependable. Each is able to give to another but it is done freely and not out of demand or pressure. They act for the good of each other.[7]

Estrangement can be extremely painful within close families, yet the strength of that bond may make it easier to close the gap. When alienation occurs, abandonment or fear come sweeping in to take up residence in our lives. It's as though a gaping hole has been created in the family and nothing can fill it.

I have seen family members literally abandoned because they have chosen a lifestyle contrary to the family's value system. I've heard statements like, "You're no son of mine," or "You're not my daughter anymore." The family is saying in effect, "If you violate one standard or area of your life, we give up on you. You're no longer one of us." Even if we feel that way at times, our calling is to stay connected.

## BLURRED BOUNDARIES

We could learn a lesson from a more primitive people. In the Australian aboriginal tribes, each family member occupies a unique physical space in the home. If a woman leaves her family for a year, ten years, or even twenty-five years, it wouldn't matter.

Her place would be there when she returns. The daughter could choose to absent herself from her family, but the family would not absent itself from her.[8]

I find this an excellent example of "bonding with boundaries." Bonding means forming an especially close relationship. Healthy families thrive on intimacy, yet each individual within that unit needs clearly defined personal boundaries. Where do I stop and you begin? What's my stuff and what's your stuff? What's my problem and what's your problem? These kinds of concerns assume greater and greater importance in direct proportion to the closeness of the relationship.

A healthy family reflects clear lines of separation between adults and children, regardless of whether one parent or two live under the same roof. Proper boundaries have been established. Yet many families suffer significant difficulties because those boundaries have become blurred and broken.

In a healthy family, parents are expected to meet the needs of their children, but the children are not expected to meet the needs of their parents. However, some parents burden their children with adult expectations and demands. Usually without realizing it, a mother or father may expect a child to perform and give at a level that is unhealthy and unrealistic.

A healthy separateness means that an adult needs to function as an adult and a child needs to function as a child. But some parents use their children as their source of identity. They don't want to let them grow up and become independent. They want to keep them attached—never cutting the umbilical cord, so to speak.

＆

*When adults have difficulty allowing their children to grow up and fail to relate to them as adults after they have reached adulthood, boundaries have been invaded and violated.*

Dr. John Townsend describes a mother who confided to her friend about the problems she was having with her eighteen-month-old son. This mother shared that she and her son had been so close ever since he was born, but their relationship had become very difficult of late. The little boy had become disobedient and disagreeable, even throwing nasty temper tantrums. She lamented that she was going to miss her "easy baby" and feared they were on the verge of entering the "terrible two's."

Her friend's response may have thrown her a bit because I'm sure it wasn't what she expected to hear. The friend encouraged her by saying that she could certainly understand the frustration, but she perceived this new stage much differently. She called it the "terrific two's." This second woman was actually looking forward to seeing her child's personality begin to emerge and blossom.[9]

I'm not sure I've ever heard anyone describe the two's as "terrific," yet here was a mother who was joyful about her child's growth and development. She was focusing upon what was going to happen with her child rather than upon what those changes would cost her. When adults have difficulty allowing their children to grow up and fail to relate to them as adults after they have reached adulthood, boundaries have been invaded and violated. Parents need to teach their children how to set boundaries. By learning this crucial lesson, they will be better able to make responsible choices later in life.

## SURVEYING OUR PROPERTY LINES

Perhaps the best way to describe what we mean by boundaries is to call them "property lines." When Iraq invaded Kuwait in 1990, the boundary lines were violated. Our states, counties, townships, and houses are all demarcated by clear boundaries which are elaborately specified in the written property titles. Once I requested that a city employee survey my lot so that I would be clear about my property lines. I didn't want to infringe upon my neighbors if I built a structure or planted some trees.

Recently I counseled a young adult who was living on his own. "Norm," he said, "when we had that recent conflict between those two countries and the one invaded the other, I just laughed. So the one country has been invaded for the first time in fifty years. I've been invaded by my parents for the past twenty-seven years. They still try to make decisions for me and tell me what to do. They want to know everything that is going on in my life and they're upset now because I don't tell them much and I don't come around. But I've got to establish myself as an adult. I've made too many mistakes already because of not being encouraged to be who I was as I was growing up. I don't want to make any more mistakes and I don't want to be overly involved with my own kids if I have any."

His experience serves as a good example of boundary invasion. What can you do as a family to encourage healthy boundaries? Here are a number of positive steps you can take:

1. Allow freedom for family members to state their opinions.
2. Make it safe to disagree without fear of recrimination.
3. Encourage every person in the family to think for himself or herself and show that you believe in his or her ability to decide.
4. Assist each person in discovering his or her talents and spiritual gifts and in developing and using them to the fullest.
5. Allow the expression of all feelings—including anger.
6. Set limits with natural and logical consequences, but not fear or guilt.
7. Allow age-appropriate choices.
8. Respect others when they say no.[10]

Ask yourself and the other family members the question, "To what degree is this true of our family life?" If someone experiences a deficiency in any of these positive steps of encouragement, write out both how you would like your family to be and the specific steps that you personally will take to make a change.

## LEARNING TO SAY NO

Some parents tell me they feel like jugglers. And they are—especially in this area on healthy bonding and setting boundaries. The task involves trying to keep family members attached in an intimate manner, yet separate at the same time.

One of the crucial lessons every parent needs to help his or her child learn is how to say no appropriately. Unfortunately, we quickly weary of hearing this word from a young child. We become convinced that "no" is his or her favorite word, rating even above "Mom" or "Dad." We wonder whatever happened to "home on the range, where never is heard a discouraging word." We begin to long for the good old days of strong parental authority.

Yet our children desperately need to learn how to use this word later on in their lives. When someone has never learned how to say no, that person feels endless confusion about his or her boundaries. In describing some of the sources for this confusion in children, Dr. John Townsend has suggested that parents who are confused about boundaries tend to produce children who are also confused. Such a premise seems logical to me.

*Source points of confusion.* We can identify several source points of confusion concerning boundaries. Consider these in three ways. First, does this situation sound familiar in the family from which you came? Second, does it sound familiar in your current family situation? And third, if so, what steps can you make to change this situation?

- Parents who feel abandoned when their children begin to make autonomous choices. These parents respond to autonomy in their children by conveying guilt or shame messages about their lack of love and loyalty to the family or to the parents.
- Parents who feel threatened by their increasing loss of control over the children. These parents use anger or criticism, not guilt or shame messages, to convey their unhappiness over the children's new-found separateness.
- Families which equate disagreement with sin.
- Parents who are afraid of the anger of their children.
- Parents who are hostile toward the anger of their children.
- Families which praise compliance in the name of togetherness over healthy independence.
- Families in which emotional, physical, and sexual abuse occur. These kinds of abuse cause severe damage to the children's sense of ownership of their bodies and themselves.
- Families in which the children feel responsible for the happiness of the parents.

- Parents who rescue children from experiencing the consequences of their behavior.
- Parents who are inconsistent in setting limits with the children.
- Parents who continue to take responsibility for the children in adulthood.[11]

*Predictable problems.* When boundaries are not clearly established and become easily permeable, a number of predictable problems can occur. Some people never learn to say no to others because of their excessive desire to please, or perhaps from feelings of guilt and fear. Still others set boundaries where none need to be set, usually in areas of personal need. They block off their own legitimate needs, often unaware of their existence. They would feel guilty asking for what they need from someone else.

Perhaps you've met someone like this—a person who adamantly refuses, vigorously objects, and becomes visibly uncomfortable whenever you attempt to do something for him or her. This person can give to others but cannot receive. By spoiling others and inadvertently teaching them they don't need to give in return, such people end up being neglectful of both others and themselves.

❧

> *Perhaps you've met someone like this—a person who adamantly refuses, vigorously objects, and becomes visibly uncomfortable whenever you attempt to do something for him or her.*

Some people have a different problem with the word no. They seem to be deaf to it. When others say no, it literally has no effect. They violate the boundaries of others by projecting their own responsibilities onto others. In one way or another, they get other people to take responsibility for them.

A final way in which boundary violation occurs is in the neglect of others' needs. Such an individual neglects to show love, care, or concern for others. This person is often critical of others and absorbed with his or her own life. Scripture instructs us, "Do not withhold good from those to whom it is due, when it is in your power to do it" (Prv 3:27, NASB). The admonition in Galatians 6:2 is to "bear one another's burdens." A multitude of passages exhort us to express love to others.[12]

Consider these typical problems which stem from the lack of proper boundaries and identify any person within your family who fits the description. Perhaps you can direct the person to some helpful reading on this subject or to get counseling to help them overcome this tendency. Remember that the sooner a problem can be identified and the younger the person, the easier it will be to make a course correction.

## WHO OWNS THE DEED?

Perhaps the best way to sum up this issue is to ask you a question: Do you know what is yours and what isn't? Or to put it another way, do your family members know what is theirs and what isn't? Lack of boundaries is essentially a problem of ownership.

We now own two dogs, an aging Sheltie and a young Golden Retriever. When the Sheltie takes the Retriever's rope toy, she violates his boundaries and discovers just how possessive he feels about that toy!

Every family needs to ask the question, "In what way do my boundaries need to be repaired?" Consider how well the following statements describe the family from which you came and then your current family situation. A simple check beside each one will do. Be sure to ask other family members to answer these as well. Sometimes it helps to try and anticipate how you think the others will answer!

1. I felt much closer to one of my parents than the other as I grew up.
2. One of my parents leaned on me for emotional support.
3. I was a "best friend" to one of my parents from childhood on.
4. One of my parents shared secrets and confidences with me.
5. One of my parents gave me special privileges or gifts and let me know that I was a favorite.

6. One parent thought I was better company to him or her than the spouse was.
7. Sometimes I felt uncomfortable or guilty when I spent time away from my parents.
8. I was aware that a parent didn't want me to marry or move out.
9. When I did move out, my relationship with my parents didn't change.
10. No one I dated seemed to be accepted or good enough for my parents.
11. I felt that I was put on a pedestal by one of my parents.
12. It was difficult to have my own privacy at home.[13]

If you checked several of these statements, what does that say to you about boundaries when you were growing up? About the boundaries in your present family?

## KEEP OUT! NO TRESPASSING!

People with clearly defined boundaries fence off certain areas of their lives with a "KEEP OUT! NO TRESPASSING!" sign. Intimacy is by invitation only to certain trusted individuals. Others find their private territory constantly invaded and wonder why. Without realizing it, these folks may have in one way or another posted a sign saying, "TRESPASSERS, WELCOME!" Many allow others to invade by not taking any action, not stating what they prefer, explaining too much, or living in fear of offending someone.

ప

*Without realizing it, these folks may have in one way or another posted a sign saying, "TRESPASSERS, WELCOME!"*

If you feel this pattern of ongoing invasion describes your own relationships, you may want to consider posting a new sign. What might you be doing or saying to invite or at least allow others to invade your territory? Sometimes you even need to go a little overboard at first to find the right balance in establishing your personal boundaries.

A friend of mine had an intrusive sister who expected her to come for every Christmas. Instead she called her sister and said, "I'm planning on going to a friend's this year, so I won't be there." As her sister started to press her for reasons and poured on the guilt, my friend simply repeated her statement one more time and then guided the conversation to other subjects.

One man in his fifties had struggled with an invasive and critical mother for years. During a typically unpleasant conversation he said, "Mother, from this point on I would appreciate it if you would not criticize me or my brothers when you call me. I want to talk with you, but if you criticize I will not continue the conversation any longer. It doesn't do you or me any good. Now, what would you like to talk about?" After this man had repeated the same statement on three consecutive phone conversations, his mother no longer directed critical remarks his way. I wonder if his brothers fared as well.

Begin to observe how other people ward off intruders. What has worked well for them may sound terrifying at first, but anyone can learn the same skills. One successful approach is to state your decision in as few words as possible. Do not even attempt to give any reasons or overexplain. Simply state your intention and then go on to the rest of the conversation. Be sure to clarify that you are not breaking off all contact with the person who tends to invade your boundaries, but simply establishing limits on some topics that you would rather not discuss any more.[14]

Here are some examples of healthy boundaries and unhealthy extremes.[15]

---

**TOO PERMEABLE**      (Inappropriate)

---

- I talk at an intimate level at the first meeting.
- I am preoccupied and overwhelmed with other people and their needs.
- I can fall in love with a new acquaintance.
- I let others determine my reality.

- I let others direct my life.
- I don't ever notice when others invade my personal boundaries.
- I sacrifice my values in order to be close to other people.

**PERMEABLE** (Appropriate)

- I don't overwhelm people with personal information, but allow time for trust to develop.
- I am able to keep relationships in perspective and function effectively in other areas of my life.
- I know love is based on respect and trust, which take time to develop.
- I believe my perceptions are as accurate as anyone's.
- I make decisions for myself based on God's guidance.
- I notice when others try to make decisions for me, are overly helpful, and/or don't consult me about planning my time.
- I am not willing to do "anything" to maintain a relationship, but have biblical values that are not negotiable.

**IMPERMEABLE** (Inappropriate)

- I don't ever open up, even to people I know to be trustworthy and caring.
- I don't let myself even think about another person I'm interested in.
- I don't ever let loving feelings develop for anyone.
- I am unwilling to listen to others' perceptions.
- I refuse to consider the opinions of others.
- I never allow anyone to help me or give me ideas and suggestions, even when helpful and appropriate.
- I am never willing to change anything I do to please anybody.

৯৯

## BRINGING IT HOME

As you seek to strengthen and improve your present family relationships, you may be concerned that someone is going to recommend some extensive surgical procedure requiring massive blood transfusions. The condition of the average family is usually not so critical, but most can certainly use a realignment such as a chiropractor might give.

Have you ever sat in a chiropractor's office and watched the patients creep in? Some put one foot in front of another very slowly; others walk in with a tilt. Pain has made each of them off-center in some way. Usually an adjustment to the spine brings the rest of the body into balance.

The spine of a family system is the adults and especially the parents. A husband and wife in balance with one another can lend stability to others who may be leaning away from the family. Often a push or a pull in one direction or another will help the family walk straight again as well.

We can all learn to respond differently in our relationships. What is not possible to determine is how the other person(s) will in turn respond to us, but that is not our responsibility.

Who do you want to improve your relationship with in the future? What specific steps will you take? How will this help your family life and the functioning of the family?

What are some of the obstacles or difficulties you will have to overcome? Describe the specific ways in which you are willing to be different. How will God be involved in this process? What will you do in order to increase your bonding with the Lord?

Listen to the story one client shared with me. Perhaps this mother's journey can give you some direction for your own life.

"Norm, for years I've struggled with my relationship with my second oldest daughter. We just never seemed to click or hit it off. We're not getting any younger, so I decided it was up to me to make some changes and try a new approach. I wish she would have taken the initiative, but perhaps my expectations were too much.

"My first step was to figure out what beliefs I had developed over the years about myself, about Sharon and about our relationship. Many of them had been cast in concrete after twenty-three years and not only that, many were negative and self-defeating. I actually began writing down what I thought or believed, and then either challenged the belief or stated what I was choosing to believe for the future.

"I used to believe it was useless to share my feelings and ever be vulnerable. So I started with this and it actually gave me more courage to initiate a close relationship. It was difficult at times to break out of some of my defensive patterns. But by praying each time before I went to see her—and actually rehearsing some new approaches and statements—we began to relate better. I learned to quit giving motherly advice. I listened and reflected back what I heard more and didn't cut her off when she became angry.

"What surprised me was discovering that each of us began to be free enough to be a bit dependent upon one another. That was something new. We're now learning to bond as two adults and we're all more relaxed at family get-togethers!"

Once you've decided what changes you would like to see come to pass in your own relationships, what are the steps you need to take to make them happen? First, consider your present family situation in light of positives and family togetherness to give you added insight into the independence/dependence balance.

A. List the five things each family member does which please you the most, stressing what they *do* rather than what they *are*.

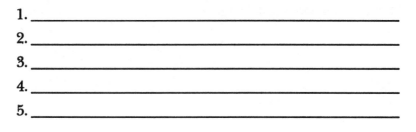

1. _____
2. _____
3. _____
4. _____
5. _____

B. List two positive and specific things which you would like each one to do more often. Be sure your answers are positive and specific. You will need to write your responses on additional pieces of paper. Take time to share your responses with one another.

1. _____

It was done _____ times in the last seven days.

I consider it:

___ very important
___ important
___ not important.

2. _____

It was done _____ times in the last seven days.

I consider it:

___ very important
___ important
___ not important.

C. If you were applying for a job as a member in your own family, how would you describe your best assets for the position to the interviewer?

1. _____
2. _____
3. _____ [16]

Next, consider how satisfied you are with the following aspects of your family on a scale from one to ten. Set aside several family times to share your responses with one another. When you hear a response that is different and more negative then yours, listen to the other person's reasons and desires rather then becoming defensive. Focus on the steps which will be necessary in order for positive change to occur.

## *I Am Satisfied:*

1. With how close I feel to the other members of my family:

0———————————————5———————————————10
Not at all    Not much    Average  Some  Yes!  Very much!

I would like to feel closer to _____

To make this happen I could _____

2. With the freedom I have to say what I want in my family.

0———————————————5———————————————10
Not at all    Not much    Average  Some  Yes!  Very much!

What I would like to be able to say is _____.

3. With my family's willingness to try new things.

0———————————————5———————————————10
Not at all    Not much    Average  Some  Yes!  Very much!

What I would like to see us try is _____.

4. With the way in which we divide up the family tasks.

0———————————————5———————————————10
Not at all    Not much    Average  Some  Yes!  Very much!

A suggestion that I have for this is _____.

5. With the way in which decisions are made in the family

0———————————————5———————————————10
Not at all    Not much    Average  Some  Yes!  Very much!

A suggestion that I have for this is _____.

6. With the amount of arguing and quarreling in our family.

0———————————————5———————————————10
Not at all    Not much    Average  Some  Yes!  Very much!

What I would like to see changed about this is _____.

7. With the way we deal with problems within the family.

0————————————5————————————10
Not at all    Not much    Average    Some    Yes!    Very much!

I would like the problems to be handled _____

_____.

8. With the way we make requests for changes in one another's behavior.

0————————————5————————————10
Not at all    Not much    Average    Some    Yes!    Very much!

I would like requests for change to be handled this way _____

_____.

9. With the way in which we show one another understanding.

0————————————5————————————10
Not at all    Not much    Average    Some    Yes!    Very much!

I would like our expression of understanding to be _____

_____.

10. With the way we support one another when we experience an individual or family crisis.

0————————————5————————————10
Not at all    Not much    Average    Some    Yes!    Very much!

I would like our support in a crisis to be _____

_____.

11. With the amount of time we spend together as a family.

0————————————5————————————10
Not at all    Not much    Average    Some    Yes!    Very much!

I would prefer the amount of time together to be _____

_____.

12. With the respect which we show for each other's opinions and ideas.

0————————————5————————————10
Not at all    Not much    Average    Some   Yes!   Very much!
I would like our level of respect to be _____.

13. With the freedom to be alone when I need to be.

0————————————5————————————10
Not at all    Not much    Average    Some   Yes!   Very much!
I would like my level of freedom to be alone to be _____.

14. With my family's acceptance of my friends.

0————————————5————————————10
Not at all    Not much    Average    Some   Yes!   Very much!
I would like my family's acceptance of my friends to be _____

_____.

To make this happen I could _____.

15. With the expectations that we have for one another.

0————————————5————————————10
Not at all    Not much    Average    Some   Yes!   Very much!
A change that I would like to see is _____.

16. With the number of enjoyable things we do together as a family

0————————————5————————————10
Not at all    Not much    Average    Some   Yes!   Very much!
My suggestions for this are _____.

17. With the level of church involvement.

0————————————5————————————10
Not at all    Not much    Average    Some   Yes!   Very much!
I would like our level of church involvement to be _____

_____.

18. With the amount of prayer and interaction we have on spiritual matters.

0————————————————5————————————————10
Not at all   Not much   Average  Some  Yes!  Very much!

I would like our spiritual life to be _____.

19. With the use of money in our family.

0————————————————5————————————————10
Not at all   Not much   Average  Some  Yes!  Very much!

I would like our use of money to be_____.

Finally, families who want to adequately bond with one another must spend enough time together. Evaluate how each family member currently spends time. What activities might you enjoy doing together (even if you have never done so before) and how often would you like to do each of them?

## Who Does What, Where, and When?

**MOTHER:**              MON TUES WED THURS FRI SAT SUN
What days and hours does she...

   work outside of the home?

   eat breakfast with family?

   eat lunch with family?

   eat dinner with family?

   spend the day at home?

   spend the evening at home?

**FATHER:**              MON TUES WED THURS FRI SAT SUN
What days and hours does he...

   work outside of the home?

   eat breakfast with family?

   eat lunch with family?

eat dinner with family?

spend the day at home?

spend the evening at home?

**CHILD:**                    MON TUES WED THURS FRI SAT SUN

What days and hours does he/she...

attend school?

work?

eat breakfast with family?

eat lunch with family?

eat dinner with family?

spend the day at home?

spend the evening at home?

**CHILD:**                    MON TUES WED THURS FRI SAT SUN

What days and hours does he/she...

attend school?

work?

eat breakfast with family?

eat lunch with family?

eat dinner with family?

spend the day at home?

spend the evening at home?

**CHILD:**                    MON TUES WED THURS FRI SAT SUN

What days and hours does he/she...

attend school?

work?

eat breakfast with family?

eat lunch with family?

eat dinner with family?

spend the day at home?

spend the evening at home?

## *I Would Like to Do This:*

| ACTIVITY | DAILY | WEEKLY | MONTHLY | LESS OFTEN |
|----------|-------|--------|---------|-----------|

1. _____
2. _____
3. _____
4. _____
5. _____

Once again it is important to compare your responses. This last evaluation chart is often a revelation for many as you see your time involvement written down.

# 6

# DRIVING ON EMPTY

WHENEVER WE LEAVE FOR A TRIP, I always make sure that the gas tank is full and that I'm headed in the right direction on the freeway. Whenever I fly, I'm even more concerned that my plane has a full load of fuel and that the radar is functioning. In either case, I want to arrive safely at my destination.

What do gas tanks and radar have to do with family relationships? People come equipped with their own personal tank of fuel for the journey—one that needs to be filled with love. Food provides energy for our physical bodies, but without love our hearts soon wither and die. People also seem to have a built-in radar system as well. We can't always see clearly where we're headed. In times of confusion or heavy storm clouds, we need that internal sense of direction to bring us safely home.

People often come to me for counseling with empty love tanks and short-circuited radars. An unhealthy family background can leave them feeling hurt, rejected, and starved for love and acceptance. Because of this deep love hunger, they often develop skewed radar that automatically draws them to others who appear able to fill their empty tanks. But so often, these starving people end up selecting a partner who turns out to be just like the parents from whom they couldn't get enough love!

I find it uncanny how two hurting individuals will find each other across a crowded room—even though dozens of others may be equally available. Their needy radar constantly works to draw two love-hungry people together.

And when they meet, do they let each other know that they are needy, hurting, and looking to the other person to fill up their empty places? Not on your life. They mask the emptiness of their love tanks. Each appears to be what he or she is not to the other person, and each tends to idealize the other. They unconsciously think, "Finally, I've found the one who can help me be complete."

ࡄ

*I find it uncanny how two hurting individuals will find each other across a crowded room—even though dozens of others may be equally available.*

People like this tend to believe "if I put my half-person together with your half-person, together we'll finally be a whole person! I'll fulfill you. You'll fulfill me." But it doesn't work that way. In order for two people to be happily married, they first of all need to be happily married to *themselves*. Otherwise they are soon disappointed and dismayed. If one person is healthy and his or her love tank is fairly full, he or she may end up feeling suffocated by this needy person.

These folks often don't even realize what's really going on in their desperate efforts to fill their love tanks. Men who do realize the deficiency of their past may try to compensate by choosing a mate who is the opposite of their mothers. But as Jim discovered, being aware of a bad pattern can carry its own set of problems.

Jim's mother was the dominant controlling force in the family. His dad never had a voice in any of the decisions for the children. As soon as high school was over, Jim joined the navy to get away.

Seven years later he met an attractive, passive woman who needed to be cared for by someone who could take charge. Just what Jim wanted!

But the relationship was anything but smooth. And over the years, the same issue kept recurring, just like a broken record. Andrea insisted that Jim make the decisions and take responsibility for their lives. Jim wanted to get away from his mother's domination and sought out a woman totally unlike her. But this meant he left behind the comfortable arena to which he was accustomed. Even though this is what Jim wanted, venturing into such a new role created insecurities and turmoil. He was full of tension in his quest to have a different relationship with a woman.

Karen's mother was cold, demanding, unloving, and quite withdrawn. Because Karen never felt sure she was loved, she gradually began to resent her mother. This void in her life caused her to seek out relationships with men who were warm, accepting, and loving—even though they lacked the qualities of responsibility and motivation.

Like Jim and Andrea, Karen was propelled toward selecting a spouse by needs and forces of which she may not have even been fully conscious. Such a choice is often guided by faulty radar. When both partners are needy, the trip can be like driving along a country road and having your car run out of gas. With no gas stations in sight, you flag down a passing motorist. You try to siphon gas from the other car to your own but discover that the other car's tank is just about empty as well. Since you already siphoned out some, now you're both stuck on empty.[1]

## EMOTIONAL FUSION

Ideal relationships blend healthy dependency and healthy independence. We constantly struggle to achieve the proper mixture between husbands and wives and between parents and children. Parenting involves a gradual process of relinquishing one's children until they are finally independent. Recently a mother of two college-age daughters cried out in anguish, "Why didn't someone teach me how to let go of my children years ago? It's so difficult to have to do it now!"

Unhealthy relationships reflect overinvolvement with the other person. As two people become enmeshed, they feed upon a mutual illusion: "As I become closer to you, I discover my own identity." This is another way of saying, "My half-person needs your half-person and then we become complete." Each one attempts to draw from the other a personal identity. But the real problem remains unresolved: neither of them has a solid sense of self to offer the other.

Hungry for fulfillment, each becomes more invested in the identity of the other. Each anticipates or mimics the partner's wants and preferences. Intent on a truly great relationship, each person pretends things are perfect when they're not. Anger, frustration, and tension begin to build but are quickly buried. After all, two people so much in love shouldn't feel that way. Sometimes the closeness becomes suffocating. If one begins to withdraw, the very identity of the other feels threatened.

≈

*Intent on a truly great relationship,*
*each person pretends things are perfect when they're not.*

The identities in a codependent relationship are similar to the birth of Siamese twins. The surgeon faces an agonizing dilemma: if the twins are separated, one or both may perish. And yet they might not survive together. In emotional codependency, each feels certain he or she cannot continue on if they are separated. And yet being together is damaging.[2]

I watched some of the Winter Olympic ice skating competition on television, and noticed especially the synchronized choreography of the pairs competition. The two skaters glide along in perfect harmony, perform their double and triple jumps in unison, and then join together again in the most intricate moves. But they are not bound to each other in any way. Each is a complete skater with individual freedom, but the hours and years of practice allow them to skate together as one.

Now imagine these two skaters trying to execute the same choreography while tied together at the waist by a rope. As they draw the rope tighter and tighter, they valiantly try to perform their dance but quickly end up tripping and falling all over one another. This same sort of dynamic is played out in a codependent relationship as each person becomes more and more closely attached to the other in search of his or her own identity.

I remember reading a description of marriage as an "emotional fusion of two personalities" into a functional whole, much like the biblical concept of "one flesh" (Gn 2:24). The author went on to illustrate the marriage relationship by talking about two lumps of clay. If you were to hold a lump of dark green clay in your left hand and a lump of light green clay in your right hand, you could clearly see the different shades. However, if you were to take both of these pieces of clay and mold and push them together, you would see just one lump of green clay—at first glance.

But if you were to inspect the lump closely, you would see the distinct and separate lines of dark green and light green intermingled through the clay. This is like the marriage relationship— two people blended together so they appear as one, yet each retaining his or her own distinct identity or personality.[3]

Healthy independence and dependence lend strength to both people. In building a platform, some people have a tendency to put the braces or pillars in a V-shape or an A-shape. But what actually works best are pillars that are not leaning on each other or touching in any way. The strongest base uses pillars that stand apart. "Sturdy, upright. Together but apart. Separate entities in a mutual role. Therein lies true strength."[4]

## CLIMATE CONTROL

When too much dependence exists in any type of relationship, one person seems to act as a thermostat for the feelings and moods of the others. If the heat is turned up, others feel it. If the heat is turned down, it affects them as well. Instead of each room having its own separate thermostat, the family can be governed by a central heating system.

For a home that's fine. For the family it is not. The members begin to react primarily to what occurs instead of acting on their own while still considering the others. I remember one mother who asked, "What's wrong with the rest of my family feeling down and depressed when I'm that way? They should feel that way if they care about me!" This woman was quite taken aback when I suggested it would be healthier if that didn't happen. Someone needs to stay strong when another person is down.

Have you ever heard of the "Independent/Dependent" family lifestyle? No, it's not a label for some new family disorder, but a term used to describe a realistic, healthy, family relationship. What would it be like if your immediate family members were each independent in a healthy way, dependent upon other family members when needed, and totally dependent upon the person of Jesus Christ? Idealistic? Perhaps. Worth working toward? Definitely. But this seems like an elusive dream for many people, especially those who come from a dysfunctional family background.

ða

*We seem to have a built-in magnet that draws us to remember the worst. And we allow this to overshadow more joyful experiences, to spread like a creeping sore and contaminate the rest of life.*

Many people go around constantly longing for change while muttering regrets and "if only's" under their breath. We often reflect upon our family of origin with this attitude. By repeating this tendency often enough, we eventually begin to project it onto our present circumstances. We look at the years spent with our spouse and say "if only." We look at the years with our children and do the same. We seem to have a built-in magnet that draws us to remember the worst. And we allow this to overshadow more joyful experiences, to spread like a creeping sore and contaminate the rest of life.

I'm certainly not suggesting that we ignore, discount, or deny our past history. When we do try to repress the terrors of our memories, they just continue to knock on the door to our present lives. Renouncing what has occurred doesn't work. Rather we must confront, cleanse, and refocus our energy to what we would like our present family to become.

With the help of Jesus Christ at work in our lives, we are never stuck. He's just waiting for us to ask for his help and cooperate by doing our part. Do you really want to be free from the painful memories of the past as well as the pain of the present? Are you willing to pay the price and really be transformed from the inside out?

## REWRITING HISTORY

Steven Covey, a motivational leader and author, talks about people who are either "reactive" or "proactive." Reactive people are strongly affected by their surroundings, whether it be events or people. They constantly build their emotional lives around the responses of others, which allows the weaknesses of others to dictate their own behavior.

Even the weather can make or break their day. If the sun is shining, they feel good. But if dark clouds fill the sky, they feel gloomy. Proactive people carry their own weather around with them. While the weather might alter their plans a bit, they have learned not to let it affect their basic attitude toward life.

Many are reactive when it comes to thinking about their family of the past and their family of the present. Some continue to react to experiences from their past as though they are currently happening. Having never made that important transition of shedding the impact of those painful memories, they end up feeling like a victim for the rest of their lives.

Proactive people can be just as aware of what is going on around them—whether it is related to the past or present—but they have learned to respond in a new way. As the adage goes, it's not *what happens to us* but *our response to what happens to us* that can hurt and hinder us.[5]

I remember one person's struggle to cope with some of the current frustrations in his family. "I feel as though I've never had a chance with my marriage or my children," he said sadly. "My past family keeps getting in the way, even though my parents are dead and we hardly ever see my younger brother. I wish I could rewrite my past! I'd like to rewrite history!"

"You can," I said to Richard. That stopped him in his tracks. He was literally stunned.

"You've got to be kidding. There is no way you can rewrite history... is there?"

My reply did not swerve. "Yes, you can, if you learn to reinterpret that history and begin to discover the positive experiences that have been denied, forgotten, or overlooked. Would you like to learn how?" Of course, Richard was eager to begin.

I used an analogy from the book *Chosen for Blessing*, which calls the reader to become a "tomorrow person" rather than a "yesterday person." I think these terms are pretty self-explanatory. Jack Hayford, a well-known pastor, describes how millions of people experience life in a rather unique way:

> Predecessors, plain people such as our parents, teachers or friends (even those disposed to our best interest) can cast shadows over our tomorrows. They may have set boundaries on our lives, limiting our view of ourselves or our potential. Or they may have been confined by boundaries of their own which found exact or mirrored images in us. But in either case, our predecessors often shape us, leaving an imprint which may be the source of our own present frustration.
>
> How can we deal with this?
>
> First, though God wants to free us unto tomorrow, He won't allow us to blame yesterday. Neither will He allow us to cast blame on anything or anybody who seems to restrict our tomorrows.[6]

Many of our memories are slanted and biased, appearing gloomier than reality because we view them through the dark glasses of grief. And the most negative and painful are usually granted an overabundance of power—like a massive complex radar which has the power to disrupt other local radar systems.

One of the exercises I recommend to a person in counseling is to pick a painful, disruptive experience from his or her past (this will work for current situations as well). I ask the person to describe it as an objective observer would, trying to stand on the outside looking in and responding to the facts of just this one event. As people force themselves through this process, they begin to discover features about that particular event which they failed to see or perhaps had forgotten. Work through this with a past episode that you feel is interfering with your family life. It's worth the effort.

## INDEPENDENCE: A DOUBLE-EDGED SWORD

In addition to breaking our own pattern of overinvolvement with others, we must also help our children become increasingly independent of us. But that often feels like a double-edged sword. The child may experience freedom and equality, while the parents may suffer separation and loss. Such growth can bring mutually supportive relationships, while at the same time bringing along in its wake a lifetime of conflict.

In the highly practical book *Leading a Child to Independence*, the authors compare the growing independence of a youngster to America's Declaration of Independence. Independence is something that happens "in the course of human events." And since it is so inevitable, we would be better off to prepare for it and foster it. As much as possible, parents need to be in charge of the process rather than be buffeted willy-nilly by the stormy winds of blustering rebellion.

When parents do not let go, the entire family can suffer dire consequences: "It leaves emotionally crippled parents living their lives through emotionally crippled children who then feebly try to perform as adults while avoiding the responsibilities of determining the destiny of their country, offspring, and society. The results are a loss of independence for all—past, present and future."[7]

Another phrase in the Declaration of Independence states that it becomes necessary "for one people to dissolve the political bonds which have connected them with one another." Sometimes a child decides that it's time to leave home. Sometimes the parent reaches that conclusion first. Each party holds the power to make the decision. And when the implementation is handled properly, the bonds can dissolve in a way that is congenial and healthy.

The Declaration goes on to say that independence is a *separate and equal* station or position in life. For a while, our country was politically and economically dependent upon England. We needed the security and protection of an established power. But America gradually grew to desire a life of its own. England naturally wanted to protect this budding colony. Because it was unwilling or unable to let go, the bloody and costly American Revolution had to be waged to sever the bonds. Unfortunately, some families end up suffering casualties in their own smaller version of the revolutionary war in the children's quest for independence![8]

**ॐ**

*Unfortunately, some families end up suffering casualties in their own smaller version of the revolutionary war in the children's quest for independence!*

## HARD WORK PAYS OFF

Here is the story of how one set of parents, Paul and Jeannie McKean, helped their children move toward independence:

As the children got older, we began studying Scripture together.... Then we started to talk about their quiet times and the things we were learning in our walks with the Lord. From our journals we shared what the Lord was teaching us. If we had a hard week, we felt free to talk about it and soak up the affirmation of our family. We took our concerns to the Lord in a spirit of oneness.

We also helped Tanya and Todd develop goals for their own lives. We felt part of being independent is knowing where you are going. In 1983, we became familiar with MasterPlanning Associates, which helped us consider questions such as "What are you dreaming of accomplishing five to twenty years from now?" Or "What needs do you feel deeply burdened by and uniquely qualified to meet?" We helped our children assess the milestones they had already passed and the ideas they would like to see become reality. We talked about colleges and careers and our purpose in life. Together we were able to dream dreams, some of which have already come true.

As the children became more independent, Paul and I let them organize some of the family days. Each of the four of us planned one Sunday each month. Todd's favorite activity was cross-country skiing; Tanya enjoyed relaxing at Dana Point Harbor.

One of the most practical things we did during our family times was talk about events to come. Each week we got out the calendar, looked at the commitments, and then planned the rest of the week. When the children were little, they were most interested in free time for play; but little by little their activities began to match ours. Looking at the calendar together has helped us take an active interest in one another's lives and avoid the miscommunications which plague busy families. Therefore we were better able to pray for each other and to understand the pressures and opportunities we shared.[9]

When asked about her parents' approach in helping them grow toward independence, Tanya replied: "My parents have made a lot of decisions for me and yet have made me make a lot of decisions. They have given me freedom when I've shown I can handle it responsibly—and even when I haven't been responsible, just to let me know I'm an individual who has worth and importance. I know now that I am quite intelligent and I can make decisions. Later on I will become responsible in certain areas that I might not be doing well in right now."

Todd also expressed his appreciation:

"As I look back, I know my parents have really cared about our lives and what we've been interested in. They haven't said, 'Kids, we're going to do this because your father and I want to do this,' or anything like that.

"They consulted us about activities we wanted. We spend at least an hour or two doing something with our parents each weekend—different kinds of activities that kids usually do. My dad and I got a little airplane that we put fuel into, and we held it by a string as it flew around in the air. We also got interested in train sets and spent some of our activity time on them. That was really fun! I know most of my friends' parents never took time for special activities with them; so I feel that really shows my parents' interest in my life."[10]

In a letter to his father, Tony, Bart Campolo reflected on how his parents helped him grow:

... That's what real freedom is, I think: the understanding that in a world filled with choices and decisions, under tremendous pressure from other people and our own desires, amid the paralyzing fear of mistakes or failure, loving God and loving His people are the only things that really matter, and doing those things is a decision that we genuinely have the ability to make in every situation.

You and Mom didn't let me do whatever I wanted to, Dad, but you gave me my freedom nonetheless. I think I finally appreciate it.
Love,<br>Bart[11]

## SAYING GOODBYE

Change can occur. Mid-course corrections can happen. But be aware! The most minor relationship adjustments will inevitably upset the delicate balance or equilibrium of family life. Even positive changes will at first create discomfort and tension. Every member of the family may be saying, "Yes, I want to change." But change carries a price tag. We creatures of habit tend to become locked into patterns of relating that frequently resist new behaviors.

In eliminating a negative pattern of behavior or relationship response, many people have found that actually saying goodbye can be very helpful. I've seen family members write down a list of what they used to do and then hold a farewell ceremony as a definitive step in breaking with their past. They literally say goodbye to each statement on the paper out loud. They commit to the Lord their new way of relating and then cut up or burn their old list.

**ᕘ**

*The most minor relationship adjustments will inevitably upset the delicate balance or equilibrium of family life.*

Saying goodbye is one of the steps recommended in the process of grief recovery. Whenever we make a significant change in how we relate to others or ourselves, we experience a loss as well as a gain. Sometimes the feelings of loss will loom larger than the gain—especially as we move through the initial stages of adjustment. No matter what loss we may have suffered, we need to grieve over that loss.

Perhaps such a change will produce an identity loss. Learning how to respond in a new and healthier way is risky. As we begin to question ourselves, our emotions may seem attached to a roller coaster. This particular kind of grief can be especially difficult because no one else may even recognize our loss; no public gathering or ceremony comforts our mourning.

Saying goodbye is not morbid, pathological, or a sign of hysteria. We say goodbye in many ways to many things in our lives, without even being aware of it. Why not take charge of it, face what we are losing, identify how our lives will be different, and feel the pain over the adjustment? Then we will be able to move on with greater freedom in our individual and family life.

Don't expect to move through this farewell process rapidly and in a straight line, as though you were traveling on a four-lane expressway. You will be forced to take some detours from time to time because the highway is under reconstruction. Traveling some bumpy roads is more normal than smoothly sailing along. Rebuilding a relationship means reinvesting in your family life. A new level of satisfaction is possible. But for a while, you may very well feel uncomfortable with whatever is new.

## THE NATURE OF CATERPILLARS

We all tend to resist changing. We come up with reasons (excuses) as to why it won't work and especially why the other people won't change even if we try. Most of us will go to great lengths to avoid unnecessary pain. If we see a loss coming down the road, why deliberately suffer the pain? So we play mental tricks on ourselves to soften its impact or to sidestep it altogether.

According to God's perspective, change is a crucial part of the package. As one author expressed it:

> You are a caterpillar, and so am I. Just as caterpillars are in metamorphosis, we are "in-process" people. That is what we are intended to be. That is what we will always be.
>
> Throughout our personal metamorphoses, God sees us as complete and perfect if we are Christians. And God is neither surprised nor disappointed that we are not completely perfected in our current lives on earth. God loves us so much that he *accepts* us right where we are. But he loves us too much to *leave* us right where we are.
>
> God has a plan for us caterpillar Christians, and he calls it transformation. According to Romans 12:2, this transformation is the result of a lifelong process of mind renewal.[12]

Cooperating with this process of transformation means actively looking more to the future, rather than passively allowing the effects of the past to dictate how we live in the present. But isn't that what we are called to do as Christians? We are to be people who allow hope to draw us ahead in life instead of being driven by fear.

I often counsel people with so much potential yet who are crippled in some significant way from making progress. Living in fear of the future is why many dreams remain dreams. We are called to enjoy the present and live in it to the fullest. We are also to continue looking to what the future has in store for us. But to fully embrace the present and the future, we need to relinquish our hold on the past.

❧

*We are to be people who allow hope to draw us ahead
in life instead of being driven by fear.*

Does the fear of "what if it doesn't work" dominate your life? Years ago I found some thoughts from an anonymous writer on the topic of risk-taking. Consider how they apply to any changes you are seeking to make in your family life at the present time.

To laugh is to appear the fool.
To weep is to risk appearing sentimental.
To reach out for another is to risk involvement.
To expose feelings is to risk exposing your true self.
To place your ideas, your dreams, before the crowd is to risk their loss.
To love is to risk not being loved in return.
To live is to risk dying.
To hope is to risk despair.
To try is to risk failure.
But risks must be taken, because the greatest hazard in life is to risk nothing.
The person who risks nothing, does nothing, has nothing, and is nothing.
He may avoid suffering and sorrow.
But he simply cannot learn, feel, change, grow, love, and live.
Chained by his certitudes, he is a slave.
He has forfeited freedom.
Only a person who risks is free!

—Anonymous

❧

## BRINGING IT HOME

How can you reverse a marital or parent-child relationship which has become too dependent? *First, you need to admit that you have a problem.* For some, that can be difficult. None of us easily declares that what we have been doing hasn't been the best. That takes courage. But the painful admission becomes easier as we focus on finding a healthier way to relate, rather than wasting energy moaning and groaning about the problem.

The next step is similar to what faces an explorer or pioneer. *You will need to discover just how your relationships have been too involved or intertwined.* The best way I have found is to do a written inventory describing your overinvolvement with the other person. In what way are you together too much? In what way do you invade one another's lives? In what way could you be more separate or independent? Do you do things for the other person or do they do things for you which could be done on your own? Put all of this in writing—including the steps you will take to change and the new ways you want to respond.

Another very helpful tactic is to tell someone else about the changes you want to make. Accountability to others is essential. In many ways that is what I end up doing in my counseling; I help people change by making them accountable to me. I do not at all mean shifting dependency from one person to another. It is simply inviting another person to help you succeed by praying and encouraging you, and asking from time to time, "How are the changes going?"

The following inventory will help you to look at your relationships. Check the statements that are true of you. What do your answers tell you about yourself? Are you satisfied with those relationships? Do any of your responses tell you, "It's time to change?" Remember, change *is* possible.

## *Relationship Inventory*[13]

1. My good feelings about myself depend on having the approval of others.

| NO! | SOMETIMES | YES! |
| --- | --- | --- |

2. I believe my main purpose in life is to solve the problems and relieve the pain of others.

| NO! | SOMETIMES | YES! |
| --- | --- | --- |

3. I value the opinions and preferences of others more than my own.

| NO! | SOMETIMES | YES! |
| --- | --- | --- |

4. I feel uneasy and "empty" if I am not in a close relationship.

| NO! | SOMETIMES | YES! |
| --- | --- | --- |

5. I sacrifice my own values and standards in order to stay connected with others.

| NO! | SOMETIMES | YES! |
| --- | --- | --- |

6. My fear of anger, criticism, and rejection dictates what I do and say.

| NO! | SOMETIMES | YES! |
| --- | --- | --- |

7. My own interests are usually put aside so I can pursue the interests of others.

| NO! | SOMETIMES | YES! |
| --- | --- | --- |

8. I believe I am being selfish when I want to do something just for myself.

| NO! | SOMETIMES | YES! |
| --- | --- | --- |

9. I give money and gifts as a way to feel more secure in relationships.

| NO! | SOMETIMES | YES! |
| --- | --- | --- |

10. I spend a lot of mental energy trying to get others to do things *my way*—without having them know or get angry (for their own good).

NO!                                SOMETIMES                                YES!

11. I try to anticipate others' needs and desires and meet those needs and desires before the other people have to ask.

NO!                                SOMETIMES                                YES!

12. My mood and sense of well-being are directly related to those of others; I can't feel good if someone else feels bad.

NO!                                SOMETIMES                                YES!

13. I spend so much time helping others that my job, family, health, etc., suffer.

NO!                                SOMETIMES                                YES!

14. I spend little time or energy considering my own emotional state and a great deal considering that of others.

NO!                                SOMETIMES                                YES!

15. I often have to explain or excuse the person closest to me to myself or friends.

NO!                                SOMETIMES                                YES!

16. My needs never seem as important and urgent as the needs of others.

NO!                                SOMETIMES                                YES!

17. I have changed my hairstyle and/or way of dressing just to please others.

| NO! | SOMETIMES | YES! |
|-----|-----------|------|

18. I believe many of the people in my life would be lost without me, because I protect them from the effects of their stupid, silly, and/or sinful choices.

| NO! | SOMETIMES | YES! |
|-----|-----------|------|

19. I have remained in one or more adult relationships without seeking help to change it, even after being slapped, punched, kicked, or otherwise physically abused.

| NO! | SOMETIMES | YES! |
|-----|-----------|------|

20. My most significant relationships seem to have a regular pattern. For instance, they begin and/or end the same way, leaving me with the same bad feelings about myself.

| NO! | SOMETIMES | YES! |
|-----|-----------|------|

# SNAPSHOTS IN LIVING COLOR

Have you browsed through your family albums lately? The memories usually come flooding back... some filled with laughter, some drenched with tears. Happy times and sad times dot the landscape of family life. What kinds of photos fill your albums? Do they match your memories?

Our mental snapshots need to remain true to life. Black and white photos carefully posed with perfect smiles pasted on every face? Or living color of vibrant reds and dreary blues with slightly crooked teeth peeking through a slightly sour smile?

Is it possible to be a perfect parent with a perfect family? For perhaps a minute or so. After that, reality hits. In all my years of counseling, I have yet to see consistently perfect parents, perfect children, or perfect families. Each person and every family lives in a state of continual growth and change. Threads of uncertainty and questioning weave in and out of our security blankets in every phase of family life.

Feeling overwhelmed by stress and doubt, individuals and couples often raise the question, "Do I have the personality or emotional stability and patience to be a competent parent?" My answer usually throws them: "Yes... and no." But it's true. The answer is not black or white. Every person walks around in living color, reflecting strengths and weaknesses. The best we can do is to build up our strengths and use them to shore up our sagging weak spots.

## THE MYTH OF PERFECTION

Parenting can sometimes feel like a roller coaster ride. One day a father or mother may feel competent and self-assured; then the next day everything seems to fall apart. Every person possesses characteristics or gifts that come naturally. Some are beneficial to raising children; others are not.

You can't be everything to your children. Your unique personality characteristics will affect your interaction with other family members in various ways. You may be a fast emotional reactor, a trait which prompts you to share your irritation openly and quickly. Yet that same temperament also enables you to be very demonstrative. Or you may be more like a pressure cooker that slowly builds up steam before finally blowing its top. Yet your children will benefit from your capacity to listen carefully without immediately flaring up. Any personality trait always cuts both ways.

৵

*Doing our best with what we have is all that is required.*

Some people miss out on the joys of family life because of a misplaced commitment to do everything "just right." Doing our best with what we have is all that is required. Even if we could do everything perfectly, we have no assurance that the rest of the family will respond the way we want. Because of that secret ingredient in the human race called free will, none of us can totally control the thoughts and behavior of others.

Parents are not going to be graded on the way their children turn out. I shudder whenever someone remarks, "They did such a marvelous job as parents! Just look at the way their four kids turned out!" It makes me wonder what they'll say ten years later when one of the adult children is arrested for selling drugs and another divorces his wife to marry his secretary.

We are responsible to love, care for, and surround a child with a positive, nurturing environment. But we are not responsible for the direction they choose to pursue as adults.

All parents vary in their own estimation. Sometimes they congratulate themselves on being a roaring success; other times they touch bottom in the pit of despair, wondering what they could have done so wrong to make such a horrible mess out of things.

I would describe this vacillation with just one word: *normal.* Those feelings—and many more in between—will flood most parents on different occasions. Some feel successful most of the time; others struggle with feelings of failure much of the time. Neither may accurately reflect reality.

Our personal evaluation usually rests in three areas: the level of self-esteem of the parents; whether a parent is a perfectionist or not; and expectations the parents have for themselves and their children. Those with low self-esteem tend to be overly hard on themselves. Perfectionists will always be disappointed, as will those with unrealistic expectations.

All parents will do a better job when they stop trying to be a perfect mother or father. Perfection is a myth. I've never yet met a successful perfectionist. They end up living a life of failure, guilt, and anger—and usually project their inevitable frustration outward onto their family members.

A perfectionistic parent is a driven person. Yet when accomplishing some outstanding achievement, he or she usually cannot enjoy the results. Picture a dissatisfied pole-vaulter in a major track meet. Every time the bar is raised, he clears it successfully. Gradually, his competitors are eliminated and he wins the event. But does this guy rest and savor his victory? No. Competing against his own high standards, he asks the officials to raise the bar three inches higher. He tries again and again to clear the bar, but knocks it down each time. Feeling like a terrible failure, he cannot experience the joy of winning first place. He must do better.

Unfortunately, many parents are like this dissatisfied pole-vaulter. Are you a Christian perfectionist? Do you struggle with a cry of desperation that rises within you: "What if I fail? What if I'm not perfect?" Relax! I have a perfect answer for your dilemma:

- You have failed in the past.
- You are failing now in some way.
- You will fail in the future.
- You were not perfect in the past.
- You are not perfect now.
- You will not be perfect in the future.

I like what pastor David Seamands says about Christians who struggle with the question of failure:

To ask the question, "What if I fail?" is once again to attach strings to God's unconditional love and to change the nature of grace as undeserved and unearned favor. If your failure could stop grace, there would never be any such thing as grace. For the ground of grace is the cross of Christ, and on the cross we were all judged as total failures. It was not a question of an occasional failure here and there. As far as our ability to bridge the moral canyon and win the approval of a Holy God, we are all total failures. In the cross we were all examined and we all flunked completely.[1]

A perfectionist is still living under the law, a person who has never learned to enjoy and appropriate the grace of God. In spite of being a failure and not being perfect, we are still loved and accepted by God. We are still recipients of his undeserved grace. That's good news for all of us.[2]

All parents fail at one time or another. I have made mistakes. So have you. Why do we equate "mistakes" with failure? They are not one and the same. You and I will make plenty of mistakes. Failure occurs when we don't learn and make a course correction as a result of our mistakes. We also fail when we give up the fight and surrender to the status quo.

## RUNNING A MARATHON

Have you ever had days when you wanted to resign from your family? Probably! Totally overwhelmed by the ongoing battle, you're tempted to just give up trying so hard. Children feel that way at times. So do parents... and spouses... and siblings... and even grandparents! When everything falls apart, we all have those fleeting thoughts—and sometimes lasting ones too! Sometimes we don't even *like* that other person, even though we still *love* them.

Recently I saw the title of a book, *Where Does a Mother Go to Resign?* One woman put it this way:

Parenthood is like a marathon race. It's long, demanding, and exhausting. Few pursuits, though, give a greater sense of accomplishment or "high." To carry the analogy a little further, three quarters through the race, marathoners get to a point called "hitting the wall," when their body is screaming, "Stop, I'm out of gas," just prior to getting their second wind and moving on strong again.

Parents, too, hit the wall—sometimes literally—most often about three quarters through the race, when they're raising teenagers, although it can happen at any time with any age child. You can reach the limits of your energy to cope raising a baby with colic, a two-year-old whose every third word is *no,* or a ten-year-old who has decided that schoolwork isn't for him. As we will soon see, strong parents, like strong runners, have found that if they can persevere past the point of near-exhaustion, a smoother going often follows. Stamina is a core quality of successful parenting.[3]

Other factors enter into running this marathon besides sheer stamina. Our efforts will not always be recognized, appreciated, or even liked. Parenting is definitely not a popularity contest. If it were, we would lose much of the time.[4] Being a mother or a father can be very tough going. Consider the parenting pressures mothers can experience:

> In her daily experience with a child, a mother's time is not her own. She has to respond constantly to unclear verbal and pre-verbal demands from her child. Often she has no idea what to do; many times no good solution is available, so she'll suffer guilt and anxiety no matter what she does.
>
> The child constantly explores the boundaries of her patience and power. When the child's control lapses, her own control is required. She must consider using force on a helpless human being who sometimes invades her bodily privacy and psychological integrity like a monstrous, consuming enemy.
>
> She deals with the world of child rearing, where hundreds of experts give contradictory advice; the outcome can't be measured for fifteen to twenty years. She has to process this advice through her intuition and a constant stream of her own childhood memories dredged up by her child's dilemmas.
>
> And she must do all this with others—mother, mother-in-law, neighbors and school teachers—looking over her shoulder, marking her report card, measuring her against their own standards. Though it would be a relief to give up and follow some set of packaged rules, she must dare to be different—the fate of her child depends on her decisions. Besides, no set of rules seems exactly right.[5]

Being a family member involves making constant adjustments and course corrections. Trial and error is a consistent part of parenting. Mistakes don't always equate with being wrong. We just weren't right on target! But the honest effort yields the information we need to hit the target the next time. Yes, some responses and behaviors are clearly negative and wrong. But many of our responses are not so black and white! In any case, one of the best ways to deal with any "mistake" is to recognize it, admit it, and state what you will do differently the next time.

When attending a parenting seminar, one mother shared a terrific insight with her group. She said,

> "I used to be so uptight as a mother. My kids just weren't responding the way I wanted. One day I was down on the floor

playing with my two-year-old and looked up at the table and the shelves. All of a sudden I discovered something. This is what it looks like to my children. Everything around them is huge and overwhelming.

"And at that moment it hit me. I started to see life through the eyes of my children. I've been wanting my children to see life through the eyes of their parents. And that just won't work. I began to listen to them more and concentrated on seeing their perceptions. I think it's hard for us to realize that not everyone else sees things the way we do."

એ

*Fact: We can guide our children.*
*Fallacy: We can control and shape their lives*
*the way we want them to turn out.*

## PARENTS: ARCHITECTS, EXPLORERS, OR FARMERS?

What can parents do to help their children grow and mature?

Fact: We can guide our children. Fallacy: We can control and shape their lives the way we want them to turn out. I have seen parents so obsessed with having their child become what they wanted, that they are still pursuing this exercise in futility when that child is in his or her thirties! These parents remind me of an architect.

Have you ever seen an architect at work? He goes to the drawing board and, in very intricate detail, designs the end product, whether it be a new home or a shopping mall. There are still parents who believe they are totally responsible for what the child becomes. Architect parents mentally design all aspects of their child's life, including the end product. They have a very clear and definite picture of what they want their child to become. They carefully dictate and control their child's activities, choices and relationships. They screen what he is exposed to and make sure he plays and socializes with the "right" children. The words "ought" and "should" are frequently heard in this family.

We all have a tendency to mold our children to match the design we have for their lives. If their unique tendencies threaten us, we try to make these differences disappear. Basically, we are comfortable with others who are like us. Thus we unwittingly attempt to fashion our children into a revised edition of ourselves. We want them to be created in our image, but that puts us in conflict with God who wants them to be created in His image.

It is very easy to abuse parental authority by compelling children to deny their individuality and conform to behaviors which violate their identity. As parents, one of our great challenges and delights is to honor our child's uniqueness and accept what cannot be changed in him. We are called to guide them, not remake them.[6]

A modified architectural approach can be used as long as the plans are very flexible and custom designed to fit the child.

*Explorers.* Since 1992 marked the five hundredth anniversary of his arrival in America, Christopher Columbus filled the news. When we think of explorers, his name often comes to mind, along with the pioneers of the 17th and 18th centuries in this country. Such people are risk-takers.

Anyone who becomes a parent takes on the role of an explorer as well, whether he or she wants to or not. In order to properly teach, guide, encourage, or nurture a child, parents must patiently observe and study that person to discover his or her unique personality traits and learning characteristics. And the better parents know those, the better equipped they will be to prepare the child for life.

The same process of exploration happens when two people marry. The amount of new information to discover and process can be literally overwhelming at times. The spouses who put in the necessary time and energy to explore their partner's uniqueness have a much better time adapting and adjusting, and consequently enjoying marital fulfillment.

What is the role of explorers? They search and ask. They're inquisitive, but they learn in a way that doesn't violate the boundaries of others. Explorer-parents are in a good position to implement and encourage the maturity and independence of their children.

*Farmers.* Once many explorers or pioneers found what they were looking for, they gave up their search to become farmers. Parents can learn to make this role change as well. Farmers consider each plant variety unique; they don't force potatoes to be tomatoes, in other words. Farmer-parents will recognize the uniqueness of each child and nurture that person to full maturity and fruitfulness. Likewise a spouse will not attempt to make the partner conform to a former romantic interest or an ideal created in his or her imagination.

I have many relatives who own large farms in Minnesota, Iowa, and South Dakota. They have all discovered the importance of timing, planting the right varieties, the proper soil, and the essential ingredients to put into the soil. They also realize that they cannot do it all themselves. Many farmers know that success at growing good crops is the result of a partnership.

> The idea of a partnership in farming is a strong one. We realize that not much will happen if the farmer doesn't throw himself wholeheartedly into bringing crops to fruition. That's his responsibility, and all his efforts lead to a productive harvest. But, it is equally true that nothing happens at all if God doesn't do His part. The farmer works with an absolute dependence on God to provide sun and rain. Even the farmer who does not believe in God knows, too well, the limitation of his powers.
>
> The active farmer wants pears to be pears, spinach to be spinach, avocados to be avocados and peas to be peas. He rejoices in the identity of what is planted and does everything to nurture each crop according to its own nature. While farmers are highly active in the nurturing of their crops, they must also learn to yield to circumstances over which they have no control. In the full knowledge of God's splendid grace, they must sometimes face the inexplicable.[7]

In partnership with God, farmer-parents are able to empower their children to mature and release them to independence. They rely in large measure upon encouragement, and those who are encouraged usually develop confidence.[8]

All three of these models—the architect, the explorer, and the farmer—provide an atmosphere which fosters growth. As parents diligently explore their children to discover their unique qualities and gifts, they are better able to cultivate and nurture their individuality without forcing the child to become something he or she is not. Spouses would benefit from following this approach with their partners as well.

## PLANTED IN GOD

In our efforts to nurture and guide others, how do we know where we are going? How do we keep from being lost and confused about which direction to pursue? A former student and friend wrote a very helpful book a few years ago entitled *Parenting Without Guilt.* She touched on the crucial issue of self-esteem which so many parents struggle with over the years. Consider her thought-provoking questions about what we have to offer as parents.

> Who do you consider trustworthy in this world? Are you generally a "trusting soul" except when the facts indicate you should be wary? Or did your early childhood experiences leave you distrustful of most people or of certain ethnic or social groups? Are you passing these same perceptions on to your children, either consciously or unconsciously?
>
> How do you view your own capabilities? Do you have a healthy self-esteem, viewing both your abilities and limitations in a realistic way? Or do you constantly try to build yourself up in your own eyes by criticizing other people? Do your children never quite measure up—academically, physically, mentally, or socially? Will your criticism affect their perceptions of their own self-worth?
>
> Who are you in your own eyes? Do you see yourself as a creature of worth placed on earth by a loving God who sent His son to die in order that you might live? Do you really believe that God loves you unconditionally? Or do you feel that you never quite measure up in God's eyes or anyone else's for that mat-

ter? Do you believe God loves your children unconditionally? Do you love your children unconditionally? In what ways are you conveying this to them?

The old adage that you can only lead a person as far as you have gone yourself is certainly true in the area of perception. If you wonder what perceptions you are transmitting to your children, ask them. You may be surprised at their answers.[9]

>

*When we base our picture upon how God views us,*
*we discover how valuable we really are.*

How do you feel about your capabilities, your value, and your worth? Because of false information, traumatic experiences, and wrong teaching, many people struggle with their self-perception. Healthy self-esteem is as vital and necessary for human beings as a strong root system is to a plant. When we base our picture upon how God views us, we discover how valuable we really are. Consider these facts about God from Scripture and sink your roots more deeply into the Father's special love for you:

- He is the loving, concerned Father who is interested in the intimate details of our lives (Mt 6:25-34).
- He is the Father who never gives up on us (Lk 15:3-32).
- He is the God who sent his Son to die for us though we were undeserving (Rom 5:8).
- He stands with us in the good and bad circumstances (Heb 13:5).
- He died to heal sickness, pain, and our grief (Is 53:3-6).
- He has broken the power of death (Lk 24:6-7).
- He gives all races and sexes equal status (Gal 3:28).
- He is available to us through prayer (Jn 14:13-14).
- He is aware of our needs (Is 65:24).
- He has created us for an eternal relationship with him (Jn 3:16).
- He values us (Lk 7:28).
- He doesn't condemn us (Rom 8:1).
- God values and causes our growth (1 Cor 3:7).

- He comforts us (2 Cor 1:3-5).
- He strengthens us through his Spirit (Eph 3:16).
- He cleanses us (Heb 10:17-22).
- He is for us (Rom 8:31).
- He is always available to us (Rom 8:38-39).
- He is the God of hope (Rom 15:13).
- He provides a way to escape temptations (1 Cor 10:13).
- He is at work in us (Phil 2:13).
- He helps us in temptation (Heb 2:17-18).
- He wants us to be free (Gal 5:1).
- He is the final Lord of history (Rv 1:8).[10]

Who holds you in highest esteem? God. Who holds each family member in high esteem? God. Who is so concerned about you and sees so much value in you that he sent his Son Jesus Christ to die for you? God. If you have a different view of yourself, you are telling God that he is wrong. Consider what affect that would have on your parenting.

## ADDING SNAPSHOTS TO OUR FAMILY ALBUMS TAKES TIME

Building a healthy family requires both quantity and quality time. Quantity time without quality is empty. I've seen families who spend an abundance of time together at home, but the hours mostly boil down to five individuals going about their separate lives.

Times of playing, sharing, working, traveling, learning, and worshiping together are vital. One quality hour is much better than ten empty hours. Sometimes we just need the knowledge that our family members are available if we need them.

A friend of mine made it a priority each week to give each of his four children one hour, exclusively to do as they wanted and he followed their lead. Needless to say, this father found himself doing things he never anticipated doing as an adult. Another friend took each child out for lunch or breakfast (yes, even McDonald's counts) once a month and continued this commitment until each child left for college.

Nothing can take the place of one-on-one times between a parent and child. I have a storehouse of memories of my many fishing adventures with my daughter, Sheryl. Josh McDowell shares one of his wife's projects with their children:

Dottie enters into the world of her own children by keeping a record of each child's life on monthly calendars. I'm talking about those calendars that have at least a one inch square for each day of the month and into those squares Dottie puts brief but special notations about what happened that day and what it meant to the child and the rest of the family.

Every year Dottie buys four calendars, one for each of our children. She tries to pick out photographic themes that fit each child. For example, one year Sean was into biking so she bought a calender with pictures of ten-speed bike events. Because Sean's current big interest is basketball, this year he has a basketball calendar.

Kelly, Sean's older sister, seems to be into everything, so Dottie wound up buying her a calendar that has a lot of pictures depicting shopping—a favorite sport of most teenagers. Katie, our ten-year-old, loves horses, so you know what is featured on her calendar.

Little Heather, only four years old, loves cats and, naturally, every month of her calendar has another picture of cats or kittens.

As each month unfolds, Dottie tries to fill in each day with a brief synopsis of what the child has done, what happened of note, and other brief remembrances. She doesn't always manage to cover each day, but she fills in an amazing number of days every month for all our kids.

The notations are simple ones—sometimes that even sound a bit mundane—but they're very meaningful to the children and to us their parents. For example here are some entries from last fall:

Heather—you went to school today. Daddy picked you up after school and you went to the drugstore for an ice cream sundae.

Then the next day's entry read:

*161*

You helped Dad and me at our family garage sale. Then you and I watched Boston lose the second playoff game with the Oakland A's. Sean—you got voted president of your freshman class today. I am sooooooooo proud of you! Luke came home with you to spend the night. He killed a scorpion that we found.

Along with making the notations on the squares for the day of the month, Dottie collects snapshots, certificates, news clippings, ribbons, and any other items that help record what the children accomplished or happened to them during the month. All of this memorabilia gets clipped, taped, or pasted on the photo/picture page that appears above the days of the given month.

As each month passes, the scenes of cats, horses, basketball players, or shopping slowly disappear as Dottie adds a record of what has happened in the lives of our kids. You could say her calendar serves the same purpose as a scrap book, but there is something intriguing about recording things day by day. It helps remind all of us of the value and meaning of time and how even the simplest things make up what life is really all about.

Like the notations, the photos and other memorabilia are often simple—but priceless. For example:

Sean is pictured with two different basketball teams he was playing on at the time. And along with those photos are some illustrations he drew for the science fair where he won a first-place ribbon.

On Kelly's calendar is a picture of Kelly with her "new car"—a 1957 Chevy that she got for a steal. If you're into cars at all you know that '57 Chevys are something of a "classic," but what's more important is that this photo records a classic time in Kelly's life—when she got her license and her own wheels and started using new freedoms and responsibilities.

Tucked in the back of every calendar are photos and other items that Dottie hasn't had time to record yet. But she works on her project every day—for at least ten minutes, when she makes her notations and tries to sort out photos and other items to display in their proper places. Dottie says that the calendars aren't a chore, but something that she really enjoys. I asked her what she might say for this book regarding the calendars and their value and she told me:

I would say the calendars are one of my biggest priorities because they're something that give us and the kids an invaluable record. I've often thought about when I would give these calendars to the children. When they get married? No, I don't think so. I believe I'll give them the calendars when they have children of their own. When they get married, they'll be so busy getting their homes together the calendars might be lost in the shuffle, but when they have children then they'll realize the incredible value of a record like this.

The reason I got started was because I was given a baby shower gift when Heather came—a calendar with the stickers that said, "The first time I sat up," "The first time I smiled," and so on. I got such a kick out of filling out those stickers for Heather I decided to start making calendar records for all the other children, and that's what I've been doing ever since.

I admit the calendars are a lot of work, but they are also a lot of fun. As I collect the different years, I can see month by month how the children grow, what they were into, what their interests were, what they left behind and what they continued on to do. There's tremendous satisfaction in that.[11]

## HOW DO YOU MEASURE SUCCESS?

What is the criteria you use to measure whether or not you're succeeding in your family life? A couple named Jerry and Rita were asked the question, "What were the best of times in your parenting?"

"We are still in the midst of the best of times," said Jerry. "Talking to my children like adults and watching them begin college are the best of times. My daughter called the other night from college and said, 'Dad, you talk to me like a parent, but you write letters like a friend.' What a feeling! I am experiencing adulthood with my children."

Rita likewise took a wide-open view of the best of times with her children. "The best of times as a parent is parenting. I tell people who don't have children, 'You can't know what you are giving up when you say you don't want to be a parent. There is no way you can sense what you would be missing unless you are a parent.' I am so glad this is what we've given our lives to—to raising our children and to loving each other."

When have they failed as parents? Rita: "The times I fail most are when I get angry. When I get angry, I cease to function. Feeling what the kids are feeling is the most important thing to me. When I'm angry, I don't listen. Then I am totally ineffective. All the things that make someone a good parent are gone when they are angry. At my angriest times, I try to go off privately, sometimes cry, then come back and talk to everyone like I should have in the first place."

Jerry also sees his biggest parental failure as anger, not toward the children, but toward Rita. "If I am angry at Rita around the children, I feel I have not been in control as father of the household. I don't know how the kids see it, but I see it as a parental failure."[12]

~

*"The times I fail most are when I get angry. When I get angry, I cease to function."*

This same couple was asked the question, "If you were to write a book on parenting, what would you include in it?" They suggested giving an abundance of praise and encouragement, consistently letting their kids know they are great kids, focusing on the positives, and making the love relationship in the family the most important item. They said that relationships are the most important ingredients. Gift-giving was essential—not material gifts, but the gifts of time, traditions, music lessons, travel, and hobbies.[13]

Another family told me what they especially valued in their family was openly sharing the entire range of feelings with one another. They could cry, hug, touch, and be angry. When distance occurred between members, they would each take the initiative to return, talk about the issue, listen to one another, apologize when necessary, and extend forgiveness. Each would conclude their part in the discussion by saying, "... and this is what I will do different the next time!" What an important and family changing statement!

What are your criteria for family success? Use the space provided to list six to eight of the criteria that you are using to measure success in your family.

1. _____

2. _____

3. _____

4. _____

5. _____

6. _____

7. _____

8. _____

Is each one consistent with Scripture? On a scale of zero to ten, how realistic is each one? Most of us would like to see progress in our family. Here are some suggestions and ideas that individual parents have found helpful in spending individual time with their children:

- Create for each child a never-ending story. Using him as the main character, each evening before bedtime weave a tale about him and his adventures. Ask him what things he'd like to do, see, explore, and learn about in his ongoing fantasy.
- Whenever a young child shows you proudly what she did—a puzzle, a picture, a house of blocks—ask her if she'd like to do it again so you can watch.
- While you are enjoying a hobby—gardening, woodworking, crafts, painting—invite a child to watch and introduce him to the basics. Provide him tools of the craft with which to copy you. One mother described herself as "an avid gar-

dener. All my kids, even the two-year-old, know how to pull a carrot."

- Use a tape recorder to produce a sound diary for each child. Record his earliest sounds—laughing, cooing, crying. Continue with his first words, songs, counting. In essence, create a permanent time capsule of his development through language. Set aside "recording sessions" for each child to tell his diary what he's learned recently.
- Allow a child to select her own special day of the week. On that day, show or teach her how to do something; for instance, sing a song, write a poem, plant a flower, bake cookies, fry an egg, make toast, tie a ribbon, wrap a gift, sew on a button, sort laundry, pump her own gas, discriminate a weed from a flower, identify a tree by its leaves, bait a hook, read a road map, program the VCR, tie a tie, play tic-tac-toe. Said a youngster now in college, "Thursday was Dad's day off. He would always do something special with me. He taught me to tie my shoes on a Thursday."
- Periodically pull out the family photo album and tell a youngster about himself from his birth forward. Describe his antics as a toddler, his early questions about life, his first days in school. Kids love time trips into the past through pictures, especially about them and all that makes them special to you.
- Carry a camera with you or keep one nearby so as to catch a child in her own special moments with Mom and Dad.
- Take a child to visit your workplace. If possible, let him spend time with you as you move through your day. Indeed, the chance to "see where Mom/Dad works" was ranked at or near the top of favorite parent-child activities by these children.
- On a rotating basis, ask each of the children if she would like to go with you as you run errands, go to the store, visit a friend, or take a drive somewhere. The car is a prime vehicle for moments of privacy between parent and child. The destination of the trip is typically less important than the time taken getting there. Said a son about car trips with his father, "I loved my times *alone* with him, regardless of where we went."

ॐ

*"I'll never forget how my dad would just let me stop
and smell the flowers, look at the trees, pick up the stones,"
said one daughter.*

- Establish a weekly walk day during which you and one child take a leisurely walk. "I'll never forget how my dad would just let me stop and smell the flowers, look at the trees, pick up the stones," said one daughter. "Start young" is the advice of these parents. Introducing a walk day to a fifteen-year-old who fusses about taking the trash thirty feet to the end of the driveway may trigger a look that says, "Walk? I'll be ready to drive in six months."

- Ask your daughter or son, depending whether you're a mom or dad, on a "date." Agree on the day, set the time, and plan the evening to its completion. Said a seven-year-old daughter obviously in love with her daddy, "When my daddy gets me flowers and we go out is the best, because he loves me!"

- Pick a day, say the third Monday of the month, as breakfast day, to spend with your son or daughter. Before school or work or athletic practice you and your child go to breakfast together. Or let each child choose a lunch day or ice-cream day. Many of the children spoke enthusiastically of a parent coming to school to eat lunch with them or taking them out to lunch.

- If your child practices a musical instrument, every so often quietly sit and listen. Your attention, punctuated by a complimentary word or two now and then, is a motivator and a display of pride. "If I had to choose one memory with my father, I'd say it was the time I came home from college on spring break and told him about the opera I was in at Indiana University. I remember relating to him the entire story of *Rigoletto* as we listened to the music. He'd never had any exposure to opera, but I was so pleased he shared with me this lovely discovery I'd made."

- Step in occasionally and help your child with his chores— drying the dishes, raking leaves, shoveling snow, doing laundry, dusting, setting the table. In addition to giving a lesson in cooperation, you will stimulate some natural camaraderie. "Working in the garden or yard with my parents was a lot of fun for me. Other kids used to ask me why my parents made us work so much. If they only knew what fun we had at those times." It's not the chore that's fun, it's having you there, if only because you're not thinking up something else for the kids to do![14]

## &

## BRINGING IT HOME

Do you have any special family traditions? These can include what you do for holidays, birthdays, vacations, at meal time, the way you greet one another, or the way you say goodnight. For example, the Waltons family on television would say goodnight to each other loud enough from each of their rooms so everyone could hear and respond. And come to think of it, watching this program together each week was one of our family traditions. We wouldn't miss it.

Some young children will call out to one of their parents after going to bed, "You forgot to say prayers with me tonight." That's a tradition. Family traditions can become so important that the members are quite upset when they are forgotten or neglected.

Take a moment and respond to the following questions:

1. What were the family traditions that you experienced in your family of origin?
2. Which family traditions did you bring with you into your current family?
3. Which new family traditions have you created?
4. What family tradition did your spouse bring with him or her?
5. What is the purpose and value of your family traditions?

The Tremaines were a family of five. Sunday dinner was a family affair which usually involved guests or some of the children's friends. All the plates were placed face down on the table. When everyone was seated, they would turn them over. One of the plates was labeled, "You are special today." Since the plates were put on the table randomly—including one on the floor for their Husky dog—no one knew in advance who would be that day's honored. It was usually a wild time when "Blackie" was the special pooch for the day!

Some of the most special family memories have nothing to do with traditions. They're built on relationships, experiences, and the investment of time. Bart Campolo wrote this letter to his father, Tony, about his favorite family snapshots:

... The times that I remember best, though, are the times I spent with you. I love those memories best of all, Dad, and they're a big part of who I am. That's the whole point of these letters for me. My childhood is gone, and I will never be able to be with you the way I was with you as a little boy. I will never be that small, and you will never seem that big again. But I have my stories, and they comfort me when I am overwhelmed by the world, when I am too old all of a sudden, when I lose my sense of wonder. They are all I have of my boyhood, and the reason I wish we had spent more time together is that I wish I had more of them now. It isn't that you didn't do enough, you see, for I would always want more. You were the king of the world back then, the imp of fun, the man with all the answers, the one who could always fix what was broken. You made life seem magical to me.

When you die, Dad, I will surely go to pieces for a while, because I still count on you more than anyone knows, but in the end I will be all right. I will have my stories, and in them I will always have part of you, the part that tells me who I am and where I came from. I only wish there was more because what there is means all the world to me.

Love,
Bart[15]

# RIPPLES ON THE FAMILY POND

"**I** FEEL GUILTY SOMEHOW. Yes, guilty is the best word to describe how I feel about some of my family members."

"Is it normal to have closer relationships with some of my friends than my own family?"

"I get along great with my older brother, but my younger ones... forget it. We've just never clicked. What's wrong?"

"I love going to visit my favorite cousin each year. But my other cousins get upset because we rarely see them. We just don't particularly want to visit them. We have nothing in common. Am I obligated to see them as much?"

"Is it all right to enjoy spending time with certain family members more than others? It's not that I dislike them, I just prefer some more than others."

These and many other questions like them are frequently directed my way. Getting along with every member of our immediate or extended family is never smooth sailing the whole way. In relating with close and distant relatives, our ship of communications runs into stormy weather from time to time. Sometimes we run aground on a sand bar, or perhaps scrape along the jagged rocks near shore. How can we resolve these inevitable conflicts? How can we strengthen the weaker relationships with our family members?

Adjusting our perspective a bit may provide a less turbulent harbor from which to set sail. We often expect to relate to all of our kin at the same depth, even though our experience actually reflects various levels of relationships. For example, we don't usually have the same kind of relationship with fellow employees as we have with our immediate family.

Sometimes the intensity of a relationship is the result of planned activity on our part. We may purposely cultivate a friendship with a new person at church to make him or her feel included. But sometimes relationships just happen. Perhaps we feel immediately drawn to someone who enjoys the same hobby or engages in the same type of work.

Many factors come into play in forming the different levels of kinship we experience. One way to consider our varied relationships is to see them as either casual or binding. *Binding* relationships may include spouse, parents, children, in-laws and other relatives, employers and co-workers—any bond which is valued as long-term or permanent. We tend to have more *casual* relationships with neighbors, distant friends, acquaintances—anyone we relate to apart from a long-term or permanent commitment.

❧

*When we expect a certain level of commitment,*
*feeling its lack can place a great strain on the relationship.*

Our obligation to binding relationships is normally greater than to casual relationships. Since most are permanent, I see few valid reasons for terminating them. However, you may find yourself in a binding relationship—with an immediate family member or even with your spouse—which is being treated by one or both parties as more casual. When we expect a certain level of commitment, feeling its lack can place a great strain on the relationship.

Clarifying expectations, especially in binding relationships, is essential to getting along with those closest to you.[1] Like most of us, you may have some relatives that you see only once or twice in five years. That kind of casual family tie is usually not a problem. Communications with family members we see on a regular basis can create the greatest amount of tension, even if we don't live together. How can we resolve conflicts and strengthen those relationships?

## USING A DEPTH FINDER

Think about the people you are related to by blood or marriage: your parents, stepparents, siblings, children, step-children, grandparents, in-laws, aunts, uncles, cousins, nieces, nephews, and so forth. With whom do you have a casual relationship? With whom is your relationship more binding? With whom do you get along best? With whom do you struggle? What are the reasons you get along well with some but not with others?

Relationships with family members can be categorized at four different levels: minimal, moderate, strong, and quality. Let's examine each of them in order to sharpen our expectations.

*Minimal relationships.* This first category involves simple, surface-level verbal interaction which is generally pleasant instead of hostile. People in relationships at this level tend not to give or receive help, emotional support, or love from each other. They just speak and listen to each other when necessary.

We usually have a minimal relationship with those with whom we are uncomfortable, but with whom we must relate to some degree. The key to getting along in a minimal relationship is to determine in advance how much you need to interact with this person, and then strive to make that interaction as healthy as possible.

*Moderate relationships.* This second level contains all the characteristics of a minimal relationship, but includes one more: an emotional attachment. In moderate relationships, we want emotional support and are willing to give it in return. A certain openness enables both parties to listen to each other's hurts, concerns, joys, and needs. Ideally, this openness is a two-way street. Regardless of the other person's stance, Christians are called to respond with love.

Emotional support is the foundation upon which deep relationships can be built. For example, a marriage that is not based upon an emotional bond between the two partners will be less fulfilling. The emptiness which prevails often leads to destruction of the relationship.

Often we become the catalyst for moderate relationships by taking the initial steps of emotional openness and support. The other person may follow suit, or else be threatened by our openness. Individuals who suffer unresolved pain from previous relationships tend to find it difficult to open up and trust anyone. In that case, all we can do is take the risk to reach out. Be patient when a loved one moves slowly toward emotional openness. Moderate relationships take time to build.

This depth of relationship reflects the scriptural model of how we are to love one another (Jn 13:34), bear with one another and make allowances for one another (Eph 4:2), serve one another (Gal 5:13), be kind to one another (Eph 4:32), and strengthen and build up one another, (1 Thes 5:11)—just to mention a few.[2]

*Strong relationships.* The difference between a moderate relationship and a strong one is found in the word help. Strong relationships develop when we become personally involved with someone by reaching out to love and care in some tangible way. We express the readiness to provide help when they need it, and we accept help from them when we need it.

For some people, the helping aspect of a strong relationship can be easier than the emotional aspect. In fact, many people bypass the emotional attachment and focus purely on helping. Less personal investment means less personal threat. Yet, strong relationships must be based on emotional support for the caring to be meaningful. Short-circuiting emotional support leads to shallow relationships. Offering emotional support builds stronger ties than merely helping.

*Quality relationships.* All the elements of the previous levels combine to reach the deepest of all. Quality relationships include the added element of *mutual trust.* We feel safe with these people when we reveal to them our inner needs, thoughts, and feelings. We also feel free to invite them to share their inner needs, thoughts, and feelings—and they feel secure in doing so. Quality relationships can exist between friends, spouses, parents, children, and even co-workers. We experience very few secrets or barriers.

Here are two conversations between a father and his adult daughter. The first conversation is an example of a more minimal relationship:

**Father:** "Mary, I just got a phone call. Your favorite cousin, Denise, just died."

**Mary:** "Oh, no. I can't believe it. We used to have such a great time together. I'm devastated. I'm going to miss her so much."

**Father:** "If you felt that close to her, why didn't you ever call her or get together with her?"

**Mary:** "You know how busy I've been with the new job, and she lived so far away. But I did call her now and then."

**Father:** "You knew she had been sick for awhile, and that she wanted you to come see her. You should have..."

**Mary:** "I told you why I couldn't go see her. You're the one with all the time on your hands. Why didn't you go see her? Quit blaming me. I'm upset enough over losing her."

A supportive conversation? Not at all. More of an attack. The daughter immediately focused on her own grief rather than her father's, and then her dad began to berate her. Let's consider the same conversation from the level of a moderate relationship:

**Father:** "Mary, I just got a phone call. Your favorite cousin, Denise, just died."

**Mary:** "Oh, no. What a shock! That must have hit you hard, Dad. She was your favorite niece."

**Father:** "Yes, she was. I knew she was sick, but her death was so unexpected."

**Mary:** "You're going to miss her and so am I. We had such good times together at the lake."

**Father:** "I think we'll all miss her. I know you were close, too. The two of you used to double date together years ago, didn't you?"

**Mary:** "Yes. I wish I had spent more time with her over the past few years. I have such good memories of Denise."

**Father:** "We're both hurt and empty over this loss. I just wanted to be sure you knew."

Notice the difference. Mary immediately responded to her father and nurtured his feelings. The father in turn verbally expressed concern for his daughter. Many times, we wish the other person would reach out to us first, but it doesn't always happen that way. We may need to take the initial step. The other person may not be capable of meeting our expectations in a particular area. But we still have the ability to nurture them. Perhaps our example will encourage him or her to respond in kind.[3]

☙

*Many times, we wish the other person would reach out to us first, but it doesn't always happen that way. We may need to take the initial step.*

*A personal evaluation.* The following exercises will help you evaluate and identify the levels of relationship you presently experience with your relatives and in-laws. Write the names of the fifteen relatives and in-laws with whom you have the greatest contact. Check the quality of the relationship you have with each person: minimal, moderate, quality, or strong. Then, using a different mark, indicate the level of relationship you would like to achieve with each person in the future.

As you review these marks, you will realize that you have relatives you love, some you only like, and others you may not like at all! That's not abnormal. But hopefully none of those are your immediate family members. Any difference between the two marks will indicate the amount of work ahead to improve each relationship.

## *Relative Relationships Inventory*

| Name | Minimal | Moderate | Strong | Quality |
|------|---------|----------|--------|---------|
| 1. _____ | | | | |
| 2. _____ | | | | |
| 3. _____ | | | | |
| 4. _____ | | | | |
| 5. _____ | | | | |
| 6. _____ | | | | |
| 7. _____ | | | | |
| 8. _____ | | | | |
| 9. _____ | | | | |
| 10. _____ | | | | |
| 11. _____ | | | | |
| 12. _____ | | | | |
| 13. _____ | | | | |
| 14. _____ | | | | |
| 15. _____ | | | | |

Let's take this personal evaluation one step farther. Circle the name of the particular relative who is the most difficult for you to get along with. Perhaps answering the following questions will help you determine the reasons for your problems:

1. Do you live with or near this relative? Why?
2. How do you feel about the amount of personal or telephone

contact you have with this person? How would you like the amount of contact to change?

3. How do you think this person would describe your relationship to someone else?
4. How might this person describe you to someone else?
5. What are the positive qualities of this person?
6. When do you get together with this person? Is it pleasant? If so, why? If not, why not?
7. How does this relative respond when you do something you want to do rather than what he or she advised you to do?
8. How do you respond when this person does what he or she wants to do instead of what you advise?
9. Do you need this relative's approval? If so, why? How do you try to gain approval from this person?
10. Do you get together with this relative at significant family gatherings such as birthdays, anniversaries, holidays, etc.? If so, what are these times like? How would you like them to be different? What could you do to change your relationship?

## CLOSING THE DISTANCE

A common family problem involves adult children leaving home to live on their own. Some parents find it difficult to release their adult children. If they continue to give unsolicited advice or interfere in other ways, feelings of anger may arise. The two alternatives seem to be either to stifle the anger or let it out inappropriately. But there is a healthier option: to discover an effective solution to the problem. In fact, this should be the main goal in any strained relationship.

Many people say to me during counseling, "Now that I'm an adult, I thought life would be different. I assumed that I wouldn't have to deal with these family tensions any longer. I don't want to be involved with some of my irritating relatives. In fact, I would be happy never to see some of them again. But then I feel guilty and obligated."

Have you ever felt like this? Of course, as adults we can ignore the family members whom we find particularly difficult. But we usually pay a price for avoiding relationships with relatives or in-laws. We need to evaluate the cost to ourselves and others before deciding not to resolve family conflicts. Consider these common responses.

First, by failing to resolve issues of family conflict, we may experience recurring anger and tension every time we come into contact. We don't plan to; it just happens. Furthermore, our negative feelings will usually spill over onto other family members, complicating the problem and contaminating the entire family atmosphere—much like an ugly oil seepage.

Second, unresolved conflicts could cause us to dread family get-togethers or reunions for years to come. Many people anticipate being with their families and spend months planning for those special occasions. But if we harbor unresolved conflicts, our anticipation for these events is anything but joyful. Our stomachs turn into a knot every time we think about it. Anxiety builds as the date draws nearer. Then we may wear a fake smile to get through it, while our insides churn. Is not getting along worth this kind of tension?

Third, we become guilt collectors. Many people are filled with guilt and regret because they have failed to resolve significant conflicts with relatives who died unexpectedly. Why wait to clear up problems until it is too late? I've talked to so many individuals who said, "I'm so glad I reached out to that person when I did. If I had waited another week it would have been too late."

One man told me, "I feel so much better having worked through my relationship with my father. I was crushed when he was killed in an accident. But I knew that healing had taken place between us and I have no regrets." Will you be able to say this about your problem relationships?

A fourth major difficulty with choosing to ignore relationship difficulties is the effect it could have on our children. Some adults who will not relate to family members deny their children the opportunity to relate to their extended family. I've seen the pain of this in the eyes of everyone affected. Restricting a child's relationship with family members may rob him or her of enjoying valuable interaction with aunts, uncles, cousins, grandparents, etc.

Fifth, unresolved family conflicts lead to overreactions and self-fulfilling prophecies. We become supersensitive to the problem relative. We tend to read into his or her comments and responses meanings which may not be true. We anticipate the worst and make it happen in our own minds. We may even begin responding negatively to anyone who even reminds us of this person, dumping anger and bitterness on unsuspecting and undeserving people.

Finally, perpetuating unresolved relationships means that we end up carrying an excessive emotional load, laboring under unnecessary anxiety. We know this person will be a part of our lives—whether we like it or not. And we carry the image of what the relationship should be or could be, but is not. The tension between the two creates an emotional burden that will cause difficulty until resolution occurs.[4]

## HOW *NOT* TO RESOLVE FAMILY CONFLICTS

An important element in getting along with relatives and in-laws is resolving family conflicts and not letting them continue to escalate. But first, let's consider some ways which do not work very well. Dr. Leonard Felder guarantees the following methods will make a relationship worse instead of better.[5]

ﾃ･

*Behind the frozen smile, they stifle a desire to scream*
*at the enemy. They sit calmly, but inside*
*they're thinking they'd rather be anywhere else but here!*

Some use the *Frozen Smile* approach. They sit with their relatives at a family gathering, forcing a smile to mask negative feelings about being in the same room as their adversary. Behind the frozen smile, they stifle a desire to scream at the enemy. They sit calmly, but inside they're thinking they'd rather be anywhere else but here! They try to fool their families and themselves with a calm exterior, but does such an act really solve anything? Not really. The fires keep smoldering, and one day they may finally burst into flame.

Then there's the *Reform School* approach. People may always attempt to change some of the irritating relatives they have to see. They give them advice and tell them what and how to change. But how often have you seen this approach work? It seems whenever we approach relatives with some constructive criticism, they know what's coming, shut down their hearing aids, and put their minds on hold so that nothing penetrates.

Have you ever had any relatives try to change you? Probably. We can defuse these encounters in a positive way. One thirty-year-old business man told me this story:

> The last time I saw my overbearing uncle, I knew he wanted to harp on me like he always does. So I started the conversation by telling him everything I knew he was going to say to me—in a pleasant tone and with a smile on my face.
>
> Then I said lightly, "If that's what you were going to tell me, Uncle Jim, you can see that I already know it. I haven't followed that advice in the past, so I won't now. Thus I don't need to hear it again. Since we've settled that issue, what else would you like to talk about?" He didn't know what to say next, but we ended up having one of the best conversations we've ever had. I think he respected me more after that. He began to treat me as an adult instead of his little nephew.

The *Distraction* approach allows people to avoid interaction with relatives they don't like. A common distraction used to avoid conflicts at a family gathering is food. Individuals may either hide out in the kitchen eating, or at meal time keep their hands in constant motion from plate to mouth. Eating makes them feel better and keeps the mouth busy, offering an excuse not to talk. This approach may work for awhile, but sooner or later the stomach rebels, the pounds accumulate, and they realize that nothing positive was accomplished by this dangerous avoidance technique.

Another ineffective approach to resolving family conflict is the *Excuse Search*. Some individuals actually spend time looking for another excuse to confront an irritating relative. They think, "If that aunt of mine brings up that subject one more time, I'm just going to tell her how I really feel." And what happens? She *does* bring it up again, perhaps because that person may be consciously or subconsciously directing the conversation back to that topic. Having found the desired excuse for rekindling a family feud, the searcher often comes away looking like an innocent victim, even honestly believing that he or she has been victimized.

I've also seen family members use the *Sacrificial Lamb* approach to conflicts. They give the appearance of making sacrifice after sacrifice for others—but always with a hidden agenda. They even keep score. They use these sacrifices as opportunities to plant seeds of guilt in the other person to get what they want out of the relationship.

The last approach is typically used by martyrs: the *It Doesn't Hurt* approach. Probably the most common mistake family members make is denying the hurt they feel in the relationship and rationalizing it away. But despite the denial, the emotional wounds remain raw and festering.

When we bury our hurts instead of exposing them, we bury them alive to resurface in other unpleasant ways. Many cases of obesity are directly related to family anger that has never been resolved. Overeating is one attempt to cover or block the inner pain. Hypertension and stress are also symptoms of buried hurt. So is depression.

Do any of these ways of responding to family conflict sound familiar? Can you identify anyone in your family who uses them? Have you been guilty of complicating family relationships by employing these faulty approaches yourself?

## POSITIVE STEPS TOWARD POSITIVE RELATIONSHIPS

Let's consider a number of positive steps which can be taken to help turn our negative family relationships into positive ones.

*1. Learn to empathize with family members.* Empathy is one of the major characteristics of positive relationships. In relating to family members, personal values, standards, and expectations often become the basis for conflict. Each person attempts to project his own values, standards, and expectations on other family members.

We often bristle and become defensive when others come on strong with differing opinions. We can either attack them for their opinions, or else exercise empathy by discovering what lies behind their beliefs. Empathy is a quality which means "to feel into or to feel with." It involves trying to view life through the other person's eyes, attempting to feel as another feels and hearing life through their perceptions.

Scripture calls each of us to be empathetic: "Rejoice with those who rejoice and weep with those who weep" (Rom 12:15, NASB). Empathy means walking with another person in their experiences and footsteps. This process may help us regain a desire to be around or help a family member whom we would rather ignore at the moment.

A rather vivid illustration of the love that underlies empathy is found in Lorraine Hansberry's book, *Raisin in the Sun*. Walter, a grown son, squandered the family's money, forcing everyone to live in an undesirable environment. His family was justifiably furious with him. Walter didn't seem to offer any loveable qualities. His mother was deeply hurt and disappointed. Fortunately, she was wise enough to know that love can persist even when a person appears unlikable. She reminds the family of this at a very tense moment:

> "There is always something left to love. And if you ain't learned that, you ain't learned nothing. Have you cried for that boy today? I don't mean for yourself and for the family 'cause we lost the money. I mean for him; what he been through and what it done to him. Child, when do you think is the time to love somebody the most; when they done good and made things easy for everybody? Well then, you ain't through learning—because that ain't the time at all. It's when he's at his lowest and can't believe in hisself 'cause the world done whipped him so. When you starts measuring somebody, measure him right, child, measure him right. Make sure you done taken into account what hills and valleys he come through before he got to wherever he is."[6]

That's empathy: seeing life through another person's perspective. We don't necessarily need to agree with our relatives' opinions, but we can at least give them the courtesy of listening and understanding their perspective. We can also learn to explain our perspective *calmly*—that's the key word—while demonstrating love and respect for them and their opinions.

∂∙

*In family relationships,
expectations often fall into the categories of
who people should be and what they should do.
But how did we get to be experts on other people?*

*2. Identify expectations.* We need to identify not only the expectations we hold for other family members, but identify the ones they hold for us. We all have such a list, but often it's hidden. I advise candidates for church staff positions to request a list of expectations from the board members. Then I suggest that the candidate supply the board with a similar list of personal expectations for the church. A specific list helps to dispel myths before they grow into major disappointments and problems.

In family relationships, expectations often fall into the categories of *who* people should be and *what* they should do. But how did we get to be experts on other people? Problems occur because family members are not living up to each other's expectations. What's more, everyone grows tired of making the effort. Unmet expectations lead to anger, which leads to resentment. Unmet expectations also harden into demands. When resisted (as they almost always are), these demands unleash a barrage of negative feelings and reactions. No one walks away happy.

When someone doesn't fulfill our expectations, how do we see that person? Probably as being in the wrong. At the same time, he probably sees us as being demanding. And the more we try to prove each other wrong, the more we each respond by trying to prove ourselves right. Family conflicts like these have been going on for thousands of years. Don't think you will escape them if you fail to identify hidden expectations.

*3. Clarify how you would like the relationship to be.* If you completed the exercise earlier in this chapter, you have identified some of your family relationships as casual or binding, and then as either minimal, moderate, strong, or quality in nature. The second step is equally important: deciding where you want the relationship to go from here. Deciding what you want the relationship to become establishes your path for growth. Be aware that you must be ready to take the initial step to see anything happen. Waiting for the other person to lead merely places you under his or her control. That individual may never take the first step. But you can.

*4. Emphasize the positive times in your memory.* Spend time thinking about occasions in your life when your relationships with irritating family members were pleasant. What made those occasions pleasant? What can you do to recreate those happy memories? How have each of your lives changed since that time?

*5. Spend time getting acquainted.* You may be related to someone but nonetheless strangers for the most part. How much do you know about your relatives, their personal history and background? What events contributed to their being the way they are today? What can you do to find out more about them and their past? I know some individuals who have sat down with their relatives to discuss individual and family history. Others have leafed through a family photo album with a relative as a means for asking questions about their life experiences. And in most cases it helped.

*6. Discover why others are critical of you.* If another family member has been interfering in your life for some time, or is constantly critical toward you, investigate why you have allowed him or her to continue to do that. Too often we tend to reinforce behavior or reactions we don't want. Perhaps you are relating to the person as a parent or a child instead of a peer.

*7. Become aware of your feelings.* Have you ever made a list of all your feelings toward this person? If not, make one and then indicate which feelings you want to keep and which you would like to eliminate. List the positive feelings you would like to develop which didn't appear on your first list. Determine what you will need to do to eradicate your negative feelings and nurture your good feelings.

Carrying a load of anger or resentment toward a difficult family member is more destructive for you than it is for them. But you can take some positive steps toward resolution. If you experience an unpleasant encounter that leaves you feeling angry, immediately write a letter to this person—a non-mailed letter!

Take time to describe all the feelings you presently have, the feelings you would like to have, the type of relationship you think is possible, and how you will pray for this individual during the next week. Sit down in a room by yourself facing an empty chair and read the letter aloud as if your relative were sitting there listening. Then destroy the letter. You will find that releasing your anger in this way allows you to continue on without unnecessary emotional baggage.

*8. Give the gift of forgiveness.* If you have been offended by a family member, forgive that person. Allowing those hurts to live inside you through unforgiveness hurts you even more deeply. Make a list of the benefits of forgiveness and unforgiveness, then compare lists. The advantage is obvious.

*9. Introduce new approaches.* When you get together with your relatives, can you predict what will be said, what is going to happen, what foods will be served, and so on? Many do. And their predictions are often correct. No wonder families don't get along. Sometimes our family traditions are so predictable that people are bored, and boredom often leads to irritation and conflict.

I know what that's like. For the past twenty-seven years, our family Thanksgiving dinners were fairly predictable, always served in one of our homes in Southern California. But one year we tried something different. Joyce and I took our mothers with us to a cabin in the mountains and spent the night, celebrating Thanksgiving there. Other relatives dropped in during the day and we had a wonderful time. Joyce's mother, who is in her eighties, actually saw snow falling for the first time in her life! And several of us went trout fishing in the lake during a snow storm. That's different!

What can you do differently to introduce some variety into your family gatherings? Some families have potluck suppers when they get together so no one is stuck cooking a big meal for everyone else. Some families meet at restaurants and leave the cooking and cleanup to someone else.

And what about those boring family conversations? Sometimes invoking a "gag rule" on one favorite subject will allow new topics to be introduced and discussed. One family began the tradition of each member introducing a topic for conversation which the family had never talked about before. Others tape a question to the bottom of each person's plate, which has to be answered before they can pile on the food. Many now have family gatherings that are rich and enjoyable, anticipated instead of dreaded.

*10. Anticipate changes for the better.* It is possible for your family relationships to get better. The changes may not happen in the relatives you have trouble with, but that's all right. Changes in you will be sufficient. Maintain the expectation that all of you can change.

I have heard so many reasons over the years as to why a family relationship will never change:

"I really have tried everything!"

"You don't know this person. She's *so* stubborn."

"How can I get along with my aunt when no one else can? I can't work a miracle!"

"It's not worth the effort. I'll just continue to avoid him. That's the only solution I can see."

"She's been this way for sixty-eight years. Do you really think she'll change?"

♨

*When you expect people to stay the same,*
*and when you expect yourself to stay the same,*
*those expectations will be fulfilled.*

These could all be true. But perhaps a new way of responding might change your relationship. Anyway, if what you have been doing hasn't been working, why keep doing it? It is senseless to keep on doing something that is failing. So you don't have anything to lose by trying something new, do you? The worst approach is to give up and to do nothing.

When you expect people to stay the same, and when you expect yourself to stay the same, those expectations *will* be fulfilled. It's so easy to focus on the negative characteristics in others. Instead, we need to see them as God sees them. Every negative trait, quirk, or liability has a positive side. Look for the strengths and undeveloped potential in your family members. Your belief in them could be the catalyst which helps their hidden gifts to unfold. Your calling in difficult family relationships is not to contribute to the problem, but to contribute to the solution.[7]

## FRANK'S STORY

Frank was a thirty-four-year-old who had lived with his mother until he was married four years earlier. He said he did this to save money, which makes sense. Sixteen months after the wedding, Frank and his wife Bev came into my office. Tension was developing between them over Frank's mother. Bev felt she was continually interfering in her son's life. (Incidentally, many people think that most in-law problems occur between the husband and his wife's mother. In most instances, in-law conflicts arise between the wife and her husband's mother, as in Frank's situation.)

Frank's mother phoned him or visited him often to contribute unsolicited advice. Frank tended to ignore what she said, except that he erupted with anger after she left. He refused to confront the problem head on, but took it out on Bev.

After listening to Frank and Bev tell their story, I looked at Frank and said, "Is the way you are handling this problem with your mother working?"

"No," he answered dejectedly.

"Then you really don't have anything to lose by trying a different approach, do you?" I suggested.

"You're right," he agreed. "I've got nothing to lose and a lot to gain. I really love Bev and my mother, but I feel caught in the middle. I know Mom's intentions are good most of the time. Perhaps I've added to the problem by not moving away from home sooner and taking her advice much of the time before. Now I've got to handle this situation."

I offered a suggestion which has proven quite effective for most problems like Frank's. It required that Frank take a new approach to the problem. He didn't have to wait long to try out his new plan. The next week his mother called him at home and gave some suggestions for his vacation.

Frank listened to her patiently, then said, "Mom, I need to share something with you. I become a bit upset when you make so many suggestions on what Bev and I should do. I realize that you love us and want the best for us. And I love you, too. Now that I'm on my own and married, I need my independence. I enjoy some of our interaction, but too many suggestions bother me. I would like you to do something for me. I think it would work better if I called you once a week and you called me once a week. We can share what's going on in our lives. If you have a suggestion, please ask me first if I would like to hear your ideas on that subject. I think this way we will enjoy the relationship better."

Frank had prepared himself for several possible ways his mother might respond to this initial conversation. She could react with hurt. She did. She could become defensive and say she was just trying to be helpful. She did. She might withdraw by not calling for a week or two. She did. Or she could respond with statements of self-pity. She did. But, in time, the relationship became much better. Frank had to repeat his request on two subsequent calls before it finally "took" with his mother. But it began to work.

&

## BRINGING IT HOME

Do you have any relatives who respond in this way? Who are they and how does it affect you? How do you respond? As in Frank and Bev's case, there may be times when you need to sit down with an objective third party to discuss problems with relatives or in-laws. The neutral observer may be able to point out previously unseen ways of resolving the issue.

Often role-playing a potentially troublesome confrontation

can ease much of your discomfort. I've done this many times in counseling, taking the part of the problem relative. It allows you the opportunity to walk through the event in a safe environment and practice responding in advance of the actual encounter.[8]

The approach that Frank took can be applied to the immediate family members who live in your home, perhaps a spouse, child, sibling, or parent. When you talk with them, don't accuse them of being a drain on the family. Accusations are not usually accepted. Begin a statement with, "I have a concern that I would like to share with you."

What else can you do? Be an encourager in your family. Much more will be said about this in a future chapter. Paul wrote: "... encourage one another and build each other up" (1 Thes 5:11, NIV). What better place to apply this verse than among your relatives and in-laws! You can change yourself. You can change your family relationships.

I love the Old Testament story of Caleb and Joshua. After twelve spies returned from the Promised Land, they gave a conflicting report. As Chuck Swindoll says, "Ten saw the problem; two saw the solution. Ten saw the obstacles; two saw the answers. Ten were impressed with the size of the men; two were impressed with the size of their God. Ten focused on what could not be accomplished; two focused on what could easily be accomplished by the power of God."[9]

At times we feel like the ten doubters when it comes to believing that we can get along with people. But the response of Caleb and Joshua works for us as we view our relationships. Fight to enter the Promised Land as you rely on God's power. Give yourselves and others the benefit of the doubt. Withdrawing in fear accomplishes nothing. Facing the issues and obstacles of relationships is the only way to grow past them. Let God lead you and empower you in your relationships and you'll discover that changes can happen.

# 9

# SWIMMING
# IN DEEPER
# WATERS

R IPPLES ON THE FAMILY POND are one thing. But
how do we stay afloat—much less make any
headway—when storms make the water really deep and muddy? I
mean the ongoing storms of serious family relationship problems. Major ones! Long-term ones! The ones that look like they'll
never be resolved. You know what I'm talking about. We all have
them.

Sometimes we wonder what went wrong. Why are we stuck with
that particular person in our family, someone who doesn't meet
our expectations and is so difficult to be around? We naturally
wish for healthy family members, especially if they are our own
parents, siblings, or children.

In the previous chapter, we considered a number of steps to
take to resolve conflicts or strengthen weaker relationships. But

some family problems are deep-seated issues. Let's consider how we can cope with these more serious difficulties that seem to defy resolution.

So many people seem to believe in magic. They cling to the illusion that someone's faults will suddenly disappear. Unfortunately, it usually doesn't work that way. And no matter who the person is who causes us difficulty, the character flaws that we find the hardest to accept are usually the ones that wounded us most deeply during childhood. Our present struggle and pain are often magnified by the pain we experienced in our early years. We sometimes feel like we're trying to swim with a bowling ball strapped to our backs.

Every time we have an encounter with a difficult family member, we are not responding just to the present interaction. We bring along with us all the years of history with this particular individual. This same dynamic often plagues marriages. When a sticky situation arises, each spouse reacts to the other—not so much about what is occurring at that moment, but for what has happened throughout the years of marriage. The present has been contaminated by the past! What positive steps can we take to resolve such long-term conflicts?

ào

*You may have some family member who is like a boxer on the defense—constantly sparring with you, arguing, having a reason for everything, and trying to wear down your attempts at resolution. How do you get through to someone like this?*

## ELIMINATE DEFENSIVENESS

So often when we are engaged in conflict with a family member, we end up fighting ourselves more than anyone else. Why? It's simple. We immediately become defensive. We erect an invisible barrier or barricade to protect ourselves from further harm. We shield our low self-esteem and feelings of insecurity from other people's judgments, expectations, and criticism. We even become defensive against our own critical thoughts.

From time to time we are all defensive. That's normal. But constant defensiveness cripples progress and growth. We lose any desire to even consider the insights and perceptions of others. You may have some family member who is like a boxer on the defense—constantly sparring with you, arguing, having a reason for everything, and trying to wear down your attempts at resolution. How do you get through to someone like this?

Here is a sample monologue a mother may use with her rebellious teenage son. These comments demonstrate several effective shifts in such a stalemate:

*Reflection:* "John, I am getting the impression from what you are saying that you're angry and feel that what I've asked is unfair."

*Empathy:* "I think I understand your feeling. I too feel that way when I'm overwhelmed around here with a lot to do and someone doesn't come through."

*Self-expression:* "But right now I am frustrated with what you're saying and how it is said."

*De-escalation:* "Your car is important to you and its condition is important to me. I don't want us to be at odds over this again and again. I guess we both would like to see this issue settled."

*Modeling defenselessness:* "I know I've tended to get upset, become loud, and overreact to you."

*Expression of hope:* "I want to be very clear about my feelings and what I want now."

*Sharing:* "I think we can work out a solution. Here is how I will respond differently from now on regardless of what you say and do. What are your thoughts and feelings? Would you like some time to think about what I've said?"

Do such statements sound stilted and contrived? Perhaps at first. Easy to pull off? Usually not. But by considering what hasn't been working before, identifying what you could say along these lines, and practicing it in advance, you can begin to make a difference in a problematic relationship.[1]

Go back and reread these comments. Think of what you could say to express the same empathy, self-expression, de-escalation, defenselessness, hope, and sharing. Even though you may feel silly doing it, rehearse your monologue in front of a mirror. Then watch for an opportunity to try out your new lines.

## ACCEPTANCE AND PERMISSION-GIVING

Someone who is struggling with a very difficult person often bristles or becomes angry or sits back in a defensive posture when I suggest the need to accept that individual. His or her perception of acceptance may involve liking or approving of what that other person does. That's not it at all.

Acceptance means giving up our dream of other people changing and becoming just who we would like them to be. After we have creatively and patiently tried everything we can think of, another person may just be determined not to change. Even when some people want to change, they may feel incapable of doing so. Instead of fighting it, you can choose to accept their resistance or incapability and live with it.

I recently made this suggestion to a woman who was telling me about her dad's latest phone call. Judy had initially come in for counseling because of her struggle to cope with such a critical and non-affirming father. Every phone conversation ended up with his daughter being on the receiving end of his negative remarks. Judy would be upset for days, have difficulty sleeping, and take out her anger on those around her.

In an attempt to resolve this impasse, I began asking some questions. "Judy, how often does your father call you each year?"

"Maybe twenty to twenty-five times."

"How many of the calls are the way you would like them to be? How often is your dad positive, not critical, perhaps even affirming?"

Judy hesitated a minute and said, "You may find this hard to believe, but I would say maybe one phone call a year. That's all, just one."

"So overall, how would you describe your father over the past few years, negative or positive?"

"Negative. I've shared that with you ever since I have been coming here. He is so critical!"

"But you expect him to be positive when he calls. Is it realistic for you to expect that with the past history you've described for me?"

"No, I guess not."

"So why be surprised when he's negative? He's usually this way, and you've survived each phone call even though it's been upsetting."

Judy actually finished what I was going to say: "So, I ought to just figure this is Dad being Dad. Why should I expect anything different at this point, unless there's some dramatic change in his life? He's who he is."

I also suggested that in her heart and mind, Judy try to give her father permission to be who he is—to be negative. If she could learn to respond to his criticism in new ways, she would be better able to cope with the painful interaction. Accepting her dad as he is and giving him permission to be a certain way could significantly free her to move ahead in the relationship.

Then I asked Judy one other question: "When your father is positive and affirming that one time during the year, do you compliment him? Do you say something like, 'Dad, thanks for being so positive and affirming today. It meant so much to me'?"

Judy sat quietly and then said, "No, I guess I never have."

All I said was, "It's worth doing. You may be surprised at the results."

Whether your long-term difficulty involves a parent, sibling, grown child, young child, or spouse, perhaps a new level of expectation and a new way of thinking would help. With whom do you seriously struggle? Identify the person by name and then make a list of his or her specific behaviors or responses that bother you the most.

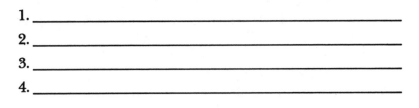

1. _____

2. _____

3. _____

4. _____

Now, consider what one step you could take in learning to accept the fact that this person has these negative traits. One man formulated a specific statement to help him become accepting: "My older brother is critical of me. I recognize that and I'm fairly sure that he will be the next time we talk. I can accept that he's this way. I'm coming to realize that this is his cover or protection against some hurt or defeat in his life. I don't understand why. I may know someday, and then again, I may not. Right now at least, I can't expect any more than this."

Perhaps the most likely way to effect a change is to specifically pray for this individual. Ask God to give you a heightened degree of understanding, patience, and acceptance for him or her, and especially for the traits or responses that you do not like. Ask God to begin healing this person of the root causes of the problem.

One counselee told me an amazing story one day. Not every situation will turn out this well, but many do.

> The last time I saw my older sister—the family perfectionist and keeper of the faults of others—I simply told her that it was perfectly all right for her to attempt to be perfect and expect us to be that way. It was also all right for her to point out our faults and we would accept her doing this. But I also said that I was concerned about her, because if she was this way toward us, she was probably the same way toward herself. I told her I would be praying for her that the Lord would help her discover the root cause of her being so hard on herself.
>
> I concluded by saying that I was more concerned about her way of treating herself than the rest of us. She didn't say anything and I thought she was going to cry. She called yesterday and I thought I was talking to a stranger. She wasn't critical; she was actually friendly. I can't believe the change.

Someone's negative characteristics often assume such a prominent position in our thinking that they soon overshadow the positive traits. Sometimes we need to get another person's perspective or interpretation of an encounter with a difficult person. A more objective observer may be able to help us identify the positives, as well as reinterpret what have always appeared as negatives.

Take a minute now to identify some of the positive characteristics of the person you find most difficult. Ask for input from someone else if you have difficulty doing so. Write down four of the person's positive qualities in the space provided. It may even help to let the person know that you are aware of these positive elements in his or her life.[2] After all, what do you have to lose?

1. _____

2. _____

3. _____

4. _____

ॐ

*Huge uproars and angry confrontations*
*begin to erupt when someone does something wrong.*
*The destructive disruption of the delicate family*
*balance leaves everyone defensive, reacting, and polarized.*

## ASK *WHAT*, NOT *WHY*

Many people become exhausted in their struggle to cope with long-term relationship difficulties. Huge uproars and angry confrontations begin to erupt when someone does something wrong. The destructive disruption of the delicate family balance leaves everyone defensive, reacting, and polarized. If you recognize this pattern in your own family, the following advice will help you learn more constructive ways of dealing with wrongs and correcting them.

One of the greatest mistakes families make when someone violates a major standard of behavior is to ask the *"Why?"* question.

*"Why* in the world would you do such a thing? Didn't you know you'd be expelled from school for fighting in the halls?" *"Why* did that happen? I can see no sense at all in your not finishing that project on time. You knew how important it was to your boss!"

*"Why* didn't you think first? You know how your mother reacts when you say that to her."

Why questions rarely lead to satisfying answers because they immediately put the person on the "hot spot." Some immediately clam up; others just start talking without considering their response. *"What"* questions work so much better.

*"What* do you think happened that sparked the fight?"

*"What* kinds of delays did you run into at work?"

*"What* did your mom say that made you so upset?"

One therapist has suggested having the persons involved write down their answer to the question, "And then what happened?" After they share their responses, the same question is asked again and again. Focusing on what happened next—instead of trying to pin blame upon another or digging defensive trenches—produces a calming effect upon the family. The primary purpose is to examine the sequence of events and learn so it doesn't recur.[3]

The next vital step is to ask, "What do you think you will do differently the next time?" Always leave as the last thought in a person's mind something positive or a different way of responding, rather than the behavior which has been the problem.

These kinds of questions have proven helpful when attempting to resolve serious family issues and conflicts. Not all will be applicable to your situation, but having several responses at your fingertips increases the possibility of resolution.

"Could you share with me what you were thinking when you responded in that way?"

"How else could you have responded?"

"How did you hope things would turn out for you?"

"Were you surprised by the outcome?"

"What do you think you can do to make things better now?"

"Do you have any ideas on a possible solution to this problem?"

For each of these questions, it may be beneficial to add, "Why don't you take a minute to think about it?" Especially if the other individual is a quiet reflective sort or a true introvert, this statement can help to eliminate the "I don't know" responses.[4]

Four other suggestions will greatly improve your listening ability, assist in calming down the participants, and promote understanding.

1. Turn off all interfering appliances including a noisy dishwasher, television, radio, stereo, or telephone so that no one

will be unnecessarily distracted.

2. Make sure that you have heard and understand the four "W"s and the one "T" of what the other person is saying to you—*who, what, when, where,* and *then* what happened—before you give your own response.

3. Discover whether the other individual wants you to give advice and suggestions or just listen. By asking them this question, you may help calm him or her down.

4. Repeat back what the other family member has said to you and ask if that is what he or she meant. If not, ask the person to tell his or her side of the issue again so you can be sure you heard it accurately.

None of us fully hears what others say without sustained effort on our part. Even though I've already quoted this Scripture, it bears repeating here. Be sure you practice what the Word of God says, "... be... (a ready listener)" (Jas 1:19, AMP); and, "He who answers a matter before he hears the facts, it is folly and shame to him" (Prv 18:13, AMP).[5]

## NURTURE AND AFFIRM

One of the most frequent responses in families is that of fault-finding, an approach with several major drawbacks. Rather than bringing correction, it usually reinforces the problem and strengthens its foothold. As a form of belittlement, persistent faultfinding is classified as verbal abuse. It is a way to wound the other family member. Constant criticism says, "I don't accept you for who you are at this time in your life. You don't measure up and I cannot accept you until you do."

Faultfinding also wounds the faultfinder. The victim usually responds in fear or anger and retaliates through some sort of withdrawal, resentment, or even aggression. Somewhat contagious and self-perpetuating, faultfinding teaches others how to respond in a negative way. When correction is necessary, the way in which we express it can make all the difference.

God's Word guides us in the way we are to respond to one another.

Do not judge and criticize and condemn others, so that you may not be judged and criticized and condemned yourselves. For just as you judge and criticize and condemn others, you will be judged and criticized and condemned, and in accordance with the measure you deal out to others, it will be dealt out again to you. Mt 7:1-2, AMP

Then let us no more criticize and blame and pass judgment on one another, but rather decide and endeavor never to put a stumbling block or an obstacle or a hindrance in the way of a brother. Rom 14:13, AMP

Any correction within a family needs to be firmly coupled with nurture. Nurturing messages convey to our family members that we value them, and that we believe in the other individual's capacity to learn, change, and grow. We demonstrate our awareness of the kind of positive self-image that we want the person to have.

2a

*Nurturing messages convey to our family members that we value them, and that we believe in the other individual's capacity to learn, change, and grow.*

Nurturing means affirming more than correcting. But such messages can come only from a person whose own self-esteem is intact, whose thought life is more positive than negative, and who is relying upon the person of Jesus Christ to teach them to love unconditionally.[6] Here are some nurturing affirmations:

- "You treat your friends very nicely."
- "You have a wonderful ability with tools."
- "Thanks for doing such a good job on your chores today."
- "Your schoolwork has really improved."
- "I liked the way you cleaned your room. Thank you."
- "You're a very special person to me."
- "I'm so glad you're my husband/wife."
- "I love you because you deserve to be loved. You don't have to earn it."

- "You make my life more complete just by being you."
- "I'm glad I have you. You teach me so much about life."[7]

And here are some examples of nurturing statements of correction:

- "Here is a way you can do it that you might like better."
- "It sounds like it's hard for you to accept a compliment."
- "Perhaps you need more practice accepting compliments, and I need more practice giving them."
- "I'm not sure you heard what I said. Tell me what you heard, and then let me repeat what I said if you heard differently."
- "Listen to the help and care I'm giving you right now."
- "You can't do that any longer, but you can do this instead."
- "That was a poor choice you made, but I have some good ideas you may want to consider for getting back on track."
- "You're not paying attention. Something must be on your mind, since you are so good at listening and thinking. I wonder what it is."[8]

Whenever very destructive and detrimental wrongdoing threatens a marriage or family relationship—such as infidelity or abuse —one of the best approaches is to take a firm stand against the behavior. Often this may mean issuing an ultimatum. Since that goes counter to many years of certain patterns of behavior and response being reinforced, such an approach is not going to be easy.

Dr. Dobson's book, titled *Love Must Be Tough*, is very appropriate in these circumstances. We must be tough but loving. For the sake of everyone involved, we must take a stand. An individual who is an abuser, adulterer, alcoholic, gambler, and so on, is helped the most by being confronted with his or her behavior and given a loving ultimatum. The person is not helped by being allowed to continue such behavior and having a spouse or parent cover for him or her.

Before confronting a spouse about a severe marital problem, there are several steps you need to take. First of all, spend a good amount of time in prayer, seeking God and considering what to do. Second, it may be helpful to discuss the alternatives with a qualified person who believes in "tough love." Third, write down the typical responses to a spouse's bad behavior, including specific statements. Then write out and rehearse out loud what to say instead. Try to anticipate the spouse's response to be better prepared.

Are you familiar with the "broken-record" technique? It has proven to be very effective in certain cases. This approach involves being persistent, saying over and over again what you want without becoming angry, obnoxious, irritated, loud, or out of control. Stick to your point as though you were a record with the needle stuck. Ignore all side issues which are brought up, as well as any request for reasons behind the confrontation ("Why are you doing this to me?"). Do not be thrown by whatever the other person says, but continue to be persistent. Here's an example:

**Joan:** "Jim, I'm concerned about the amount of time that you've been gone and I thought it might be helpful for us to look over our schedules."

**Jim:** "Oh, good grief. There you go again, griping about my schedule. You like the money I bring home, don't you?"

**Joan:** "I understand you're making good money, but I am concerned about the amount of time that you're gone and would like to talk about it."

**Jim:** "Well, my schedule is set and that's that. What about you? What do you do with all the time you spend around here? The house could use some cleaning."

**Joan:** "You could be right about the house and I will work on it. I am concerned about the amount of time that you're gone and feel it would be good for both of us to look at our schedules."

**Jim:** "Look at what? Why should I be here more? We don't ever do anything!"

**Joan:** "Jim, I am concerned about your time away and would really like to discuss this with you."

**Jim:** (pause) "Well, what's there to discuss? Go on."

When we are repetitive and persistent, the other person often realizes that he or she is not going to sidetrack us and perhaps reluctantly begins to discuss the issue. George and Sally, a couple in their mid-thirties, provide another example. Their fairly healthy marriage would have been even better except for George's parents. They were very demanding and often dictated where George and Sally would be for holidays and even for some of their vacations.

Sally was becoming more and more upset and George was also reaching the end of his rope. They began to talk about how to handle his parents in a more effective manner, as well as how to deal with the manipulation and ensuing guilt feelings which always seemed to occur. George and Sally talked with several other couples and read two or three books on how to be assertive. Here is the first positive shock George's mother received over the phone:

**Mom:** "Hello, George, this is Mom."

**George:** "Hi, Mom, how are you doing?"

**Mom:** "Oh, all right I guess." (She sighs.)

**George:** "Well fine, but how come you're sighing?"

**Mom:** "Oh, well, I guess I haven't been doing too good. I don't know what's wrong. Anyway, are you coming over this weekend? I was hoping to see you. You know it's been several weeks since you and Sally have been here."

**George:** "I'm sorry you're not feeling too well, Mom. No, we won't be coming over this weekend. We have some other things that we have already planned to do."

**Mom:** "Well, what's more important than seeing your dad and mom? Aren't we important to you anymore?"

**George:** "I can understand that you want to see us, Mom, and you are important, but we won't be coming over this weekend."

**Mom:** "Well, we sure are disappointed. We were positive that you would be over, and I already have a turkey for dinner. Did you know that?"

**George:** "No, Mom, I didn't."

**Mom:** "Both your father and I are disappointed. Here we were expecting you to come and we have the turkey already bought."

**George:** "Mom, I can tell that you're disappointed, but we won't be able to be there this weekend."

**Mom:** "You know your brother and sister come over to see us all the time. We don't even have to ask them!"

**George:** "That's true, Mom. They do come over more and I'm sure they are a lot of company. We can plan for a visit another time and work it out in advance."

**Mom:** "A good Christian son wants to see his parents often."

**George:** "Does my not coming over make me a *bad* Christian son?"

**Mom:** "If you really loved and cared for us, you would want to come and see us."

**George:** "Does my not coming to see you this weekend mean that I don't love you?"

**Mom:** "It just seems that if you did, you would be here."

**George:** "Mom, not coming over does not mean I don't care for both of you. I love you and Dad. But I won't be there this time. I'm sure you can use the turkey now or freeze it for another occasion. Now, let me check with Sally and you look at your schedule and see when we could all get together."

By planning and rehearsing this approach in advance, George was able to take a stand with a minimum of guilt feelings. As he and Sally continued to be more assertive, they became much more comfortable with their relationship. As George's parents began to back off, George and Sally felt freer to initiate get-togethers they could all enjoy. And his parents began to enjoy the visits more since they were no longer the pursuers.[9]

え

## *"If you really loved and cared for us, you would want to come and see us."*

Perhaps these approaches are foreign to you, but they can be effective in promoting a positive atmosphere. I've worked with numerous families on various issues and have learned many unique approaches. Some people have found it effective to first share their thoughts and concerns initially in writing or even on tape. After all, it's difficult to argue with a written or recorded message. It gives the sender and receiver time to reflect upon what is expressed before interacting. Raising an issue in this way may eliminate the possibility of becoming tongue-tied in a face-to-face encounter.

In dealing with behavior or attitudes that are interfering with the growth or health of the family, certain accusatory statements usually draw an instant rebuttal—for instance "You should..." or "You never..." or "You always..." Try instead: "Recently I wanted you to..." or "It would have helped if you had..." These comments are likely to be greeted with more receptivity. Be sure to describe fully your own desires at the present time. Use statements like, "I want..." or "I would (or we would) appreciate it if you would..." or "Can we count on this?"

## STOP THE SEEPAGE

Deep and ongoing conflicts in family life often center around an individual who overtly or covertly disrupts the overall functioning of the group. That person acts like a drain on the family rather than adding to it.

Picture the family as a reservoir with several tributaries or streams feeding into it. But instead of expanding, the reservoir is slowly diminishing in size and function. Why? Even though it may not be apparent, a seepage exists somewhere. Unless the leak is stopped or new resources discovered, this drain will continue. In some cases, change may not be possible, but every attempt should be made to plug the hole.

For example, having raised a profoundly mentally retarded son has provided opportunities to work with a number of families who have handicapped children—ranging from Down's syndrome to cerebral palsy or spina bifida. Caring for a seriously disabled person requires an inordinate amount of time, energy, and patience. Because the tasks and emotions easily become overwhelming, between 70 to 80 percent of couples with handicapped children divorce.

In this situation, additional resources can be discovered and implemented to help the family not only remain intact, but grow and develop because of the hardships. What are these resources? Certainly social and medical agencies can offer assistance, but most crucial are God's grace and strength in the midst of pain and sorrow. Our own family has personally benefited from this grace.

In such difficulties, we learned to cherish the words of comfort which come from Scripture:

> Blessed [be] the God and Father of our Lord Jesus Christ, the Father of sympathy (pity and mercies) and the God [Who is the Source] of every consolation and comfort and encouragement. 2 Cor 1:3, AMP

> Moreover—let us also be full of joy now! Let us exult and triumph in our troubles and rejoice in our sufferings, knowing that pressure and affliction and hardship produce patient and unswerving endurance. And endurance (fortitude) develops maturity of character—that is, approved faith and tried integrity. And character [of this sort] produces [the habit of] joyful and confident hope of eternal salvation. Rom 5:3-4, AMP

How do we survive serious disruptions that come sweeping into our family life? We need to learn to worship. The figure of Job always stands out as one who practiced this principle in the midst of extreme turmoil and suffering.

> Somehow, joy arises from loss and suffering and toil as much as it does from pleasure and ease. It is much deeper than the surface of existence; it has to do with the whole structure of life. It is the perfume of the rose that is crushed, the flash of color in the bird that is hit, the lump in the throat of the man who sees and knows, instinctively, that life is a many splendored thing.

> Don't misunderstand me. I am not suggesting that God sends adversity to enhance our appreciation of life or to make us more aware of his nearness. Nor am I implying that the fullness of life comes only to those who have passed through deep waters. Rather, I am saying that God is present in all of life, including its tragedies. His presence transforms even these agonizing experiences into opportunities for worship.

> In one day, Job lost everything—his servants, his livestock, his wealth and his children. "At this, Job got up and tore his robe and shaved his head. Then he fell to the ground in wor-

ship and said: 'Naked I came from my mother's womb, and naked I will depart. The Lord gave and the Lord has taken away; may the name of the Lord be praised.' In all this Job did not sin by charging God with wrongdoing" (Jb 1:20-22, AMP).[10]

Richard Exley continues this thought:

We don't worship God because of our losses, but in spite of them. We don't praise him for the tragedies, but in them. Like Job, we hear God speak to us out of the storm (Jb 38:1). Like the disciples at sea in a small boat, caught in a severe storm, we too see Jesus coming to us in the fourth watch of the night. We heard him say, "Take courage! It is I. Don't be afraid" (Mt 14:27, NIV)....

If you've lived for any length of time, you've probably had opportunity to see the different ways people respond to adversity. The same tragedy can make one person better and another person bitter. What makes the difference? Resources. Inner resources developed across a lifetime through spiritual disciplines.

*If you haven't worshiped regularly in the sunshine of your life, you probably won't be able to worship in the darkness.* If you haven't been intimate with God in life's ordinariness, it's not likely that you will know how or where to find him should life hand you some real hardships. *But by the same token, if you have worshiped often and regularly, then you will undoubtedly worship well in the hour of your greatest need.*[11]

*Other leaks.* A family can also become seriously drained when one member is significantly disruptive, perhaps by being consistently unhappy, critical, faultfinding, angry, resentful, pessimistic, or suffering low self-esteem. Consider whether the following descriptions characterize any of the members of your immediate or extended family.

- Constantly complains.
- Sulks to gain control.
- Shows disregard for daily schedule of others.
- Uses negative non-verbals.

- Throws temper tantrums.
- Gossips about family members.
- Uses the silent treatment to control others.
- Will not share their true feelings.
- Threatens to leave the family.
- Plays one person against another and manipulates.
- Never forgets past mistakes of others; resurrects them.
- Consistently tells lies.
- Takes their own personal unhappiness out on others.
- Does not respect others' personal privacy or boundaries.
- Demands that family life revolve around them.
- Does not take others' needs or feelings into consideration.[12]

The most effective approach is for each individual to evaluate the family separately, and then have everyone come together to discuss each problem. Such a process will not be easy or comfortable, but it is necessary to corporately identify problems and stimulate change and growth. One family member may be more sensitive to particular areas, so every individual needs to give input.

Several members of a family are commonly identified on this list. As one mother said, "It was painful to find that I identified myself in several of these categories and two of my children identified the same areas as I did." In discussing each problem, be sure to suggest a positive alternative for the negative behavior.

After this initial step in correcting the seepage problem, go back and complete the second step. If you stopped here, you would have focused solely upon the negative. Take each person's name and list two positive qualities about them. In what way do you pray for this person with respect to both the negative trait and the positive? What insight do you gain as to how you could help them? Have you assured the person that you believe he or she is capable of changing?

In counseling individuals recovering from loss, I often find it helpful to create a timeline showing their relationship with whomever they lost. This tool helps to identify the positives and negatives of the relationship. After writing down remembered events in the form of a chart, people are amazed at how much more clearly they understand that specific relationship.

Another help in plugging a leak involves determining when the seepage began. One counselor suggests that the family members participate in creating a "family lifeline." Draw a long line on a piece of paper and allow everyone to list significant events of the year along the line. (This can be an enjoyable group activity for any family. Such a family history or diary increases in value as the years go by.)

When the timeline is completed, ask each family member to list his or her own personal reactions to each event. Then search for differences in reactions, as well as over- and under-reactions. This exercise often reveals "trigger events" which may have contributed to someone's having become a serious drain on the family reservoir.[13] Finally, think about how you can love and support this family member in a way that will help him or her to grow and change.

### BRINGING IT HOME

Serious tension and estrangement can plague families for months, years, or even decades. Parents are alienated from their adolescent or adult children. Middle-age adults are distant from their own parents. Siblings haven't spoken to one another for years. Hurt and offenses often grow in our minds over time. The intense pain of physical and sexual abuse always requires years of healing; in many cases, no reconciliation ever comes to pass in the sense of a continuing relationship. But even in these areas, people can recover, go on with their life, and learn to forgive the perpetrator.

*Even if our attempts at reconciliation don't work out, at least we will be able to look back and say, "I did all that was possible."*

When a family has become bogged down by difficult relationship problems, someone needs to take the initial step toward reconciliation. We would prefer that the "other person" do the dirty work, and we often perceive someone else as more to blame. Even if our attempts at reconciliation don't work out, at least we will be able to look back and say, "I did all that was possible."

In working toward a healing of any relationship, I would suggest five simple steps.

The first is to begin to pray specifically for the other individual, for yourself, and for the relationship. Share with God what you would like to see happen, but then ask him for specific guidance as to his desires. Ask for wisdom to change any negative thinking toward this person and/or situation, and for the words to say when you do reach out. Then be sure to listen.

The second step is to plan out word for word what you would like to say. Write it down so that you can refine it and rehearse in advance. This will provide you with what you will be sharing in the next three steps. In your heart and mind, give the other person permission to be defensive when you approach them.

The third step occurs when you reach out to this family member. State the purpose of your discussion. Make it clear and specific. Some examples might be: "I have been concerned about our relationship for some time and I would like it to be better. I want to work toward that and I have been praying that you would like that as well." Or, "I've been bothered for some time about our relationship and I would like to make it better."

Think through the fourth step carefully beforehand: state honestly and accurately how you see your role in the problems that have transpired. Since we tend to focus more upon what that individual may have done to us, rather than our own part in whatever has happened, this is often the most difficult statement to make.

Some examples might be:

"I imagine it must have been difficult for you when I didn't want to talk on the phone."

"You probably wondered why I didn't return your calls or want to come by anymore. That must have upset you."

"I know that when I was growing up I caused you some headaches, especially when I didn't want to tell you what I was doing."

"I know I reacted to you with anger. I did that to keep you from giving me advice anymore. I didn't want to be angry and I know it wasn't easy to hear."

Most books and resources on this subject make similar suggestions like this and then move on. But just stating what we have done is only part of the healing process. Even in minor infractions or altercations in an immediate family, the crucial phrase remains: *"I would like to ask your forgiveness."* But if we are going to reflect the presence of Jesus Christ in our family life, this phrase must be asked sincerely when we know that we have not responded in a good way. Asking forgiveness is an important step in freeing both parties. Before you go on to the next step, ask for forgiveness.

The fifth and final step in the process is stating how you would like your relationship to be with this individual in the future. It doesn't necessarily have to be just the way it was before the offense occurred. You may not spend a great amount of time with the person. In some cases you may not even choose to have an ongoing close relationship. You are merely stating the changes that you would like to see, and what needs to occur to make them happen.

"I would like us to be able to talk together on the phone. What could we do differently to make this happen?"

"I would like us to begin building a new relationship. What can we both do to make it different this time?"

"I would like us to be able to get together again for Christmas. What can we do that would be different and comfortable for both of us?"

"I would like us to be in contact each week on the phone. Tell me what would make it comfortable for you and then I can share what I would like to see happen."

1. If you have a difficult family member, identify what it is about the relationship that makes it so hard. Write down your thoughts.

2. Describe what you will say to this individual when you engage him or her for reconciliation.

3. Share what you will say about your role and responsibility in the difficulty and how you will ask forgiveness.

4. Describe how you would like your relationship to be different with this individual.

5. Describe how you have been praying for this person and how you will pray in the future.

If you end up with the feeling that focusing on strengths and praying for others is the answer… you're right.

# THE TRANSFORMING
# POWER OF
# ENCOURAGEMENT

ROWDS LINED BOTH SIDES OF THE STREET, all eyes peering in the same direction. Many of them had already been waiting for over an hour. Finally, in the distance, they saw a tiny speck moving slowly but steadily along the highway. In another minute, the speck had grown. Everyone began to clap and cheer when they could actually make out the shape of a person propelling his wheel chair. The cheering intensified as the smiling marathoner reached the edge of this small midwestern town.

This courageous paraplegic was traveling from one end of the country to the other. At a reception for him later on in the day, someone asked him, "What keeps you going? Why go through all the pain and agony of pushing yourself day after day on those highways? How do you do it?"

He replied simply, "Didn't you hear it?"

"Hear what?" the man asked.

"You heard what keeps me going when I came into town. All those people clapping and cheering. That's what does it. All those cheerleaders. They're my encouragement. They believe in me. And then I believe I can make it. We all need someone to believe in us."

One of the crucial functions of the family is to encourage each other. The word encourage means "to inspire to continue on a chosen course; impart courage or confidence to; embolden, hearten." Scripture calls us to "encourage... edify... build up" (1 Thes 5:11, AMP). Everyone needs a dose of encouragement. Everyone needs a dose of courage.

Families who sail through the years without upsets, crises, and even traumatic tragedies are the exception rather than the norm. Without courage, we would all fail.

Picture this scenario. The long anticipated birth of your first child is at hand. Everything is going according to plan, the delivery is normal and easy, your son is alert and healthy... except... he has no arms. This tiny baby is born with a rare disease called bilateral upper extremity amelia.

Can you imagine how you would feel? The shock! The fear! The concern! How can he survive or function? Won't he have to be taken care of the rest of his life? How will our family make it? Should we have any other children?

Instead of some wild fabrication of my imagination, this is a true story. Sixteen years later, this family's story was told in the *Los Angeles Times*.[1] The boy lives with his mother, stepfather, and two younger siblings. Not only did his family survive, his story portrays incredible courage. This sixteen-year-old boy maintains a 3.5 grade-point average and runs on the cross country team. Even more amazing is the fact that he learned to use an acetylene torch for welding, using just his feet. He learned to use scissors at the age of four, dress himself, swim, and use a computer.

This youth learned to overcome tremendous obstacles. And that is the key to making it as a family today. Who are the people in your family of origin, family past, or current family who have overcome obstacles? Who encourages them?

What have you overcome? Who encourages you? Often we don't even realize what huge feats we have accomplished in the past. What are some of the current obstacles in your family? What could be done to overcome them now? Who needs a dose of encouragement from you right now?

## SILENT EXPRESSIONS OF ENCOURAGEMENT

Beyond offering praise or reinforcement, encouragement means accepting each family member as a person of worth and letting them know it. It involves paying attention to them, listening, and letting them know you understand.

One of the maladies that can infect a family is what I call "empty talk." Some people talk a lot, but say very little and do even less. In time such behavior can create a discouraging environment, along with disbelief and mistrust in those who constantly breathe this smog of empty words. We soon begin to tune out and turn deaf.

ॐ

*The gift of our undivided attention is a treasure.*

"Silent talking" offers proof of what an individual says verbally. Family members need to express interest, love, and concern through listening, touching, and hugging. We may need to put down something we're doing or turn off the stereo or TV, turn toward the person, and look him or her in the eye. The gift of our undivided attention is a treasure.

My daughter drove home this lesson one day when she was about eleven. I had just arrived home from a trip and gotten out of the car. Sheryl came bursting out of the front door crying out in excitement, "Daddy, look at my new coat that Mommy bought me!" She twirled around in front of me several times. I remember saying, "Yes, it is nice and it looks pretty on you." She twirled around again and I made another comment, picked up my bags, and went in the house.

Later on that evening as we were sitting in the family room,

Sheryl looked at me and asked, "Daddy, even though you didn't look at my coat very long, do you really like it?" I gulped. I realized that I should have paid her more attention, especially at a time when I wasn't that tired or pressed for time.

Encouragement involves validating another person's intentions as well as their responses, showing respect, and believing in them. It means purposely choosing to focus on the person's strengths rather than weaknesses. This is encouragement![2]

Expecting the best out of each person is far different from expecting perfection. When you see a family member excelling at something, take time to notice, affirm, and reinforce their achievement. But don't begin to expect this behavior every time. Each of us will fail and make mistakes. There is no such creature as a perfect person.

One young man shared these very encouraging words with me: "Fortunately, I came out of a home where I was accepted for who I was at all times. I was accepted when I achieved and when I blew it. I knew I was loved at all times. That was probably the best gift that my family ever gave to me. And I want to be able to do this with the people in my life as well."

During the 1992 Winter Olympics, a former Olympic skater named Scott Hamilton served as one of the commentators for the ice skating events. At one point, Hamilton shared about his special relationship with his mother who had died prior to his winning an Olympic gold medal. "The first time I skated in the U.S. Nationals, I fell five times. My mother gave me a big hug and said, 'It's only your first National. It's no big deal.' My mother always let me be me. Three years later I won my first National. She never said, 'You can do better,' or 'Shape up.' She just encouraged me."

## FALLING FORWARD

Failure branches off in two directions. We can fail and fall backward; or we can fail and fall forward. We can learn from each failure. Family is the place to fail and experience the grace of God as the other family members bathe us in acceptance and love. Husbands make mistakes. Wives make mistakes. Parents make mistakes. Children make mistakes. Everyone does.

Just like pruning stimulates new growth in a rose bush, mistakes foster growth when a family focuses on the strengths rather than the defects and weaknesses of others. Understanding and accepting the unique personality God has created within each family member applies precious fertilizer to the roots.

You probably have a checking or savings account at a local bank. But do you keep a family strength bank account? Do you search for the strengths of each person in the family as well as the strengths of the family unit in order to make regular deposits? Such a practice will encourage the family unit to grow, impart stronger values, and deepen the reality of love and security.

Some families meet on a regular basis for family strength sessions, perhaps weekly or bi-monthly. All those who attend are encouraged to tell of a new strength they have discovered in their own lives, as well as in the life of another family member. They keep an account by recording both individual and family strengths in a ledger.

Using banking terminology, Joe Batten suggests that a strength can be a quality, ability, skill, or area of knowledge. The assets for a family are the individual members' strengths, which are discovered and then used within the life of the family. Since liabilities are usually present within the family, these are the strengths that are missing. Identifying these and then working to build them is an important step.

In any investment program, capital is important. A family's capital is the strengths of all of the family members. In a sense, this is similar to the individual and spiritual gifts of a body of believing Christians. Each with his or her gift fills the vacant places. Investments happen by discovering the strengths and gifts, then sharing them and developing them in the various members of the family.

Creating a bank of encouragement will bring a greater degree of cohesiveness, unity, and joy to the family. Rather than encouraging prideful boasting, focusing and directing their attention upon these strengths benefits the entire family.[3]

I talk to many people today who are desperately looking for solutions for family problems. I'm not sure there are any guaranteed formulas, but there are proven guidelines that are essential.

You can't go wrong by encouraging one another through acceptance and appreciation.

*Unconditional acceptance will build any relationship.* Have you ever been the recipient of unconditional acceptance? The feeling is terrific. Do you actively express love to your spouse, child, or parent—no matter what they do or say, no matter how bad they mess up or hurt you?

ह

*Being loved in this way imparts a feeling of security. It gives the feeling, "I have value and it doesn't depend on what I do! I'm loved for me!"*

Acceptance means consistently showing love even when a spouse isn't returning it, even when a child turns his or her back on our teaching and Christian values and lives a life of sin for several years. Being loved in this way imparts a feeling of security. It gives the feeling, "I have value and it doesn't depend on what I do! I'm loved for me!"

This kind of agape love comes from God. And we cannot really be consistent in expressing it without the presence of Jesus Christ invading and guiding our lives. Otherwise we will sink into the deadly trap of spooning out performance-based love.

*Appreciation is a second essential ingredient in building healthy relationships.* All of us need to be recognized for who we are and what we have done. Appreciation imparts a feeling of significance. Josh McDowell describes the importance of appreciation in one of his books:

> It's funny how one little phrase can bring a concept or principle to life. I was sold on giving my kids unconditional acceptance, but I had been struggling with learning how to appreciate them. It isn't that I never praised them for what they did; it was simply a matter of praising them *after* I was sure I had corrected all the things they had done wrong. Naturally, because kids have a tendency to make mistakes, it was just too easy to

find them doing things wrong. Mix that with their intuitive ability to perceive that the best way to get my attention was to do something wrong and I had a real problem.

One side of me had been trying to accept my children, and the other side had been trying to correct them for doing things wrong. It was no wonder that I often felt a little schizophrenic! But all that changed when I turned the emphasis upside down. Instead of concentrating on what they were doing *wrong*, I started to make a conscious effort to look for what they were doing *right*. My new goal was to find at least two things about each child that I could appreciate every day, and then be sure to compliment each child on what I saw.

I'm not sure my children noticed any "overnight difference," but I know I did. My whole perspective on parenting changed.

I would look over and see Kelly studying and then stop a moment to say, "Honey, I appreciate the way you study." When I saw Sean taking out the trash, I would stop him and say, "Sean, thanks for remembering to take the trash out."

I'd find little Katie picking up her toys, and I'd say, "Katie, sweetheart, Daddy really appreciates how you take care of your toys."

Another thing I began to do was try to find all of the children in the same general area—our family room for example —and stand in the middle of all of them for an "appreciation session." In this case, I wouldn't necessarily say anything out loud, but I would consciously stop for three minutes to ask myself, *How many things can you appreciate about your kids if you stop to think about it right now?* Then I would try to mentally list fifteen or twenty things I appreciated about the four of them. That meant finding about four or five items per child, but I always made it well within the three-minute time limit I set for myself.

This little exercise helped remind me of just how much I have to be thankful for about my kids, and it kept me primed for saying appreciative things at the proper time. You see, it isn't a matter of not being able to find things to appreciate about your kids; what it's all about is programming yourself to *speak up and tell your kids what you see*—to give them honest praise for their effort.[4]

Teaching children to express appreciation for their parents is also an encouraging factor in a family. Josh tells how he taught his oldest daughter this lesson:

I even show my love for Dottie in the way I discipline the children. Several years ago, before our oldest daughter had moved into the teens, she and Dottie got into a period of "my mother/myself" tension. They just kind of grated on each other. Today it's just the other way around and they get along beautifully, but back when Kelly was about eleven, she began sassing Dottie and talking back to her in general.

After observing this a few times, I decided that enough was enough. I grabbed Kelly by the shoulders, gently swung her around, looked her in the eye and said, "young lady, you might talk to your mother that way, but I will never let you talk to my wife that way. I love that woman, and I will not only protect her from people outside the family, but I will also protect her from you kids. Don't ever talk to my wife that way again!"

Kelly blinked, mumbled something, and walked away. But the results of my brief speech about how I wanted people to talk to my wife were unbelievable. It helped break Kelly of her habit of sassing back to Dottie. A few times she would start to make some smart remark, catch herself, and look over at me and say, "Oh, I can't talk to your wife that way, can I?"

"No, Kelly, you can't," I'd reply with a twinkle in my eye. Even in disciplining your children you can reinforce the idea that "I am committed to my mate."

Something else I've done with the children is to read Proverbs 31:28-31, which talks about a husband praising his wife and the children praising their mother. I've done this with Dottie present and then we all discuss and think of things we can thank and praise Mom for. This little exercise accomplishes two things. First, the children have to think of something specific and positive to say about their mother, rather than just taking her for granted. For that matter, so do I. And second, the children hear me praising their mother and again they see that I am committed to her—my wife.[5]

## SETTING ASIDE TIME FOR FAMILY ENCOURAGEMENT

Aside from individual responses, certain approaches prove useful for an entire family in providing a source of encouragement. Some families use a weekly or bi-monthly encouragement meeting of fifteen to thirty minutes to help everyone develop a more positive perspective upon the family as a unit as well as each person.

The rules are simple. The meeting is to occur at the same place and time without any interruptions. Each person is given a chance to speak positively about every other person. It may be helpful to reflect before the meeting and jot down some positives. No negative feelings, gripes, or blame are allowed at this meeting. This is not a problem-sharing session. When one member is sharing positives about another, he or she needs to look at that person and speak in the first person.

One family used the following statements to help guide their thoughts toward positives. After each description, the various family members can give their opinions as to who reflects the content. Perhaps no one fulfills it, or someone feels he or she does it best, or it could even be the family pet!

This person gives me hugs.
This person is available for me to talk with.
This person is on time a lot.
This person shows me he or she believes in me.
This person expresses anger in a healthy way.
This person is a calming influence around our home.
This person gives compliments.
This person shares personal feelings.
This person helps me find solutions.
This person remembers special things I like.
This person greets me when I come home.
This person is generous.

Another approach or addition is to ask who in the family best reflects the teaching of certain passages in Scripture, e.g., Proverbs 16:32; 17:17; 17:27; 18:13; 20:3; and 28:23. Another variation is to have a different person ask each week at the end of the meeting: "In what way can I be more of an encourager to you during the coming week?" A helpful reply would be, "I would appreciate it if you would…, and when you do, I will acknowledge what you have said or done."

This type of meeting may seem contrived, unnatural, and even awkward. Some may even say, "Why do we need this? Just give an occasional pat on the back or a compliment now and then and we'll do all right." That's just the problem—*the occasional now and then*. True encouragement happens all too infrequently in this busy world. A specific meeting scheduled for this purpose offers many positive benefits. It helps to eliminate power struggles in the family, provides healthy memories for the members, creates a positive atmosphere, and encourages each person to feel significant. The family as a whole is enabled to see itself in a more positive light.

ह

*"Why do we need this?*
*Just give an occasional pat on the back or*
*a compliment now and then and we'll do all right."*
*That's just the problem—the occasional now and then.*

## STEMMING THE TIDE

But how can you encourage someone with an obvious problem behavior? Is it possible to still speak kindly to someone who drips incessantly like a leaky faucet? Do you have some type of behavior that you would like to corral like a herd of wild horses? Asking this question to a group of parents usually leads to some interesting responses. Listen to some of them.

"I wish we could control the griping and complaining that goes on in our family."

"What I don't like are the sarcastic put-down comments that all of us make."

"Blame. That's what gets to me. Blame, blame, blame. Nobody admits to their part in a problem, they just point the finger at others."

We first need to identify and confine a negative behavior which we would like to eliminate from the family's interaction. Then ask each family member when and where it usually occurs, in which room of the house. Is it done when people are sitting down or standing up, far from one another or close together? Is the television off or on? Does it continue if the phone rings or if someone drops over? Who is best (or worst) at this particular behavior?

After you have gathered the needed information, suggest a new approach. Here is what one father said to his family.

I've noticed that we have a number of complaints that we like to make and get off our chest. That's understandable since all of us have things that we would like to see changed from time to time. But we need a better way to deal with our complaints, so we will begin to have a Family Complaint Time. The only time this will occur is Tuesday and Thursday night from 7:15 to 7:30. It will be held in the den. This will be our complaint time and complaint room.

We cannot make complaints any other time so I suggest that you write them down so you can remember them. We are not to complain to anyone at any other time. When you do have a complaint to share we will all listen to you, not interrupt and not defend ourselves. We will consider your complaint, but when you share it you also need to come up with a positive solution or suggestion that you would like us to consider as well.

During the first two weeks, a number of complaints slipped out of various family members. Each time, they were told, "Write it down and save it for the meeting." After a while they remembered and the dinner times especially became more enjoyable and livable.[6]

When the complaints are in the form of sarcasm or put-downs, it may be helpful to explore hurt feelings. Healthier ways of expressing anger could be suggested, as well as more constructive ways of responding to family members.[7]

## THE DEADLY RUT OF ROUTINE

When problems are resolved in a family, everyone feels encouraged by the progress. And encouraged families tend to be more creative in their shared activities. What have you done recently to generate new life in your family? The rut of routine can so easily creep into our busy lives. We soon become captive to regular patterns, schedules, discussions, entertainment, or activities.

Add to this problem the "Hurry Up And Rush Through Life Syndrome." "Frantic" is the way one father described the atmosphere in his family. "Everyone seems to be on this schedule where we've always got too much to do," he said. "We all collapse at the end of the day. It's at the point where we don't enjoy anything or anyone anymore! That's not the way it should be!"

How is your family life? Does it feel hectic, driven, in a rut? What can you do to make it more fulfilling and encouraging?

The James family established a pattern of sharing at least one meal together five days out of the week. Sometimes it was breakfast; other times it was the evening meal. Each Sunday they would talk about their upcoming week and plan the meal schedule, agreeing to rearrange activities and rise earlier some mornings as necessary. During the meal time, three very important conditions were implemented: all TV's, stereos, and radios were silenced; a "do not disturb" sign was placed on the front door; and the phone was taken off the hook.

The Kellys were another family that struggled with busyness and overinvolvement. To evaluate how they were spending their time, they each made a list of all of their activities and then rated them using the following criteria: very crucial; very important; important; and good.

Any activity that landed under the "very crucial" column was viewed as essential to a person's life. Anything that fell under "very important" would probably stay, but could go if necessary.

Anything under "important" could either stay or go. Any activity that fell under "good" would be dropped.

The Kelly family was quite surprised to discover all they were doing. Each activity was evaluated by asking, "Why am I doing this? What is the purpose?" A number of activities were dropped, some with reluctance. But interestingly enough, in a couple of weeks, they were barely missed. How would you and your family fare with such a chart?

## A TIME MACHINE

In another family, the parents announced to their kids that they would all be entering a time machine in just three weeks. In order to prepare for the week-long journey, each person would have to take a trip to the library and read about what it was like to live as a family one hundred years ago! They were to discover what items families didn't have in their homes at that time and how they functioned from day to day.

As they began their investigation, the family members were really shaken to discover they wouldn't have a TV, radio, refrigerator, electricity, dryer, or washing machine. One child came home and asked his mother, "When you were younger, did you use a washboard to wash clothes?" Everyone began to catch a glimpse of how their grandparents and great-grandparents had lived. As the family members gathered information, they had to either make or adapt items to use for this week-long journey.

Are you aware that before 1945, the following items were not available: television, frozen food, contact lenses, microwaves, CDs, penicillin, polio shots, radar, ballpoint pens, pantyhose, clothesdryers, electric blankets, FM radio, or electric typewriters? Young people assume that the gadgets we have today always existed!

Friends and relatives were informed of the family's time-machine venture, and offered helpful advice on where they could obtain the necessary equipment. Antique stores and collectors were contacted with requests to either borrow or rent certain items. In exchange for this, the stores hoped to receive publicity through the family's friends, and perhaps even coverage from the local paper about this wild adventure.

The entire family plunged into problem-solving with great enthusiasm. The questions seemed endless. How do you open a can? What can we use for an ice box? What's a kerosene lantern?

Different foods were also selected which fit those times—a major shock to the digestive system of the kids. A trip to a home for the elderly provided an opportunity to interview several people in their eighties and nineties. While the information gleaned was helpful, the family's perspective and attitude toward the elderly was the greatest benefit.

In many ways, a new sense of vitality and togetherness came to this family by their willingness to break the routine of their daily life. Their time-machine venture into the past was filled with many humorous events, adjustments, lessons in patience, and newly gained appreciation for the past and the present. After the week was over, they held a debriefing session to discuss what they liked, didn't like, and what they had learned. While perceiving the past more clearly, they discovered ways their current life would now be different. They all agreed that the three weeks of preparation had been just as valuable as the actual week itself.

How would a similar experience impact your life? Are you ready for the challenge? The past year I've been subscribing to a magazine called *Reminisce,* "the magazine that brings back the good times." Many of the articles reflect not only the time of my childhood (the late thirties and forties,) but also my mother's, who is now in her early nineties. This magazine has added much to our understanding of our family's past.[8]

## LEARNING NEW PATTERNS

A less venturesome approach has helped a number of other families, one which reminds me of what my dad and I used to do. We would sit and listen to the radio each evening. Listening to adventure stories or music together was a pattern of our family life. Some families now spend a portion of one evening a week listening to a program on the radio, ranging from some of the older suspense and comedy programs to music to Garrison Keillor's "Prairie Home Companion."

Each family member takes turns selecting a program. Country music, hard rock, classical, blue grass, oldies from the fifties and sixties may require some ear adjustments. This radio time provides an opportunity to experience an event together without watching it or doing something. Some families ask one another what they liked about a particular selection, or what memories the programs elicited.

Have you ever noticed a sign in a store indicating an employee of the week or month? The person is simply given recognition for an outstanding job. Some families have established this same practice. One specific individual is named "Family Member of the Week," although the selection is based not upon performance but just rotates in alphabetical order.

The purpose is simply to recognize who the person is and perhaps defer to them a bit more than usual or show care for them in special ways. Such an activity helps to teach the important principle that family members are to be treated as special *all the time.* By the way, cats and dogs are eligible for this award as well!

The Wilson family consisted of two parents and five children, ranging in ages from seven to sixteen. One of their unique rules had a profound effect upon the family. When anyone arrived home at the end of the day—whether from school or work—everyone was to be greeted in a positive way. No griping or negative comments could be shared right away. They would show interest and concern to each one, as well as share hugs and kisses. The Wilsons believed that what occurs during the first four minutes will set the tone for the rest of the evening. If the initial interactions are negative and critical, the remainder of the evening will follow suit! On the other hand, a positive start tends to continue as well.

ॐ

*After greeting the children, he and his wife would spend the next fifteen minutes alone in the kitchen without any interference or interruptions from the children.*

227

When Dad arrived home, no requests from the children were allowed. In times past, he was frequently inundated by verbal requests as soon as he hit the door. After greeting the children, he and his wife would spend the next fifteen minutes alone in the kitchen without any interference or interruptions from the children. Naturally this elicited a number of comments from the kids but they learned to respect their parents' privacy. After dinner, the children shared their requests in writing, and gave their parents a chance to consider them without pleas, arguments, and time pressure. Unrealistic? It won't work? Not true at all. Families who are creative will make it work!

## GOD'S ENCOURAGEMENT

One other step is vital to the growth of any family: learning to reflect the Word of God as it relates to family life. Each time a family meets together, they can discuss the meaning of one particular passage of Scripture. Then each person can describe how they are going to put this passage into practice during the coming week. Here are some of the passages which can be used for this purpose:

- Love one another (Jn 13:34).
- Bear one another's burdens (Gal 6:2).
- Bear with one another and making allowances because you love one another (Eph 4:2).
- Serve one another (Gal 5:13).
- Be subject to one another (Eph 5:21).
- Think more highly of one another (Phil 2:3).
- Be kind to one another (Eph 4:32).
- Show honor to one another (Rom 12:10b).
- Encourage one another (1 Thes 5:11a).
- Strengthen and build up one another (1 Thes 5:11b).
- Receive one another (Rom 15:7).
- Admonish one another (Rom 15:14).
- Have the same care for one another (1 Cor 12:25).
- Pray for one another (Jas 5:16).

Time and time again, the Word of God admonishes us to behave in a positive and encouraging way. "And become useful and helpful and kind to one another, tenderhearted (compassionate, understanding, loving-hearted), forgiving one another [readily and freely], as God in Christ forgave you" (Eph 4:32, AMP). "Clothe yourselves therefore, as (God's own picked representatives,) His own chosen ones, [who are] purified and holy and well-beloved [by God Himself, by putting on behavior marked by] tenderhearted pity and mercy, kind feeling, a lowly opinion of yourselves, gentle ways, [and] patience—which is tireless, long-suffering and has the power to endure whatever comes, with good temper" (Col 3:12-13, AMP).

I recently saw a news story about a small airplane that had been lost. The man's wife called the authorities to say that her husband had gone flying the day before and had never returned. Their first question was, "Did he file a flight plan?" Since the man had not, the hands of the rescuers were tied. They had no way to determine where this pilot was planning to fly. They couldn't even begin to devise a search and rescue plan.

Pilots usually file a flight plan to help them determine course settings and let others know their intended destination. Families are no different. Filing a flight plan would remove an added element of risk from the family journey. True, we would still run into occasional turbulence. And with no automatic pilot, we would begin to drift off course if we don't keep our eyes on the compass and our hands on the controls at all times.

Can you envision using the above Scriptures as the flight plan and guiding compass for attitudes and behavior within our families? Pondering God's words of encouragement offers another important way to actively build family life.

ðŸ™¢

## BRINGING IT HOME

You may be a parent, a grandparent, never married, an uncle or aunt, but everyone has some family connections. To help you plot a course for your family's future, take some time to complete the following evaluation. You may want to come back to this several times rather than trying to complete it in one sitting.

## *Family Flight Plan*

1. Provide an example to other family members that is positive, encouraging, loving, and reflects the Word of God.

   Example of how this is done _____

   One other family member who does this is _____

   How?_____

2. Ask for the opinions and suggestions of others, listen and hear what is said.

   Example of how this is done _____

   One other family member who does this is _____

   How?_____

3. Help to create a vision of how each person can fulfill his or her potential, as well as what the family can become.

   Example of how this is done _____

   One other family member who does this is _____

   How?_____

4. Trust others and expect the best from each person.

   Example of how this is done _____

   One other family member who does this is _____

   How?_____

5. Let others know that you believe in them and pray for them to become all that God has for them.

   Example of how this is done _____

   One other family member who does this is _____

   How?_____

6. Allow and encourage others to make their own decisions and only suggest when you think they may need help.

Example of how this is done _____

One other family member who does this is _____

How? _____

7. Share with other family members all you know about your background, tradition, or family "roots."

Example of how this is done _____

One other family member who does this is _____

How? _____

8. Assume that others are truthful and right unless there is clear evidence to the contrary.

Example of how this is done _____

One other family member who does this is _____

How? _____

9. Believe and practice the principle that your words as well as actions have the potential to build up or destroy another family member.

Example of how this is done _____

One other family member who does this is _____

How? _____

10. Model openness, vulnerability, and the sharing of your feelings, and encourage this in others.

Example of how this is done _____

One other family member who does this is _____

How? _____

11. Work toward assisting the family to work together in making decisions and respecting the feelings and thoughts of others.

    Example of how this is done _____

    One other family member who does this is _____

    How? _____ [9]

   While certainly not an all-inclusive list, these will help you identify the positive steps that you can take toward stronger family life. Do you find it difficult to identify anything that you are doing or that another family member is doing? The next step is to consider what you need to do in your own life to make this a reality. Then think about how you can encourage others to work toward this goal in their own lives.

# 11

# PERILOUS
# PASSAGES

"FAMILY LIFE? Sure I can tell you what it's like. It's mostly like driving on a bumpy road in a car with no springs. Other times, it's like riding on a four-lane highway, with everyone picking up speed. And you can't be sure what lies ahead."

"It's a journey on a road that varies from being straight and smooth to winding, steep, and rough with a few unexpected detours thrown in for good measure. And even though you thought you had packed for every possible circumstance, you soon discover you still left something out."

June was a counselee who had hit one of those bumpy stretches, with no end in sight. "Over the past few years," she said, "I've experienced stress and loss in some ways I never expected. And that's thrown me. I'm a careful, organized person. I look at life realistically. And I don't just consider what is happening now, but I plan for the future. When I was eighteen, I studied and reflected on the different transitions that I would experience. But now that some of them have arrived, they still surprised me. Why? I wasn't able to handle them as well as I thought I would. Why not? Instead of feeling challenged by them, I felt threatened. Why?"

## TRANSITIONS ALONG THE FAMILY JOURNEY

Even though our day to day experience can sometimes feel like drudgery, family life is always full of twists and turns, bends in the road, U-turns, even temporary roadblocks and seeming dead-ends. The journey uniquely blends acquiring and losing, receiving and giving away, holding and then letting go.

Another term for the losses in the family lifecycle is *transition*: a shifting from one period of certainty to another, with a time of uncertainty and change in between.[1] Within this shift, the inherent sense of loss is acknowledged by some and either ignored or denied by others.

Along with the loss, every transition carries with it seeds for growth, new insights, refinement, and understanding. But in the midst of turmoil, sometimes the positive aspects seem too far in the future to be very real.

❧

*Some people wish life were like a video player.*
*Then whenever they found a particular stage to be*
*especially satisfying, they could just hit the pause button*
*and remain there a while.*

One of the natural transitions of life begins in our first year. Our baby teeth come through after bouts of pain and crying. We have gained a valuable tool for continued growth. But one day, these hard-earned baby teeth begin to loosen and wiggle. Soon they either fall out or have to be gently pulled out. We must suffer this necessary loss to make room for our permanent teeth. Sometimes we end up losing these as well and have to be fitted with false teeth. None of these transitions is easy and painless.

Some people wish life were like a video player. Then whenever they found a particular stage to be especially satisfying, they could just hit the pause button and remain there a while. But life is not a series of fixed points. Stable times are actually the exceptions; transitions are the norm. Dr. Charles Sell uses an apt analogy to describe these normal transitions in life:

> Transitions are mysterious, like an underground passageway I once saw in a tour through a castle. The castle's rooms were gigantic, the woodwork extravagant, and the huge beams in the inner part of the towers projected massive strength. But what captivated me the most was that underground tunnel. A half-mile long, the escape route led from the castle to the stables. It was strikingly different from the rest of the castle.
>
> The vast ballroom offered its visitors the feeling of dignity. A sense of comfort overtook us in the luxurious bedroom suites. Serenity filled the garden room. But the secret tunnel was mysterious and unnerving. It held no comfortable chairs because it was not a place to rest. No artwork adorned its moist, dark stone walls. It was not a place to browse. The tunnel was not made for stopping. It was for those en route with a sense of urgency. It turned your mind to either the past or the future: either you would concentrate on the extravagant castle you were leaving behind or on the stables ahead.
>
> Life's transitions are like that, going *from* somewhere *to* somewhere. The present circumstances may seem like a void. It would be pleasant to turn around and go back to the security left behind. But because that is impossible, it is necessary to keep groping for what is ahead; then there will surely be a resting place. Uncertainty cries out "How long?" And anxiety questions, "Will I ever get through this?"
>
> Drawn to the past by warm memories and yearnings, the future simultaneously beckons with a mixture of hope and fear. Sometimes depression opens its dark pit. Above, the grass is green, the sun shining on gleeful men, women, and children. But those in transition feel distant from them, pressured by the urgency to get on, to get through and out. Each transition carries with it the death of the previous state and the birth of a new one.[2]

We are always moving from, into, through, and out of something or other. Resisting this process puts us at the mercy of what is happening. How we can feel a greater sense of control in the inevitable ebb and flow of family life?

## THE LAST STRAW

Some people seem to cope well with unexpected crises. They stay in control by taking on each situation one at a time, while delaying their response to others. Others are thrown into stressful upheaval when too many unanticipated events happen all at once. "Oh, no! Not something else!" we cry. "This is the last straw." We can begin to crumble when our resources seem to have been exhausted.

What can we do when we're in the midst of a transitional struggle? First we need to identify the focal point of our particular difficulty in making the adjustment. The problem may be a normal change of life or one of the unexpected events mentioned above. But most problems encountered during such a transition center on one of the following:

1. We could be having difficulty separating from the past stage. We might be uncomfortable with our new role at this time of life.
2. We could be having difficulty making a decision concerning what new path to take or what plan of action to follow in order to negotiate this new transition.
3. We could be having difficulty carrying out this new decision because of a lack of understanding of what's involved in making the change. Perhaps we lack enough information concerning expectations for ourselves and others. We could also be struggling with our own lack of preparation for this transition.
4. We may already be in the midst of this transition, but we may be having difficulty weathering the period of adjustment until the new changes have stabilized. Again, we could be lacking information or resources that are needed to make the change secure.

To effectively move through a time of transition, I would recommend an orderly progression of steps. First of all, we need to identify the *target problem* in terms of the specific difficulty that we feel at this time and what we are willing to work on. Second, we need to identify the *target goal,* that is, the situation in which we feel we could move ahead. This goal includes specifying what it would take to feel competent in moving forward in our lives again. The third step is to *identify the tasks* that need to be accomplished in order for a smooth transition to occur.

## INDIVIDUAL TIMETABLES

Some transitions are quite normal, but nonetheless involve major changes. People marry, have children, the children go to school, move into adolescence, and then adulthood. Other events can be more wrenching, affecting us in ways we never expected. Negative transitions may include a miscarriage, the inability to have children, separation, divorce, an infant's crib death, the death of a spouse or parent, loss of a job or long-term unemployment.

Positive events can have the same effect, such as a move, a promotion, the birth of twins, or finally having a baby after seventeen years of being without. Some adults bypass many of these natural transitions, especially if they never marry or if they die in their forties.

During any major transition, people must restructure how they view their role in life and plan how to incorporate the change. They need to put forth tremendous effort to give up old patterns of thinking and activity and develop new ones. Whether or not this transition becomes disastrous depends upon the person's ability to handle this process of change in a healthy way.

One of the greatest determinants of whether a transition involves excessive stress and crisis potential is the timing of such an event. Serious difficulties can occur when the accomplishment of tasks associated with a particular stage of development is disrupted or made extremely difficult. For example, a teenager who suddenly becomes a paraplegic because of a diving accident must rethink his or her whole life.

Even if we don't stop to think about it, we all have timetables for our lives. In premarital counseling, I ask couples when they plan to become parents, graduate from school, move to a higher level of responsibility in their careers, and so on. Some of them have developed a very precise timetable. Most people have their own expectations for when certain events will occur—a sort of "mental clock" that tells them whether they are "on time" or not in terms of the family lifecycle.

ₔ

*Most people have their own expectations*
*for when certain events will occur—a sort of*
*"mental clock" that tells them whether they are*
*"on time" or not in terms of the family lifecycle.*

When an event does not take place "on time" according to someone's individual expectations, a crisis may result. Many mothers face an adjustment when the youngest child leaves home. But this predictable stage can be planned for in advance. When the child does not leave home at the expected time for some reason, a crisis can often occur for both parents and child.

Having an event happen too early or too late in our plan can deprive us of the support of our peer group. June, for example, wanted a child early in life but didn't have one until three days after her thirty-seventh birthday. Consequently, she lacked the support of many other women her age. Surrounded by those having their first child in their early twenties, June felt unable to develop any close friendships at this stressful time of her life. Most of her contemporaries had gone off to work.

By being off schedule, we may also feel deprived of the sense of pride and satisfaction that often accompanies such an event. Some people have worked out a mental timetable for advancement in their work. But what happens if that sought-after promotion occurs two years prior to retirement rather than fifteen years earlier? We can begin to wonder: is it really recognition for accomplishment or merely a token gesture? When an event occurs later than expected, its meaning is often lessened.

Having an event occur too early can also limit us from preparing adequately. A young mother who is widowed early has to support her family during a time when most of her friends are married. An oldest son may suddenly have to quit college and take over the family business because of some unexpected event, even though he feels ill-equipped for this new role.

My wife and I entered the "empty nest" stage approximately seven years ahead of schedule. When our daughter moved out to be on her own, we should have been left with a thirteen-year-old son at home. But he was a profoundly mentally retarded child, much like an infant, who had left home at the age of eleven to live at Salem Christian Home in Ontario, California.

We had planned for his leaving for two years by praying, talking, and making specific plans and steps to follow. Therefore, his departure and that of our daughter were fairly easy transitions. But when Sheryl told us a year and a half later that she wanted to come back home and live for a while, we faced a more difficult adjustment. We had very much enjoyed being just a couple again and hadn't expected her to return.

## LOSS OR GAIN?

As teenagers move through adolescence, most of them look forward to graduating from high school as a giant step toward adulthood and independence. But this common transition also carries with it a number of losses—including status, friends, and familiarity. Because these losses are usually not anticipated, their impact can be felt even more keenly.

When we are young, some of our losses are celebrated as much as mourned. Most of the early ones are developmental and necessary. We can accept these natural transitions fairly easily. But often we focus on the gain without remembering that it usually carries some loss along with it. When we face the developmental changes connected with aging, the losses affect us much more heavily because the attached gains are often lacking.

Those over forty usually experience more of the releasing and losing part of the family journey that goes hand in hand with the gathering and accumulating. R. Scott Sullender describes this later stage of life:

> The middle years of adult life are spent building. We build a family, a career, a home and place in the community. It is a time for planting roots deep into the soil of our psyches. We build memories that last a lifetime. We form deep emotional attachments with one another. The latter half of life, however, is a time when what has been built up gradually dissolves. One by one (or, sometimes, all at once) we must let go of family, career and home.[3]

Remember the first crush you ever felt on someone of the opposite sex? Most childhood and adolescent romances are filled with painful losses—sometimes daily, even hourly! Moving from school to school, failing a grade, dropping out, leaving home for college, or just moving out—all these transitions carry an element of loss even if the change was planned. When we hit the job market, losses multiply along with the many rejections. Someone else gets the job or the promotion, deals fall through, court cases are lost, businesses fail, the economy falters, we can get stuck in a job going nowhere.

Many transitions in life are related to aging. As we grow older, the dreams and beliefs of childhood begin to crumble and change. Then come the physical losses attending the usual aging process. Ironically, one change typical of middle-age involves gain ... those unwanted pounds and inches! We gradually lose our youth, our beauty, our smooth skin, our muscle tone, our shape, our hair, our vision and hearing, our sexual ability or interest, and so on.

In the later years, the losses take on a different flavor. Now they seem to be more frequent, permanent, and in many cases, negative. Who rejoices over losing hair, teeth, or graduating to bifocals or even trifocals? We don't usually call these "growth experiences." Our losses now seem to build on other losses.[4]

In our younger years, we may have one or two physical problems, which are often correctable. But later on, bodily ailments accumulate faster than our ability to resolve them. Muscles don't work as well or recover as quickly. Our response time slows down.

Our eyeglass prescription needs to be changed more often. One day we suddenly notice that people seem to be talking in softer tones. We soon have to turn up the television volume along with the thermostat!

The nature of the losses is compounded by their growing frequency. We don't usually lose many of our friends through death early in life. But in our later years, such loss becomes much more frequent. The longer we live, the more friends and relatives we usually lose. Visits to the funeral parlor become almost second-nature.

We seem to handle loss best when it is more infrequent. But after mid-life, we typically move into a time zone of accumulated losses. It can be difficult to handle the next one when we are still recovering from the present one. Our coping skills soon become overtaxed. If they were never highly developed to begin with, serious and frequent losses can hit us like a freight train.

Losses in later life often loom with growing finality. Losing a job at age twenty-seven simply means we have to look around for a new one. But losing a job of many years' duration at age fifty-seven means big trouble. Now what, especially if demand for our skills has significantly decreased over the years?[5] These later years carry such numerous changes—many of which are out of our control—that we need to face how we feel about what is happening to our family life.

## FACING THE EMPTY NEST

One of the biggest transitions a parent faces is the time when their children leave home. Sometimes both generations look forward to this day with joyful anticipation. Greater freedom looms on the horizon for the parents as well as the child.

But once more the gain carries inherent losses. Parents must face a significant change in the amount of control they have over their kids. If they choose a lifestyle contrary to the way they were raised, many parents battle feelings of failure. Children may have been the mutual bond that held the husband and wife together. What might happen when that glue is no longer there? I've heard some parents say, "Yes, it's true our children are leaving and we're losing them from the home, but our gain will be our grandchildren." But what if the grandchildren are delayed for ten more years or never arrive at all?

Having our children leave home doesn't mean just empty rooms, but emptiness in other ways as well. When our children marry, it is their choice of when and if they will have little ones of their own. Sometimes parents seriously violate boundaries by their persistent insistence that their children "get with it" and have a child. We must always ask if our concern is primarily for the child or for ourselves.

Any major transition has the potential of becoming contaminated by side effects and personal feelings.[6] Having completed the major task of parenting may stimulate emotions ranging from relief to sadness over the loss. Some still attempt to live out their own life through the life of their child—with predictable consequences for both. For many the most painful feeling of all is no longer being needed—often a symptom of having based one's self-esteem and identity solely in the life of the offspring.

I have counseled with a number of parents who were extremely bitter when their children left. As one said, "I really feel left out now. They didn't turn out the way I wanted and now that they've moved two thousand miles away, what chance do I have to influence their lives?" Others are bitter because their overly indulged children ended up becoming takers, adults who didn't learn to give and respond in the same manner as their parents. Perhaps they were trained too well.[7]

Here are many of the typical thoughts parents have expressed when the time comes for their children to leave home. The range of feelings runs the gamut.

- "I miss the early years with my children. I was so tied up in work at that time."
- "The nest doesn't seem to empty as fast as I want. They're sure slow in moving out."
- "I looked at that small chair and started to cry. It seemed like yesterday my son was sitting in it."
- "I'm sure I'll be glad when they leave. But won't I feel useless?"
- "That room seemed so empty when he left."

- "I'm looking forward to a new job! This time for pay!"
- "Now that they're gone, we sit, we don't talk, don't look at each other. Nothing!"
- "Parenting is hard work and I want to get out of this job."
- "We married at twenty and had the first one at twenty-two. The last one came at thirty-four. He left when he turned twenty-one. Why didn't someone tell us it would take twenty-nine years until we were alone again as a couple!"
- "We're adjusted to their being gone. I hope none of them divorce or lose a job and have to move back. I like this setup!"
- "I don't want to build my happiness on when they call, write, or visit. I need my own life now."
- "They left too soon, married too young, and had kids too soon. I hope they realize I'm not their baby-sitter. I raised one family, but I'm not going to raise another!"
- "I've done what I could. They're in the Lord's hands now. And I guess they always have been, come to think of it."[8]

&

*Children pushed out of the home too soon can crash in flames. But if we hold onto them too tightly, they usually end up with an unhealthy adult dependence which hinders both personal and relational maturity.*

## SAYING GOODBYE

When people are learning to fly a plane, an instructor is constantly by their side in the cockpit until their first solo flight. That day is a huge event for most novice pilots, the time to launch out on their own and put into practice what they have learned. Both instructors and students can be scared. If a novice pilot is pushed to solo too soon, he or she could either crash or develop a pattern of mistakes that are difficult to change.

Two major characteristics within American society tend to predict potential for marital success. One is if a person has had an opportunity to live on his or her own before entering into marriage. The other is having emotionally separated from one's parents. Children pushed out of the home too soon can crash in flames. But if we hold onto them too tightly, they usually end up with an unhealthy adult dependence which hinders both personal and relational maturity.[9]

As parents, most of us pour ourselves into our children. They're one of our greatest investments. But unfortunately, I've seen many people build their lives around their children and end up feeling absolutely empty when they are no longer around. Life goes on, however. The normal life span of today means that we could spend two-thirds as much time in the period after child rearing as we do while going through it.[10]

When I was on the staff of a church years ago, we used to give a packet of materials to expectant parents called, "The Loan of a Life." That title sums up the truth that our children belong not to us but to God. Both parents and children have to learn to shift gears in this process of growing up. Sullender cites a poem which reflects this journey.

Your children are not your children.
They are the sons and daughters of Life's longing for itself.

They come through you but not from you,
And though they are with you yet they belong not to you.

You may give them your love but not your thoughts,
For they have their own thoughts.
You may house their bodies but not their souls,
For their souls dwell in the house of tomorrow, which you cannot visit, not even in your dreams.

You may strive to be like them, but seek not to make them like you.
For life goes not backward nor tarries with yesterday.
You are the bows from which your children as living arrows are sent forth.
The archer sees the mark upon the path of the infinite, and He bends you with His might that His arrows may go swift and far.
Let your bending in the Archer's hand be for gladness;

For even as He loves the arrow that flies, so He loves also the bow that is stable.[11]

I encourage parents to give a letter of release or relinquishment to their engaged child as a way to say goodbye. We gave Sheryl such a letter when she married, which I share with her permission.

Dear Sheryl,

You probably didn't expect to receive a letter from us at this time, but we have always wanted to write a letter to our about-to-be-married daughter. And that time is here—finally!

For years we have prayed for your choice of the man with whom you will spend the rest of your life. Patience does have its rewards, doesn't it?

Sheryl, our desire for you is that you have a marriage which is fulfilling, satisfying and glorifying to God. You, as a woman, have so much to offer. You have God-given talents and abilities which, with each year of your life, emerge more and more. You have a sensitivity and love to give to Bill which will enhance your marriage.

We know there are times when you get down on yourself and feel discouraged. Never give up on yourself. God never has, nor will, and we never have nor will. Treat yourself with the respect that God has for you. Allow him to enable you to continue to develop now as a married woman. Jesus Christ has started a new work in you and he will bring it to completion.

Sheryl, you have brought so much delight and joy into our lives, and we thank God that you have been our daughter for all these years. We have all grown together through learning to accept one another and through some difficult times of hurt and pain. That is life! But because of Jesus Christ, we all learn through those hard times.

We look forward to becoming parents of a married daughter. Mrs. Bill Macauley: doesn't that have a great sound!

Sheryl, thank you for how you have enriched our lives. Thank you for who you are.

We love you,
Mom and Dad

## SHATTERED DREAMS

One of the struggles which many parents experience today is the shattering of the dreams we have for our children. There is nothing wrong with dreams—as long as they are realistic and have not been set in concrete. We dream about their school performance, who they will marry, their future happiness. Sometimes our desires for our children are extensions of our own dreams, perhaps something we missed out on or failed to attain enough of. We naturally want our children to be a reflection of our beliefs, values, and standards.

I had high hopes for my daughter's academic success. I now understand the reasons for my expectations much better than I did then. When I realized that my retarded son Matthew would never progress much beyond a two-year-old mentally, my hopes for Sheryl and her academic pursuits increased dramatically. I just assumed she would attend and complete college. After all, since I had completed college and two graduate programs, why wouldn't Sheryl follow that same path?

Those were *my* dreams, not my *daughter's*. Sheryl quit college after one year and became a licensed manicurist in a nail salon. Her career choice wasn't what I would have chosen, but I was not the one to choose. And then she began to excel in her field. Sheryl applied her God-given artistic talent to her work as a manicurist by doing nail art—painting miniature scenes on the nails of her customers.

She learned most of what she did on her own, without benefit of lessons. She would just create a new idea and never stop to think that it couldn't be accomplished. Sheryl also learned the art of air brushing on her own and even designed some new nail styles. Her skill developed to the point of winning several national competitions in this field, teaching for a major nail company, opening her own nail salon in which she did her own interior decorating. My daughter eventually built one of the finest businesses in this field in her city. We are now able to share the creative challenges required of managing our own businesses.

Sometimes parents end up feeling wounded as a result of shattered dreams. When a child begins living a lifestyle which is not our own, we may end up feeling devastated. My wife and I have been there. I will never forget the day when Sheryl walked into my office and calmly told me that she understood the values her mother and I had lived by and taught her, but she had decided to take a different direction for her own life. This wasn't an adolescent in the throes of an identity crisis, but a twenty-one-year-old woman.

For the next four years, we experienced deep heartache as we watched our daughter live contrary to her own values as well as ours. Perhaps we hurt even more than others because our communication with her never faltered. Since we kept in close touch, we didn't have to wonder where she was and what was happening. These were long and painful years.

Then one Sunday morning, the three of us were in the worship service at Hollywood Presbyterian Church where we attend. At the conclusion, an invitation was given for salvation, rededication, praying for the sick, and the laying on of hands for healing. Sheryl turned to me and said, "Daddy, will you walk up there with me?" I tearfully escorted her to the altar and had the privilege of seeing my daughter rededicate her life to Jesus Christ. My wife and I witnessed the changes which took place in Sheryl's life. Two years later, I had the joy of escorting her down another church aisle to be united in marriage to a strong Christian man.

We experienced the deep wounds, but we also had the tremendous joy of experiencing the return of a prodigal daughter. Whenever the prodigal son in Luke 15 is used as an illustration, I always remind myself that each and every one of us is a prodigal in some way. It's just that some detours in life are much more apparent than others.[12]

We all need to put such experiences in the context of God's command: "Consider it all joy, my brethren, when you encounter various trials, knowing that the testing [or trying] of your faith produces endurance" (Jas 1:2-3, NASB). The word "consider" means to regard the adversity as something we welcome or are glad about. The verb tense actually indicates that we will have to go against our natural inclination to view trials as a negative force in our lives.

We all go through many times when we don't see it that way at all. Then we will have to remind ourselves, "No, I think there is a better way of responding to this. Lord, I really want you to help me see it from your perspective. And I understand that this will take some time." God created us with both the ability and the freedom to determine how we respond to the inevitable upsets of family life. We may honestly wish that a certain event had never occurred. But we can never change the facts, only the way in which we allow it to affect us. Chuck Swindoll speaks so realistically and helpfully about life's difficulties:

> Crisis crushes. And in crushing, it often refines and purifies. You may be discouraged today because the crushing has not yet lead to a surrender. I've stood beside too many of the dying, ministered to too many of the broken and bruised to believe that crushing is an end in itself. Unfortunately, however, it usually takes the brutal blows of affliction to soften and penetrate hard hearts. Even though such blows often seem unfair.[13]

ॐ

*God created us with both the ability and the freedom to determine how we respond to the inevitable upsets of family life.*

## AN OPEN WOUND

Many families go through the unexpected trauma of a divorce. Some feel it is easier to recover from the death of a spouse or parent because that loss at least offers some sense of closure. Divorce is like a death in the family that lasts forever, an open wound that never completely heals.

No one who marries ever plans on this happening. People usually divorce for two reasons. One is to escape a relationship that is either empty, destructive, or full of pain. The second is to find a better relationship with someone else. In some cases, a continuing pattern of unfaithfulness or abuse offers visible evidence of the reason for divorce. But too often, unhappy individuals tend to blame their partner for being the cause of their misery. Terminating their marriage only brings a new set of problems as they take their unhappiness with them into their new marriage.

When divorce does interrupt the normal flow of the family life-cycle, it usually becomes one of the most complex issues ever to invade their lives. One of the newest adjustments is having a child divorce and return home again—bringing along the children, of course.

The effects of a broken relationship travel out like ripples on a pond. The disturbance caused by a small pebble is one thing; staying afloat after a huge boulder has hit the water is another. One writer actually sees six distinct divorces occurring, six different overlapping stages which interact with one another.[14] If you, your parents, or your child has ever experienced a divorce personally, you will know these first hand. Let's consider these six stages of divorce.

The first stage is the *emotional divorce* which can occur years before the final dissolution. It focuses around the problems of the marriage in remission and all of the events and feelings leading up to the actual breakup. The painful conflicts can go on for years.

Second, the *legal divorce* involves the judicial procedures in formalizing the proceedings and making provision for each spouse to have a legal basis for remarriage. The angry tussle which often takes place in the legal arena adds additional intensity to the emotional stress of spouses and children.

Third, the *economic divorce* can leave both parties in precarious financial straits requiring a major adjustment in lifestyle. If younger children are involved, they may not understand the radical curtailment in resources, especially if they remain with the mother.

In her book *The Divorce Revolution,* Lenore Weitzman states that one year after a divorce, the woman's standard of living *decreases* by 73 percent, while the man's *increases* by 42 percent. She reports, "These apparently simple statistics have far-reaching social and economic consequences. For most women and children, divorce means precipitous downward mobility—both economically and socially. The reduction in income brings residential moves and inferior housing, drastically diminished or nonexistent funds for recreation and leisure, and intense pressures due to inadequate time and money."[15]

A fourth stage is the *co-parental divorce* to work out the custodial arrangements as well as the visitation arrangements for the children. This can span the range of sole custody with limited visitation rights to joint physical custody in which a child alternately spends a lengthier period of time living with each parent. To continue this arrangement, each parent is fairly well confined as to where they live for a number of years.

But the complexity doesn't stop there. Divorce reaches its long arm into a fifth arena—the *community divorce*. What happens to your mutual friends? Who continues to get together with whom? Family get-togethers and holidays can become tense and complicated. The juggling which occurs often wears down the children as they end up adjusting to each side's desires.

A sixth and final divorce has been called the *psychic or personal identity divorce*. The formerly married person now has to adjust to being alone, single without the roles customarily shared with a partner. The adjustment may seem never-ending, and the couple may not even have easy access to their normal support group. Do you know anyone who is going through this disruption of life? How can you help to meet their needs?

The trauma of divorce never goes away for the children, as attested to by the growing number of books being published on the subject. I see this kind of long-term damage constantly in my counseling practice. Recently a young couple who came for pre-marital counseling talked about the pain of divorce in their own families. Both expressed their concern that they didn't want a repeat of this in their own marriage.

Today's perspective of "family" is much more inclusive than it was years ago. Family is more than the presence of children. We now have single parent families after divorce or death, single parents who have never been married, childless couples, reconstituted or blended families. Because of all these variations, the types of transitions and losses have multiplied as well. Many families today reflect an attitude of "yours," "mine," and "ours" when it comes to children. Unfortunately, the loss of some of these different family situations may not be recognized so much as a loss by society. Then the tragedy is compounded by the lack of encouragement or support to grieve over what has been lost.

## ROLE REVERSAL

One transition which most don't expect or particularly want to occur is "role reversal." In our mid-years, our own mother or father can sometimes become the child and we become the parent. Often this shift occurs gradually. Over a period of years, we begin to realize that control has begun to swing from our parents to us. We find that responsibilities they used to shoulder have been passed along to us. Now it's our task to care for them.

You start checking to see if they're feeling all right or if they remembered to take their medicine. We have to complete household tasks for them, and take them shopping or to the doctor. One day we may find ourselves doing our parents' laundry, washing their hair, selecting their food, and restricting what they eat. We have to adjust our pace to theirs for a change.

My wife and I know about this situation firsthand. Both our mothers live near us in a retirement home. Joyce's mother is in her late eighties and mine is now ninety-two. My mother just gave up driving four years ago. With so many aches and pains, she can barely get around now. We have become our mothers' chauffeurs and overseers.

As parents become elderly, they may resist having to depend upon their children and try to prove they are still capable. If they once were strong and independent, admitting their dependency can be quite difficult. We, as their adult children, need to be careful not to take away their freedom, dreams (realistic or unrealistic), hope, and sense of usefulness. If we do, they may soon lose their will to live.

We often experience some frustration and anger as we see our parents becoming weaker and more dependent. Handling their increased limitations can be difficult, especially when they can't leave their living quarters without our help. We are vividly reminded that their time with us is growing shorter. When they don't answer the phone, we can begin to feel a sense of panic. Perhaps they are asleep or in the bathroom or...

We naturally resist the aging of our parents. The wrinkles and gray hair aren't the way we remembered our own mother or father of yesteryear. And this isn't the way we want to remember them. Perhaps their changes remind us that someday we will likely be in that same spot. Our irritation and impatience may be simply a defense against the fear we feel for our own future. While we don't like what we see happening, we can do absolutely nothing about it.

How will you handle these possible transitions of life? Helping our parents through increasing infirmities is a responsibility and privilege many of us will face sooner or later. How we handle such changes will be strongly influenced by our past involvement with our parents. Our storehouse of memories will affect our behavior and feelings, whether we realize it or not. Being a helper to elderly or infirm parents requires an abundance of patience. If our past relationship was positive, we will usually find it easier to respect them and accept their weakness. But grieving over our parents' limitations can be painful nonetheless.[16]

## THE DEATH OF A LOVED ONE

Some of the transitions in my own family life came about in ways that we could never have anticipated. Our son Matthew provided one of the biggest. For years my wife Joyce and I considered our retarded son, Matthew, a tremendous source of blessing in our lives. Our values, perspective on life, character qualities, insight, skills, and relationship with God were all refined and increased because of the presence of this handicapped child.

 è

*Parents rarely expect to outlive their children. All we have left of Matthew are precious memories.*

On March 15, 1990, Matthew was called home to be with the Lord. We felt an extremely empty place in our family. Parents rarely expect to outlive their children. All we have left of Matthew are precious memories. Anything that adds to that storehouse is highly valued. Because of the severity of his retardation, Matthew was only able to speak a few words and had very few responses. We had only one brief film of him and no audio recordings. At his death, he was still only about eighteen months old mentally.

August 15, 1991 arrived—the day Matthew would have observed his twenty-fourth birthday. Any anniversary is painful when the loss is fresh. That evening, we made contact with one of the attendants who had cared for Matthew at Salem Christian Home, his residence for the last eleven years of his life. A friend had told us that this woman wanted to tell us some of her experiences with Matthew.

As we talked with this attendant over the phone, she shared with us several aspects of Matthew's life we had never seen. She described how he had learned to put together a very simple puzzle. When she took him for a walk outside, Matthew would walk way ahead and then try to hide from her. She shared how he had learned to dry his own hair with a hair dryer, and how he would turn it around and blow it on her hair. One day she brought her own six-month-old baby into the dorm for all the residents to see. She sang "Rock a Bye Baby" as Matthew held this little baby in his arms, and noticed tears running down our son's face.

To someone who has never gone through the experience of raising a handicapped child, this might not seem like much. But when the limitations are so massive and the ordinary experiences of life so few, knowing these additional experiences of our son were immeasurable blessings for us.

I never cease to marvel at God's timing. The very next day, I received a letter from a woman who had written me a year earlier. Her first letter described how a healing had taken place between this woman and her eighty-three-year-old father. A rift between them for a quarter of a century had been mended and a new bonding had occurred. She wanted to share this with me because my book, *Always Daddy's Girl*, had helped her with this relationship. She also asked if I would pray for her father who hadn't yet invited Jesus Christ into his life as his personal savior.

In this new letter which I received, this woman shared how her father had indeed become a Christian the year before. She then went on to say that he had died just three months later and enclosed a written portrayal of her last visit with him. I share it here with her permission because it provides a beautiful picture of the passages of life through which we all move.

Midlife. A reversal of roles. Dad is the child now and I am the parent.

We got word that his heart was failing. He had made a valiant effort to come to his granddaughter's wedding, but the trip proved to be too much for him. Upon arrival at the wedding, he looked ashen gray. Everyone was concerned about him. I reassured myself that with a little rest next week, he would be fine. But next week came, and along with it the alarming news. He was listless, unable to be aroused at times, pale and trembling, and his legs and ankles were very swollen. All symptoms of congestive heart failure. He needed to be seen by a doctor.

As a daughter, my heart was heavy with the thought of losing Dad. Tears flowed freely as I prayed for another opportunity to be with him before he died. How I longed to tell him one more time how much he meant to me. You see, our relationship now as father and daughter was a very simple, yet tender one. Each time I visited him, I would remind him that he gave out hugs like no one else could, and that I still needed him to be my Dad. His face always beamed when he was reminded.

When packing my bags to make the four-hour journey to his home, thoughts turned to a book that I had recently given to my daughters. It was a children's book that told how love is passed from one generation to another. I tucked it into my suitcase, hoping to be able to share it with Dad.

Upon arriving, the doctor confirmed our suspicion—it was congestive heart failure. Dad could have another heart attack at any moment. The doctor requested that I stay with him for the next week to monitor his condition.

The second evening after dinner, I told Dad that I wanted to share something with him—a story about him and me. He responded appreciatively to my request to read the story to him. As I began to read, emotion engulfed my voice. The story began with the child as a baby being rocked in the arms of the parent, and having this song sung to him:

"I'll love you forever
I'll like you for always
As long as I'm living
My baby you'll be."

As the story unfolded of the child passing through the various stages of childhood into maturity, Dad listened with enjoyment. At every stage of development, the parent would sing the same verse to the child. He looked at the pictures with childlike eagerness, commenting on them every now and then. At that moment, came the realization that the roles had been reversed. I was now the parent, reading a story to the child. It felt strange. But it was all right, for that's the way that life is sometimes. Roles do change as we pass from one stage of life into another.

In the story, years after the child had reached maturity the parent became elderly and frail. The picture showed a frowning man holding his dying mother in his arms, rocking her and singing this song:

> "I'll love you forever
> I'll like you for always
> As long as I'm living
> My mother you'll be."

"That's how I feel about you, Dad. I will love you forever!" Tears filled both our eyes and he hugged me once again.

The days of our visit quickly passed, and it was time to make the four-hour return trip home. My family was expecting me for dinner that evening. It would be difficult to leave Dad, knowing that I may never see him again this side of heaven. But the Lord had already assured me that someday in heaven, we will be reunited. Now my calling as a parent will be to go back home to the next generation and pass on the song that Dad has sung to me in every stage of life:

> "I'll love you forever
> I'll like you for always
> As long as I'm living
> My baby you'll be."[17]

## BEING "PUT OUT TO PASTURE"

Among the later passageways of life is retirement, one which has the potential for being a long-term source of both joy and sorrow. This stage requires that we come to grips with the past and the future in terms of work. Many men suffer a severe loss of identity and self-esteem because of having used work to define their personal identity.

Retirement is ideally an eagerly anticipated event toward which we work all of our lives. Some people don't even wait for the golden age of sixty-five; they retire early in order to have enough health and energy to pursue other interests. As I talk with young couples in premarital counseling, many of them are planning to retire in their fifties! I wish them luck! For some of us, such prosperity is difficult to fathom.

How can we properly prepare for the actual rite of retirement, whether it comes early or late? When built upon a strong marital relationship and a proper sense of personal identity, this transition can be a rich time of continued growth. As people consider retirement, I encourage them to define their expectations and develop a plan by making a list of all their desires for retirement, along with their possibilities.

All of us need to anticipate not only the predictable transitions but also the unexpected and untimely events which might occur as well. One such plan I have used with counselees is divided into three parts. Plan A assumes good health and good finances, and either both spouses still together or alone. Plan B allows for the variable of poor health, and Plan C anticipates poor finances in addition to poor health. Thinking about, discussing, and preparing for as many options as possible adds to a feeling of security.

ॐ

## BRINGING IT HOME

First spend some time exploring your life to date. On a timeline stretching from birth to your present age, list the significant transitions you have experienced in your life up to this point. Then try to answer the following questions:

1. Which of these transitions in your life gave you the greatest sense of joy? Why?
2. Which gave you the greatest sense of loss? Why?

3. What transitions might you experience during the next five years? How do you think these will affect you? What can you do to prepare for them?

4. What transitions might you experience during the next ten years? How do you think these will affect you? What can you do to prepare for them?

5. If your parents are living, what transitions might they experience in the next five years? What could you do to assist them in preparing for these transitions? How do you think these transitions will affect you?

7. If you have children, what transitions might they experience in the next five years? What could you do to assist them in preparing for these transitions? How do you think these transitions will affect you?

8. What loss in your life do you feel is still unresolved?

Perhaps the following suggestions will help you feel a greater sense of being in control of the situation during a period of transition or loss. You can begin to do something more positive about the inevitable changes in your life.

*Try to identify what it is that doesn't make sense to you about your transitional loss.* Perhaps it is a vague question about life or God's purpose for us. Or it could be a specific question: "Why did this have to happen to me now, at this crucial point in my life?" Ask yourself, "What is it that is bothering me the most?" Keep a card with you for several days to record your thoughts as they emerge.

*Identify the emotions you feel during each day.* Are you experiencing sadness, anger, regret, "if onlys," hurt, or guilt? What are the feelings directed at? Has the intensity of the feelings decreased or increased during the past few days? If your feelings are vague, identifying and labeling them will diminish their power over you.

*State the steps or actions you are taking to help you move ahead with your life.* Identify what you have done in the past that has helped or ask a trusted friend for help.

*Be sure you are sharing your loss and grief with others who can listen to you and support you during this time.* Don't seek out advice-givers, but rather those who are empathetic and can properly relate to your feelings. Remember, your journey at this time will never be exactly like that of another person; each of us is unique.

*It may help to find a person who has experienced a similar loss or transition.* Groups and organizations abound for losses of all types. Reading books or stories about those who have survived similar experiences can be helpful.

*Identify the positive characteristics and strengths of your life that have helped you before.* Which of these will help you at this time in your life?

*Spend time reading the Psalms.* Many of them reflect the struggles of humanity but give the comfort and assurance that are from God's mercies.

*When you pray, share your confusion, your feelings, and your hopes with God.* Be sure to be involved in your church services since worship is an important element in recovery and stabilization.

*Think about where you want to be in your life two years from now.* Write out some of your dreams and goals. Just setting some goals may encourage you to realize you will recover.

*Become familiar with the stages of grief.* Then you will know what to expect and you won't be thrown by what you are experiencing. Remember that understanding your grief intellectually is not sufficient. It can't replace the emotional experience of living through this difficult time. You need to be patient and allow your feelings to catch up with your mind. Expect mood swings, and remind yourself of these through notes placed in obvious places. These mood swings are normal.

*The final step is saying goodbye.* Being able to say goodbye helps us move toward closure. It brings back some of the feelings of control over our life and circumstances that were diminished by the loss or the transition. When you say goodbye, you are acknowledging that you are no longer going to share your life with whatever the change was whether it is a job, a place, a person, or a dream. You will always have the memory, but now you acknowledge that you will live without whatever it was that you had.[18]

# OUR
## LEGACY

THE SEVEN OF THEM HUDDLED TOGETHER talking in hushed tones, the surrounding room reflecting the many experiences of the owner. The sounds died out when a man holding a briefcase entered the room. As he sat in a chair facing the others, all eyes were focused on him—for he was either the bearer of good news or bad news. This distinguished, gray-haired man was the family attorney who had summoned the seven together for the reading of the will.

Those who await the reading of a will are often filled with conflicting emotions. We usually find grief over the loss of the loved one, blended together with guilt or anger over the unfinished aspects of the relationship and hopeful anticipation of what might be revealed in the will. Personal expectations always exist, whether we admit them or not. These seven survivors were no different.

After the usual opening condolences and preliminary statements, the attorney began to read the will, thankfully brief and to the point. The shares for the four children and the three grand-children were equal. But what was stated in the will was not what anyone expected. No mention was made of tangible or material goods. Their absence left the seven wide-eyed. The words of the will reflected a deep wisdom which would take time to fathom.

> Since I love all of you, I want you to receive the best I have to offer. That won't be found in items or possessions or money. There is really no need for this will to dispense what I have for you, since it has already been given but perhaps not yet received or understood.
>
> I have spent a lifetime of creating and giving to each of you. There is a legacy which each of you have received. It would be clouded and even contaminated by any of my material goods. Hopefully what I have left you over the years in our interactions and experiences will fill your lives more than what I acquired.
>
> I have dispensed all of my material wealth to the poor and homeless in your names. Now you will be free to experience the blessings of that act, as well as discovering what you were given over the years. And when you realize what it is, consider what you will pass on to others.

If you were one of the seven, how might you have responded? I'm sure the reactions would vary. Some would catch the significance of this unique act, others might not. Perhaps what the creator of the will was saying is reflected in these words: "As each of you has received a gift (a particular spiritual talent, a gracious divine endowment), employ it for one another as [befits] good trustees of God's many-sided grace—faithful stewards of the extremely diverse [powers and gifts granted to Christians by] unmerited favor" (1 Pt 4:10, AMP).

## RICHES FROM THE PAST

Legacy is a word we may often use, but rarely define. A legacy is a bequest of something acquired from the past. We usually leave a will or a trust when we die so that our family members will receive those items we want them to have. Sometimes we receive legacies we wish had never been given to us. We would rather have been left out of the will!

At this very moment, you and I are in the process of creating a legacy that we will pass on to our family members. Do you know what it is? Have you planned for it—or will they receive whatever is left when you die? I've talked with counselees about their wills. Some of them said they spent an incredible amount of time and money creating an ironclad final will and testament. Wanting to be very specific about what their children would receive, some people gave it considerable thought before finalizing their will.

Do we give the other elements we pass on to our children as much time and thought? If we did, perhaps the outcome in some areas of our family life would be different. The material goods we leave behind will be remembered, but of even greater impact is who we are and how we have shaped the lives of others. Much of who we are comes from the legacy passed onto us, some of which we know and some of which we're not even aware.

*ぇあ*

*Sometimes we receive legacies we wish had never been given to us. We would rather have been left out of the will!*

I'd like to share with you the story of my family's legacy. Let's begin with my mother who was born at the turn of the century in May of 1900, the third of eight children. Little did she know that over ninety years later, she would witness more radical changes in the world than at any other time in history.

Mother survived the rigors of growing up on a farm, including running a pitchfork through her foot and sustaining back injuries when her horse raced through a low door in the barn. She learned to work hard plowing and harvesting the fields. She held a light for her father as he constructed one of the first homemade tractors. During the winter, she either walked several miles through the snow to school or skated there on the frozen Sioux River.

But my mother's roots were found in another country across the ocean. Her great-grandfather lived in the mountains of east-central Germany, in the small town of Unterellen, Eisenach. He and his family lived at the foot of a high hill upon which stood a famous castle, the Wartburg where Martin Luther translated the Bible. During the early 1800s, this family trained their children well in the values of Christianity, independence, and frugality.

My mother's grandfather immigrated to America in 1867 as an apprentice cabinet-maker, landing here with five cents in his pocket. He found his way to Iowa and eventually married another immigrant. Through many hours of hard work and frugality, they were able to survive years of harsh winters and occasional tornadoes battering their log cabins.

My mother married at age nineteen. As an airplane mechanic in World War I, her husband had flown with pilots to test the plane, but on two occasions crashed and sustained hidden injuries. After they married, they began an odyssey of moves which would eventually bring them to California. Driving an old car in which they also slept, they cooked their food in a pan on two stones over a fire. When the car broke down, her husband would take it apart and repair it himself since there were no tow trucks or repair shops. They often bogged down in the foot-deep sand which made up many of the roads.

When their car finally died, they abandoned it two hundred miles from Los Angeles, hitched a ride, and stayed with the couple who had given them transportation to this emerging city. In time they searched out the hills above Hollywood and discovered a beautiful canyon with abundant brush, trees, and wildlife. Here they began to settle like pioneers on the prairie. The down payment on the lot was ten dollars!

They rented a one-room shack in the hills while they built their first home. Constructed without benefit of a level, this house is still liveable today. Without sewers, a cesspool had to suffice. In 1925, they were able move into another house. Mother's farming background was not forgotten as she planted fruit trees, vegetables, and all types of flowers.

Both she and her husband worked hard on the homes, in addition to holding down fulltime jobs. As a manager for a bakery, the way in which my mother handled some of her experiences reflected her strength and independence. One day a man came in, ripped the phone off the hook, and demanded the keys to the safe. But she slipped out and called the police, who quickly apprehended him. When someone followed her one dark night as she walked the three miles to her home in the hills, Mother outran him. She also had to be assertive when a movie personality by the name of Hopalong Cassidy asked her out on a date. She quickly let him know that she was married.

Her first son was born in 1930. Four years later, tragedy struck when her husband suddenly died of a stroke. This young widow had to find a job during the difficult depression years and rented out rooms in her home to survive financially. During the next year, her father died unexpectedly, as well as her older sister's husband. Now both women were young widows with children to raise.

In 1937, my mother married a widower who was twelve years older. I was born when Mom was thirty-seven years of age. She worked hard raising both my half-brother and me, as well as taking care of three other houses which she rented out. Our family encouraged both the enjoyment of life as well as the values of honesty, hard work, and getting a thorough education. My parents sacrificed to give us experiences and opportunities that had not been available to them. We went on trips and were given music lessons. As a family, we saw practically every movie produced in Hollywood during the forties.

With over thirty-five cousins to get to know, visits to the other relatives were as frequent as possible. Between my mother's brothers and sister, the children, grandchildren, and great grandchildren totalled over one hundred thirty-five! And with all the other siblings on her father's side, approximately four hundred sixty family members are still living. Once a year, they still come together for a family reunion in Iowa.

Living in this canyon area was similar to growing up in the country, with the added resources of a large metropolitan city just minutes away. My brother and I developed an appreciation for animals and the outdoors while avoiding some of the pressures of city life. Mom taught us how to help repair the rental homes, including painting, tar papering roofs, laying linoleum, and cleaning out sewer pipes.

We had tough times as well. When I was two years old, Mom inadvertently gave me poison instead of medicine. Our neighbor—by the television name of Sky King—rushed me to the hospital to have my stomach pumped. Over the years we experienced devastating floods with homes and cars being washed down the sloping street. One of two major fires destroyed over twenty-five homes across the hillside from us. Once a mother skunk bore a litter of babies in between the walls of one of the homes, coyotes raided the chicken yard, and a swarm of bees built a hive under the roof. Life was never dull!

Just twenty-four years after marrying her second husband, my mother was again widowed when my dad was killed driving home from work. This was the first death of a loved one that I ever experienced. Since both my brother and I were already married and starting families of our own elsewhere, Mom poured her energies into babysitting for other families who lived in the canyon.

When she entered her seventies, my mother didn't seem to slow down but instead began to travel. She took six different world tours, included one in which she helped to smuggle Bibles into Russia! Finally in her eighties, Mom sold her houses and moved into a retirement center near me. Even into her nineties, she has continued to raise the flowers that she had always loved.

ॐ

*Mom passed on a strong legacy, a rich heritage from her side of the family. As a result, my brother and I have a better sense of who we are individually and as a family... in a world where a clear sense of family is fading fast.*

At the age of ninety, my mother concluded her own written life history with this poignant description of the retirement center: "When I first moved here, I attended all the activities such as trips and concerts and had so many friends. By 1989, I lost virtually all my friends to death and now along with crippling arthritis, I feel very lonely here. Where I'll go from here only God knows."

For a number of years, my mother recorded her life experiences. A writer by trade, my older brother compiled her material and we gave it to her on her ninetieth birthday. It is now being rewritten to include many other events and pictures from 1910-1990. Then we will pass it along to our children and many other relatives as well.

Here was a woman whose values reflected her early years as well as her family's background. Wanting us to develop our potential to the fullest, she encouraged us, helped us in any way possible when we struggled, corrected us when necessary, and demonstrated compassion. Mom passed on a strong legacy, a rich heritage from her side of the family. As a result, my brother and I have a better sense of who we are individually and as a family... in a world where a clear sense of family is fading fast.

## FATHER MEMORIES

Randy Carlson concluded his book, *Father Memories,* with his mother's eulogy to her father:

My mother called this past week and recounted some moving experiences that had come to mind as she considered her own father memories. She recalled that on her fourteenth birthday, her dad wrote in her autograph book words that reflected his character and love for his family. She still cherishes the inscription he wrote: "A good name is rather to be chosen than great riches, and loving favor rather than silver and gold" (Prv 22:1, KJV).

Her voice cracked with emotion as she read aloud the poem she had recently written expressing her appreciation of her dad. Although her dad has been dead for forty years, his legacy of love lives on. The character traits and values of my grandfather—integrity, a good sense of humor, respect from and toward others—have been passed down through the generations.

Tears came to my eyes as I considered how much my life, and my children's lives, have been enriched by my grandfather's faithfulness as a father years ago, even though I never knew him. He died when my mother was only sixteen.

I asked Mom if I could use her poem to close this book, as a

fitting tribute to fathers everywhere. I hope it is an encouragement and a challenge to you. Even if it doesn't ring true for
your dad, it certainly fits our Father in heaven.

## Dad

Dad, you gave me life,
> The family name to hold.
> You taught me humble pride,
> And purity, fine as gold.

Dad, you gave me love.
> You always held my hand.
> You gave me trusting faith,
> That in hard times will stand.

Dad, you gave me strength.
> You showed me how to smile.
> You were my constant friend,
> Down many a weary mile.

Dad, you gave me guidance,
> To always choose the right.
> To help a needy neighbor,
> Even in the cold of night.

Dad, you gave to me a goal,
> To follow all my dreams,
> And gave me loving praise;
> Today, how much it means.

Dad, you are my tower;
> You hold a special place.
> When walking in your footsteps,
> There I see your noble face.

Dad, you were a Godly man;
> You taught me how to pray,
> To love the Lord forever;
> His Word will light the way.

Dad, many years have passed away
> Since you said "good-bye" to me.

I'll look for you in Heaven,
Where we'll spend eternity![1]

I was not only was given a sense of history by my mother, but an even more extensive one by my father. Born on a farm in Maine, he quit school to go to work after the eighth grade. Dad was hardworking and responsible, grateful for having work, and cautious with his money. Even though his education was not extensive, his enjoyment of novels helped me develop an appreciation for the wonder of words. But like so many children, I didn't realize this precious gift until later in life.

My father's roots were not in Germany but in England. One of his older relatives kept extensive records. The earliest known family member was granted a barony in 1509 and entitled to a seat in Parliament. I have a handwritten listing of each relative dating back to the fifteenth century. What a treasure! This family historian even described some of the more personal qualities of my ancestors: "They were a highly intelligent, studious family supporters of religion and patriots within the Revolutionary struggle. They had rare executive ability and a strong sense of justice, and a self-sustaining spirit."

The first ancestor to immigrate to this country arrived in 1621. His son married a woman whose father came over on the Mayflower. It's been said if that ship contained all the ancestors claimed by people today, it would have sunk in the harbor! But much to my surprise, my own research uncovered a list of those who came over on the Mayflower. And yes, the individual cited in my genealogy was there!

From this union came a son who farmed two hundred acres of land in Maine, but spent most of the time away as a scout. He married an American Indian woman. While my father moved to California, the next generations continued to live on the original homestead in Maine.

My dad's historical line was traced through the males in the family. And now the name of my family will come to a halt. I am the parent of two children, a daughter and a son. Our daughter married and will carry on the line under her husband's name. But our profoundly mentally retarded son died at the age of twenty-two. Our family name stops, but the family doesn't.

## A FAMILY HERITAGE

I recently attended a memorial service for a man who died in his early eighties. The first church elder who worked closely with me, this man's gentle spirit and concern for people served as a model. During the service, quite a bit of time was spent in re-telling his family history. I thought, "What a rich history this man had and passed on to his six children. I wonder if they knew all of these details."

The next day I was talking with one of his granddaughters, a woman in her mid-twenties. She shared, "That service was so special. Granddad told us many stories about himself and his childhood, but I learned so much yesterday about our family back-ground which I didn't know. It was so helpful." Perhaps instead of waiting for the family history to be shared in a eulogy, we could discover it now and preserve it for both ourselves and other family members.

Who is the first person in your family line that you know about? During what century and in what country did he or she live? History books at the public library will help you picture the events, customs, and living conditions of that time.

৯৯

*Perhaps instead of waiting for the family history to be shared in a eulogy, we could discover it now and preserve it for both ourselves and other family members.*

In some cultures, families hand down a detailed history in oral form to the children. They are told the stories again and again until they have made an indelible impression. A family's history doesn't have to be forgotten, but often is because memories fade and no one takes the time to chronicle the events.

Who could you talk to in your family that could shed some light on your past, your history, your legacy? What do you know about the generations that preceded you? What were their quali-ties? Who is the historian within your own family? Who is the ear-liest ancestor you know anything about? What was the legacy this person passed on to you? The better you get to know those who preceded you, the better you will come to know yourself and others in your family. Some discoveries are sure to amaze you.

Ancestor-hunting can be an exciting adventure for the entire family, especially when you couple that story with historical details of that day and age. And the very process of exploration can create closer family ties with those you interview or contact.

Numerous books and resources are available in bookstores and especially in the public library to assist you in tracing your own family history. I have listed a few in the Suggested Reading List at the back of the book. If you want to read a good book on genealogies, what better place to start than the Bible. A study of Christ's ancestors will lead to some surprising discoveries.


## IF ONLY'S

Some couples in their forties and fifties say, "I can't wait to get my hands on that inheritance and spend it. I've been wanting to use it for years." Most people aren't that blunt and calloused. But when we do receive an inheritance from our parents, we usually spend it in one way or another. That's understandable. But some parents spend their children's inheritance as well! "WE'RE SPENDING OUR CHILDREN'S INHERITANCE" reads a bumper sticker I have seen on the back of recreational vehicles driven by older adults.

I have seen this same principle in operation in my counseling practice—but from a different perspective. I see many families who have gotten caught up with the values encouraged by the surrounding world. They become financially strapped because they bought into the "buy it now with your credit card" syndrome. Then they spent the next ten years paying off the cost plus the interest.

They listened to those who said children need to be in soccer, Little League, ballet, and every other imaginable activity. In so doing, they often sacrificed their own free time and placed an inordinate amount of structure on their children—which in many ways denied them the opportunity to be children.

As I work with people in the grieving process, I often help them identify the regrets they have over their relationship with the deceased. Even more beneficial would be to consider each family member while they are still with us and write down what our regrets would be if they were to suddenly die.

I commonly hear statements like: "If only we had spent more time together." "If only I had taken the time to listen to you and play with you." "I regret the silly arguments we had each day." "I regret that I didn't tell you how much I appreciate you and love you."

Why not identify these "if only's" to provide some direction we need to take in our relationships? Then if anything does happen to that family member, the "regrets" and "if only's" would be far fewer. It's worth a try.

## WHAT LEGACY WILL YOU LEAVE?

Sometimes we allow distractions to drag us off course with our family. Recently, I watched a comedy movie on television called *Battling for Baby*. The battle between two ex-friends who become the grandparents of the same baby was humorous, but at the same time contained a thought-provoking message.

The maternal grandmother—a concert pianist who was terribly uncomfortable with children—was holding her granddaughter at the baby's first birthday party. The mother of the baby looked at her and said, "Mother, it's interesting you're here for her first birthday party. You weren't there at mine. Where were you?"

The grandmother looked surprised. After a moment's reflection she answered, "Well, I guess I was in Vienna." Later on when she was alone in the kitchen, she asked herself, "I wonder what was so important in Vienna that I missed her first birthday?" All of us can ask that same question: "I wonder what was so important that I missed..."

The Word of God is very clear about our calling in a non-Christian society. "And do not be conformed to this world, but be transformed by the renewing of your mind, that you may prove what the will of God is, that which is good and acceptable and perfect" (Rom 12:2, NASB). Sometimes we can be close in our efforts... and yet so far off.

A young man's experience in college best illustrates this fact. He described a father and son who walked onto his job site one morning looking for work. They appeared to have the tools of the trade, as well as the calloused hands of those who worked in the building trade. The foreman hired them and put them to work building a foundation for the walls of a split-level ranch home. They went about their bricklaying and completed their task on time.

ૐ

*Sometimes we can be close in our efforts...*
*and yet so far off.*

But the next day, when the other workers tried to install the metal frames for the windows and doors, nothing seemed to fit. The frames matched the specs on the blueprints, but they just wouldn't go into the openings. The foreman finally came over and stretched his own tape measure across the openings and discovered the problem. Here are the words of that college student:

> I felt frustrated and sad as the foreman asked to see the bricklayer's ruler. He unfolded it and laid it on the floor. Then the foreman stretched out his own tapemeasure beside it and locked it open.
>
> Amazing.
>
> The difference wasn't much per inch—less than one-eighth—but stretched over the distance, it added up to an expensive blunder. None of the bricklayers knew it could happen. I didn't either. But it did—and it does. When quizzed about the ruler, the unfortunate man said he bought it from some "bargain barrel" at a hardware store.
>
> He had bought a lie which made his speed as a bricklayer an illusion. In the end, the vital components of the home would not fit in their rightful place.
>
> He was sincere... but wrong. He was skilled... but disgraced.
>
> His work was a monument to a man who put his faith in an unreliable standard.[2]

What do you use as your standard? What will you leave as your legacy? Maybe it's time for a course correction. It's up to each of you to decide.

## IMAGINE ATTENDING YOUR OWN FUNERAL

What legacy are you leaving? Each of us is creating our own legacy right at this very moment. I have been doing this for many years. As Tim Kimmel puts it in his excellent book, *Legacy of Love,* "Your words, your schedule, your choices, your obedience, the way you savor your victories and the way you swallow your defeats all help to define your life. It is this definition that your children rely on most as they seek to chart their own future."[3]

What are others receiving from you? What are you giving to make your family great? We don't have any option when it comes to leaving a legacy. We all leave one wherever our feet have touched as we walk through life. However, we do have an option as to the kind of legacy we leave. What you do, what you say, and who you are will live on. What will your legacy be?

I am enthralled with a story that Kimmel tells about his travels around the Bahamas by sailboat.[4] While Tim and his wife were snorkeling the reefs and exploring the various isolated islands, they headed into the harbor of Man-O-War Bay for supplies and repairs. While exploring the island, they stumbled upon a graveyard—a beautiful spot with tropical plants and flowers and a white beach in the background. But open graves which had apparently been dug months before puzzled them. They had never seen anything like that before.

Returning to the harbor, Tim and his wife met one of the pastors on the island and asked him about the open graves. He explained that since the island rested on a coral platform, digging a grave required several days. With limited facilities and refrigeration, a body could not be preserved that length of time. Since people were usually buried within a few hours of dying, the government required that two graves be kept ready for the next death.

Tim asked how they could assemble people in time for the funeral. The pastor's answer was very interesting. In the case of a sudden death, they did the best they could to get people to-gether. But in the case of a lingering or terminal illness, the funeral was held in advance!

When people were dying, their family and friends would carry them into the church or come to their house for the funeral service. Can you imagine hearing your own funeral service? In most cases, it worked out quite well and gave the dying an oppor-tunity to hear what others had to say about them. In some cases though, the people recovered. I wonder if hearing the eulogy in advance—whether good or bad—may have encouraged them to keep on living.

Would you want to hear your eulogy in advance? Do you won-der, like I do, what would be said? What would you want your friends and family to say about you? What would you change now so that your family members would be able to say positive remarks about you and the influence you had had upon their lives?

A sobering thought, isn't it? Sometimes we need such thoughts to prompt us to change the course of our lives. What better time to start than now? Here is a Family History Quiz to get you started on this exciting adventure.

1. Who is the earliest relative in your family tree that you know about?
2. What do you know about him/her?
3. Who could help you discover some of the details of his/her life?
4. Who was the oldest relative you personally knew? Parent, grandparent, great-grandparent, uncle or aunt, great uncle or aunt?
5. What were his/her nationality, occupation, personality char-acteristics, and contributions he/she made to society and to your life? What were his/her values and religious beliefs?
6. How did his/her life differ from yours today?
7. How many living relatives do you have today? Who are they? Where are they? What are they like? How often do you see them? Have you ever considered creating an extended fam-ily newsletter and sending it out once a year?
8. Which relatives are you most like?

9. What are your positive traits and qualities which you are passing on to others?
10. What do you hope will be said at your own eulogy?

## BEING IN GOD'S FAMILY FILLS THE GAP

*Family*—what does it mean to you? What images unfold in your mind as you focus upon this word? For many it means the people you can count on no matter what. Those who were there when you needed them. Those with whom you share your joys and sorrows. Those who show up at your graduation, wedding, when you're in the hospital.

Family usually includes the people that you immediately look to for help, support, love, and acceptance. The ones you want to be among the first to see your newborn baby. Those with whom you may experience your deepest emotions, your greatest joys, and your most painful hurts.

Family means times of reunion, traditional holiday gatherings, brief airport encounters when one passes through on business, and partings that are sad and painful. And family means times of stress, tension, disagreements, and sometimes painful distancing.

Family can mean welcoming a new member by marriage... and in time seeing them leave when divorce invades your family structure. Family means learning to grieve, not in isolation, but together as strength is shared in times of deepest need. A family is a grouping which expands through births and marriages and shrinks a bit when a member leaves for whatever reason.

What did your family mean to you? Who came and who went? What marks did the different people make on your life? What were the imprints you made and are making on others? Who are the people in your life that you consider family?

We are part of an even larger family than our immediate relatives. As believers, we are all related, all joint heirs in Christ. Our call within this family of God is to relate to one another, serve one another, love one another. But this family is not to be an exclusive one which keeps others on the outside. Our mission is to expand God's family by inviting others to join through a personal relationship with Jesus Christ.

At certain times in our lives, a brother or sister in Christ may fill a void left by a family member. That hope and reality can heal past hurts and lift us up. Instead of being stuck as a "yesterday person," we can be freed to become a "tomorrow person." We can change our focus from what was to what will be!

# NOTES

ONE

*The Tie that Binds*

1. David Blankenhorn, Stephen Bayne, and Jean Bethke Elstain, eds., *Rebuilding the Nest*, (Milwaukee, WI: Family Service America, 1990), 75.
2. *The Detroit News*, May 22, 1988, as quoted in Blankenhorn, et al.
3. John Naisbitt in his bestseller *Megatrends: Ten New Directions Transforming Our Lives*, as quoted in Blankenhorn, et al.
4. "The National Report on Work and Family," Fall 1989, as quoted in Blankenhorn, et al.
5. Senator Chris Dodd of Connecticut, March 1989.
6. *The Boston Globe*, April 11, 1989, as quoted in Blankenhorn, et al.
7. Daniel Seligman in *Fortune Magazine*, July 17, 1989, as quoted in Blankenhorn, et al., 11.
8. Morris Massey, *The People Puzzle* (Reston, VA: Reston Publishing Co., 1979), 27, adapted.
9. Diane Fassel, *Growing Up Divorced* (New York: Pocket Books, 1991), 181.
10. Blankenhorn, et al., 77.
11. Blankenhorn, et al., 89-90.
12. Blankenhorn, et al., 42-43ff.
13. "Heartbreak of Cohabitation Ends in Divorce," *Los Angeles Times*, November 16, 1989.
14. Mary Ellen Schoonmeker, "Marriage: The First Years, What Holds You Together... ," *Family Circle*, September 1, 1988, 99.
15. Massey, 148-52, adapted.
16. Blankenhorn, et al., 90.
17. Sara McLanahan and Karen Booth, "Mother-Only Families: Problems, Prospects, and Politics," *Journal of Marriage and the Family*, 51, No. 3, 1989. As quoted by E. Mavis Hetherington and Josephine D. Arasteh, eds., *Impact of Divorce, Single Parenting, and Stepparenting on Children* (Hillsdale, NJ: Lawrence Erlbaum Associates, 1988), 557-80.
18. Blankenhorn, et al., 44-45.
19. Randy Carlson, *Father Memories* (Chicago, IL: Moody Press, 1992), 13.
20. Willard Gaylin, *Feelings* (New York: Harper and Row Publishers Inc., 1979), 22-23. Used by permission.
21. Corrie Ten Boom, *In My Father's House* (Old Tappan, NJ: Revell, 1976), 58.
22. Ten Boom, 58.
23. Blankenhorn, et al., 100-101, adapted.

24. Questionnaire adapted from Pearsall, *Power of the Family* (New York: Bantam, 1990), 38-40.

### TWO
### *Roots Run Deep*

1. Massey, 52.
2. Massey, 281, adapted.
3. Massey, 55-74, adapted.
4. Hans Finzel, *Help! I'm a Baby Boomer* (Wheaton, IL: Victor Books, 1989), 14-15, adapted.
5. Gary Collins and Timothy Clinton, *Baby Boomers Blues* (Waco, TX: Word Publishers, 1992), 42-49, adapted.
6. Cheryl Russell, *100 Predictions for the Baby Boomer: The Next 50 Years* (New York: Plenum, 1987), 91-95.
7. Collins and Clinton, 81, adapted.
8. Massey, 80-99, adapted.
9. Massey, 99, adapted.
10. Massey, 110-27, adapted.
11. Massey, 128.
12. Massey, 143, adapted.

### THREE
### *Looking in the Rearview Mirror*

1. Mel Roman and Patricia E. Raley, *The Indelible Family* (New York: Rawson, Wade Publishers, Inc., 1980), 5-6.
2. Roman and Raley, 15-17, adapted.
3. For additional information on personality differences and birth order characteristics, see *The Power of a Parent's Words* by H. Norman Wright (Ventura, CA: Regal Books, 1991).
4. Roman and Raley, 35-39, adapted.
5. Roman and Raley, 46-47, adapted.
6. H. Norman Wright, *Always Daddy's Girl* (Ventura, CA: Regal Books, 1989), 168-69, adapted.
7. Roman and Raley, 42-43, adapted.
8. Michael Reagan with Joe Hyams, *Michael Reagan: On the Outside Looking In* (New York: Kensington, 1988), 7-8.
9. Reagan, 15.
10. Reagan, 12.
11. Carlson, 162.
12. Charles R. Swindoll, *Living above the Level of Mediocrity* (Dallas, TX: Word Publishing, 1987), 94-95.
13. Dr. Ray Guarendi, *Back to the Family* (New York: Villard Books, 1990), 43-44.
14. Josh McDowell and Dick Day, *How to Be a Hero to Your Kids* (Waco, TX: Word Publishing, 1991), 9-10.
15. Guarendi, 44.

# Notes

16. Original survey from Dr. Patricia Love, *The Emotional Incest Syndrome* (New York: Bantam Books, 1990), 111-14.

## FOUR
### Families that Flourish

1. Love, 103, adapted.
2. Jerry Lewis, *How's Your Family?* (New York: Brunner Mazell, 1979), 63, adapted.
3. Lewis, 47-49, adapted.
4. Love, 102-107, adapted.
5. H. Norman Wright, *So You're Getting Married* (Ventura, CA: Regal Books, 1985), 22-24.
6. Jeanette Lauer and Robert Lauer, "Marriages Are Made to Last," *Psychology Today,* June 1985, 22-27.
7. Mel Krantzler, *Creative Marriage* (New York: McGraw-Hill, 1988), 54.
8. Steven Covey, *The Seven Habits of Highly Effective People* (New York: Simon and Schuster, 1989), 188-89, adapted.
9. For more on this subject, see *Holding onto Romance* by H. Norman Wright (Ventura, CA: Regal Books, 1992).
10. Leo F. Buscaglia, *Loving Each Other: The Challenge of Human Relationships* (New York: Fawcett, 1984), 96-97.
11. Lewis B. Smedes, *Forgive and Forget* (San Francisco: Harper and Row, 1984), 37.
12. As quoted in Michele Weiner-Davis, *Divorce Busting* (New York: Summit Books, 1992), 45.

## FIVE
### Connected Yet Separate

1. Henry Cloud, *When Your World Makes No Sense* (Nashville, TN: Thomas Nelson, 1991), 62-64, adapted.
2. Cloud, 67-68, adapted.
3. Cloud, 68.
4. Source unknown.
5. H. Norman Wright, *Holding onto Romance* (Ventura, CA: Regal Books, 1992), 54-56, adapted.
6. Mike Mason, *The Mystery of Marriage* (Portland, OR: Multnomah Press, 1985), 84.
7. David Field, *Family Personalities* (Eugene, OR: Harvest House, 1988), 27, 36-37, adapted.
8. Fassel, 192, adapted.
9. Dave Carder, Earl Henslin, Henry Cloud, John Townsend, and Alice Brawand, *Secrets of Your Family Tree* (Chicago: Moody Press, 1991), 165, adapted.
10. Carder, et al., 172-73, adapted.
11. Carder, et al., 173-74.
12. Carder, et al., 176-79, adapted.
13. Love, 25-26, adapted.

14. Love, 171-73, adapted.
15. Sandra D. Wilson, *Released from Shame* (Downers Grove, IL: InterVarsity Press, 1990), 136.
16. Richard B. and Freida Stuart, Behavior Change Systems. Family Precounseling Inventory (Champaign, IL: Research Press Company, 1975), adapted.

SIX
*Driving on Empty*

1. Robert Hemfelt, Frank Minirth, Paul Meier, *Love Is a Choice* (Nashville, TN: Thomas Nelson, 1989), 119, adapted.
2. Hemfelt, Minirth, and Meier, 127-28, adapted.
3. H. Norman Wright, *Communication: Key to Your Marriage* (Ventura, CA: Gospel Light, 1974), 4-5, adapted.
4. Hemfelt, Minirth, and Meier, 130.
5. Covey, 71-72, adapted.
6. Jack W. Hayford, *Taking Hold of Tomorrow* (Ventura, CA: Regal Books, 1989), 33.
7. Paul and Jeannie McKean, *Leading a Child to Independence* (San Bernardino, CA: Here's Life Publishers, 1986), 21.
8. McKean, 21-23, adapted.
9. McKean, 134-35.
10. McKean, 144-45.
11. Tony and Bart Campolo, *Things We Wish We Had Said* (Dallas: Word Publishing, 1989), 63.
12. Wilson, 11.
13. Wilson, 128-29.

SEVEN
*Snapshots in Living Color*

1. David Seamands, *Freedom from the Performance Trap* (Wheaton, IL: Victor Books, 1988), 117.
2. H. Norman Wright, *Afraid No More* (Wheaton, IL: Tyndale Books, 1992), 105-106, adapted.
3. Guarendi, 85.
4. Guarendi, 78-101, adapted.
5. Roger Gould, *Transformations* (Copyright 1978. Reprinted by permission of Simon and Schuster, Inc.), 100.
6. Tim Kimmel, *Legacy of Love* (Portland, OR: Multnomah, 1989), 55-56.
7. Ralph Mattson and Thom Black, *Discovering Your Child's Design* (Elgin, IL: David C. Cook Publishing Co., 1989), 196.
8. H. Norman Wright, *Power of a Parent's Words* (Ventura, CA: Regal Books, 1991), 51-54, adapted.
9. Marilyn McGinnis, *Parenting without Guilt* (San Bernardino, CA: Here's Life Publishers, 1987), 43-44.
10. Janet Congo, *Finding Inner Security: A Woman's Quest for Interdependence* (Ventura, CA: Regal Books, 1985), 50-51.

# Notes

11. McDowell, 164-65.
12. Guarendi, 13.
13. Guarendi, 14, adapted.
14. Guarendi, 125-27.
15. Campolo, 213-14.

## EIGHT

## *Ripples on the Family Pond*

1. Wright, *Always Daddy's Girl*, 252-56, adapted.
2. Wright, *Always Daddy's Girl*, 254-55, adapted.
3. Wright, *Always Daddy's Girl*, 254-56, adapted.
4. H. Norman Wright, *How to Get Along with Almost Anybody* (Dallas, TX: Word Publishing, 1989), 152, adapted.
5. Leonard Felder, *A Fresh Start* (New York, NY: Signet Books, 1987), 98-100, adapted.
6. Lorraine Hansberry, *Raisin in the Sun* (New York: Signet Books, 1959), 121.
7. Wright, *How to Get Along with Almost Anybody*, 156-59, adapted.
8. Wright, *How to Get Along with Almost Anybody*, 150-51, adapted.
9. Swindoll, 100.

NINE

## *Swimming in Deeper Waters*

1. Randy Cotton Rolfe, *Adult Children Raising Children* (Deerfield, FL: Health Communications, Inc., 1989), 91-94, adapted.
2. Love, 162-65, adapted.
3. Pearsall, 83, adapted.
4. Guarendi, 143, adapted.
5. Guarendi, 143, adapted.
6. H. Norman Wright, *The Power of a Parent's Words* (Ventura, CA: Regal Books, 1991), 101-102, 146-48, adapted.
7. Wright, *The Power of a Parent's Words*, 147.
8. Wright, *The Power of a Parent's Words*, 149-150.
9. H. Norman Wright, *How to Have a Creative Crisis* (Dallas, TX: Word Publishers, 1986), 149-50.
10. John Killinger, *For God's Sake—Be Human* (Dallas, TX: Word Publishers, 1970), 147. As quoted in Richard Exley, *The Rhythm of Life* (Tulsa: Honor Books, 1987), 108.
11. Exley, 127-37.
12. Pearsall, 239-40, adapted.
13. Pearsall, 246-49, adapted.

TEN

## *The Transforming Power of Encouragement*

1. *The Los Angeles Times*, Metro Section B, December 22, 1991, 1-2, adapted.
2. Robert Sherman, Paul Oresky, Yvonne Roundtree, *Solving Problems in Couples*

*and Family Therapy* (New York: Brunner/Mazel, 1991), 27-28, adapted.

3. Joe Batten and Wendy Havemann, *Tough Minded Parenting* (Nashville, TN: Broadman Press, 1991), 63-64, adapted.

4. McDowell, 87-88.

5. McDowell, 130-31.

6. Sherman, et al., 233-34, adapted.

7. For additional help with anger in the family, see *When Anger Hits Home* by Gary Oliver and H. Norman Wright (Chicago, IL: Moody Press, 1992).

8. For more information, write *Reminisce*, Customer Service, P.O. Box 3051, Milwaukee, WI 53201.

9. Batten and Havemann, 132-50, adapted.

ELEVEN

## Perilous Passages

1. Naomi Golam, *Passing Through Transitions* (New York, NY: The Free Press, 1981), 12, adapted.

2. Charles M. Sell, *Transitions* (Chicago, IL: Moody Press, 1985), xi.

3. R. Scott Sullender, *Losses in Later Life* (Mahwah, NJ: Integration Books, Paulist Press, 1989), 54.

4. Sullender, 3, adapted.

5. H. Norman Wright, *Recovering from the Losses of Life* (Old Tappan, NJ: Revell, 1991), 15-17, adapted.

6. Sullender, 54-55, adapted.

7. Sullender, 61, adapted.

8. Roman and Raley, 205-206, adapted.

9. Jerry and Mary White, *When Your Kids Aren't Kids Anymore* (Colorado Springs, CO: Navpress, 1989), 39-40, adapted.

10. Thomas Bradley Robb, *The Bonus Years*, Foundation for Ministry with Older Persons (Valley Forge, PA: The Judson Press, 1968), 64, adapted.

11. Kahlil Gibran, *The Prophet* (New York: Alfred A. Knopf, 1923), 21-22.

12. Wright, *Always Daddy's Girl*, 267-69, adapted.

13. Charles R. Swindoll, *Growing Strong in the Seasons of Life* (Portland, OR: Multnomah, 1983), 274-75.

14. Paul Bohannan, *The Six Stations of Divorce*, in Bohannan ed., *Divorce and After* (Garden City, NY: Doubleday Anchor Books, 1971), 33-62, adapted.

15. As quoted from C. Berman, *Adult Children of Divorce Speak Out* (New York: Simon and Schuster, 1991), 57.

16. H. Norman Wright, *Seasons of a Marriage* (Ventura, CA: Regal Books, 1983), 132-35, adapted. Two of the most helpful resources to aid you with elderly parents are *Caring for Your Aging Parents* by Barbara Deane (Colorado Springs: Navpress, 1989) and *Eldercare for the Christian Family* by Timothy S. Smick, James W. Duncan, J.P. Moreland, and Jeffrey A. Watson (Dallas, TX: Word Publishing, 1990).

17. Used with permission of Sherrie Eldridge, Indianapolis, Indiana.

18. Wright, *Recovering from the Losses of Life*, 76-77, adapted.

# Notes

TWELVE

*Our Legacy*

1. Carlson, 201-202.
2. Kimmel, 219-20.
3. Kimmel, 215.
4. Kimmel, 199-201, adapted.

## DIVORCE, REMARRIAGE, AND BLENDED FAMILIES

Jim Smoke, *Growing in Remarriage* (Revell, 1990).

Angela Neumann Clubb, *Love in the Blended Family* (Health Communications, 1991).

Bob Burns and Tom Whiteman, *The Fresh Start Divorce Recovery Workbook* (Thomas Nelson, 1992).

Dorothy Weiss Gottlieb, Inez Bellow Gottlieb, and Marjorie A. Slavin, *What to Do When Your Son or Daughter Divorces* (Bantam Books, 1988).

Diane Fassel, *Growing Up Divorced: A Road to Healing for Adult Children of Divorce* (Pocket Books, 1991).

Laurene Johnson, *Divorced Kids* (Thomas Nelson, 1990).

H. Norman Wright, *Always Daddy's Girl* (Regal Books, 1989).

Randy Carlson, *Father Memories* (Moody Press, 1992).

Laurene Johnson, *How to Blend a Family* (Zondervan Publishers).

## PERFECTIONISM

David Stoop, *Hope for the Perfectionist* (Thomas Nelson Publishers, 1991).

David Seamands, *Freedom from the Performance Trap* (Victor Books, 1988).

Holly G. Miller, *How to Stop Living for the Applause* (Servant Publications, 1990).

## GENDER AND COMMUNICATION DIFFERENCES

H. Norman Wright, *How to Speak Your Spouse's Language* (Revell, 1986).

H. Norman Wright, *Understanding the Man in Your Life* (Word Publishers, 1987).

Deborah Tanner, *You Just Don't Understand: Women and Men in Conversation* (William Morrow and Co., 1990).

## MARRIAGE RESOURCES

H. Norman Wright, *Holding onto Romance* (Regal Books, 1992). (Previously titled *Romancing Your Marriage.*)

Frank and Mary Alice Minirth, Brian and Deborah Newman, Robert and Susan Hemfelt, *Passages of Marriage* (Thomas Nelson Publishers, 1991).

## PERSONALITY DIFFERENCES

Otto Kroeger and Janet M. Thuesen, *Type Talk* (Delta Bantam-Doubleday, 1988).

H. Norman Wright, *The Power of a Parent's Words* (Regal Books, 1991).

## FINANCIAL RESOURCES

Larry Burkett, *Your Finances in Changing Times* (Tape series—6 tapes from Christian Financial Concepts, Inc., 1990).

Russell Crossen, *Money and Your Marriage* (Word Publishers, 1989).

Larry Burkett, *Complete Financial Guide for Young Couples* (Victor Books, 1989).

## EFFECTIVE FATHERING

Three excellent books for a father to read are written by Dave Simmons and published by Victor Books: *Dad, the Family Coach,* 1991; *Dad, the Family Counselor,* 1991; *Dad, the Family Mentor,* 1992.

## SETTING BOUNDARIES

Dave Carder, Earl Henslin, John Townsend, Henry Cloud, Alice Brawand, *Secrets of Your Family Tree* (Moody Press, 1991).

Henry Cloud, *When Your World Makes No Sense* (Thomas Nelson, 1990).

Rich Buhler, *New Choices, New Boundaries* (Thomas Nelson, 1991).

## GENEALOGIES

Ira Wolfman, *Do People Grow on Trees—Genealogy for Kids and Other Beginners* (Workman Publishers, 1991). A good basic overview to acquaint you with the process.

Jeanne Eddy Westin, *Finding Your Roots* (Ballantine Books, 1977). A practical resource showing you how to find your ancestors through public libraries, specialty libraries, genealogical societies, public records, federal records, other countries, how to unite your newfound family and how to write your own family history.

William Fletcher, *Recording Your Family History—A Guide to Preserving Oral History with Video Tape and Audio Tape* (Dodd, Mead and Company, 1986). This resource has thousands of suggested topics and questions as well as suggested interview techniques. If families would take the time to respond to these questions just in their own immediate family, they would definitely have a sense of who each person is in their family. (Please be aware that the life of most video tapes is approximately fifteen years under the best of conditions. Check with the various manufacturers of the tapes for their recommendations on storage and usage in order to protect your important videos.)

# Other Books of Interest
# from Servant Publications

## When Your're Mom No. 2
*A Word of Hope for Stepmothers*
### Dr. Beth E. Brown

One in every six children in America lives in a reconstituted or "blended" family. In most of these families, much of the childrearing falls to Mom No. 2. *When You're Mom No. 2* offers practical help, trouble-shooting tips, and spiritual encouragement that will last stepmoms through the years of building strong and healthy family life. **$8.99**

## Keeping Your Kids Christian
*A Candid Look at One of the Greatest Challenges Parents Face*
### edited by Marshall Shelley

*Keeping Your Kids Christian* offers practical down-to-earth guidance from some of the most respected Christian parents today. Their failures and sucesses, woven throughout a wide variety of family stories, are shared to encourage parents today and show them how to accomplish some of the greatest feats in Christian parenting. **$9.99**

## Healing Adult Children of Divorce
*Taking Care of Unfinished Business*
*So You Can Be Whole Again*
### Dr. Archibald D. Hart

When parents divorce, the children usually grow up with unfinished business to resolve. Chances are they were left with emotional wounds, the scars of which remain with them even as adults. *Healing Adult Children of Divorce* examines the long-term effects of this traumatic event, the damaging consequences that follow children of divorce, and ways to resolve past hurts that have shaped their lives. **$16.99**

Available at your Christian bookstore or from:
**Servant Publications • Dept. 209 • P.O. Box 7455**
**Ann Arbor, Michigan 48107**
Please include payment plus $1.25 per book
for postage and handling.
*Send for our FREE catalog of Christian*
*books, music, and cassettes.*